THE RISE AND FALL OF THE ENGLISH ECCLESIASTICAL COURTS, 1500–1860

The first history of ecclesiastical jurisdiction in England covers the period up to the removal of principal subjects inherited from the Middle Ages. Probate, marriage and divorce, tithes, defamation, and disciplinary prosecutions involving the laity are all covered. These all disappeared from the church's courts during the mid-nineteenth century and were taken over by the royal courts. The book traces the steps and reasons – large and small – by which this occurred.

R. B. Outhwaite is a late fellow of Gonville and Caius College, Cambridge. He devoted much of his scholarship to the history of ecclesiastical jurisdiction of England.

CAMBRIDGE STUDIES IN ENGLISH
LEGAL HISTORY

Edited by

J. H. BAKER
Fellow of St Catharine's College, Cambridge

Recent series titles include

The Rise and Fall of the English Ecclesiastical Courts, 1500–1860
R. B. OUTHWAITE

Law Courts and Lawyers in the City of London, 1300–1550
PENNY TUCKER

Legal Foundations of Tribunals in Nineteenth-Century England
CHANTAL STEBBINGS

Pettyfoggers and Vipers of the Commonwealth
The 'Lowers Branch' of the Legal Profession in Early Modern
England
C. W. BROOKS

Roman Canon Law in Reformation England
R. H. HELMHOLZ

Sir Henry Maine
A Study in Victorian Jurisprudence
R. C. J. COCKS

Sir William Scott, Lord Stowell
Judge of the High Court of Admiralty, 1798–1828
HENRY J. BOURGUIGNON

The Early History of the Law of Bills and Notes
A Study of the Origins of Anglo-American Commercial Law
JAMES STEVEN ROGERS

The Law of Treason in England in the Later Middle Ages
J. G. BELLAMY

William Sheppard, Cromwell's Law Reformer
NANCY L. MATTHEWS

THE RISE AND FALL OF THE ENGLISH ECCLESIASTICAL COURTS, 1500–1860

R. B. OUTHWAITE

CAMBRIDGE UNIVERSITY PRESS
Cambridge, New York, Melbourne, Madrid, Cape Town, Singapore, São Paulo

Cambridge University Press
The Edinburgh Building, Cambridge CB2 2RU, UK

Published in the United States of America by
Cambridge University Press, New York

www.cambridge.org
Information on this title: www.cambridge.org/9780521869386

© Cambridge University Press 2006

First published 2006

Printed in the United Kingdom at the University Press, Cambridge

A catalogue record for this publication is available from the British Library

ISBN-13 978-0-521-86938-6 hardback
ISBN-10 0-521-86938-2 hardback

CONTENTS

FOREWORD
R. H. Helmholz

This account of the jurisdiction of the English ecclesiastical courts was the last work written by R. B. Outhwaite before his early death from cancer in the spring of 2005. It completed one part of his scholarly career. The book also fills a gap in knowledge. Many treatises on the law of the Church of England contain a historical dimension and general treatments of English law sometimes have a little to say about the ecclesiastical courts. But most of these works approach the subject from the outside, using evidence from the common law to describe what happened in the spiritual forum. That is necessarily second-hand evidence. And despite some forays into the history of the courts of the church after their restoration in the 1660s, such as the two excellent books written by Professor Stephen Waddams of the University of Toronto, there has been no overall account of the history of ecclesiastical jurisdiction itself. Little has been written from the perspective of the general historian, that is, the historian who seeks to trace the fate of the courts as they found their way forwards after the Elizabethan Settlement and then, later on, as they approached the demise of their jurisdiction over the laity in the mid-nineteenth century. Brian was that historian, and this is the gap his work fills.

My part in the production of this book has not been significant. I did both enjoy and benefit from a friendship with Brian, having had the good fortune to be elected to a fellowship at his college, Gonville and Caius, during the year I served as Goodhart Professor in Cambridge. I also

knew something about the ecclesiastical courts from my own
work on their history prior to the 1640s. For these reasons it
fell to me to read through and undertake some editing of the
typescript he left at his death. I have corrected a few
mistakes, occasionally amended the author's prose in the
interest of clarity and added a few details, bibliographic and
factual. However, this remains Brian's book and accom-
plishment throughout. I have done nothing – at least
nothing consciously – to alter his conclusions or approach.
The only real change of which I am conscious is to have
made his language slightly more 'legal' in tone and
substance.

I am sure that Brian himself would have made additions
and changes had he been spared time to do so. Indeed, he
left notes for a final chapter, in which he intended to sum up
and clarify his conclusions. He particularly wished, for
example, to stress the relative importance of the instance
side of ecclesiastical jurisdiction. Even before the end of the
seventeenth century, it was jurisdiction in contests between
private parties about tithes, testaments and defamation that
provided the great bulk of the work (and income) for the
English civilians, or ecclesiastical lawyers. The *ex officio*
side, prosecutions relating to immorality or religious
dissent, actually played a smaller role in the maintenance
of the church's place in the history of English law than some
histories of the so-called bawdy courts suggest. Of course, it
is true that court officials also profited from *ex officio*
prosecutions. Those prosecuted had to pay what we would
call 'court costs'. But Brian thought that too much attention
had been paid to the 'bawdy' side of ecclesiastical jurisdiction, and he wished to stress this corrective point.

Brian's notes show that he would also have added to his
conclusions about the several ways in which the jurisdiction
of the courts was effectively diminished. Prior to the
nineteenth century, little was lost as a direct consequence
of parliamentary legislation. Such restrictive measures as
were introduced usually removed jurisdiction that had
largely disappeared anyway. Nor did he think that emphasis

could rightly be laid on efforts from common lawyers to restrict the scope of ecclesiastical jurisdiction. Instead, he wished to stress change in attitudes among those affected by the system. Perhaps he left something out by not taking up the legal mechanisms by which ecclesiastical jurisdiction was curbed, but what he wrote is nonetheless helpful – as for example in his discussion of the unwillingness of church-wardens to present men and women for discipline even though they were required to do so in the official sources of the day.

The process by which Parliament eventually did dismantle the church's existing jurisdiction in the mid-1800s is also a theme to which his notes show he would have returned in concluding. Cases involving scandals among the clergy and long-repeated complaints against the fees exacted by the courts obviously played a part. But these were not new. They can be found in virtually every period since the courts were established in the second half of the thirteenth century. However, the pressure for reform was building in the first half of the nineteenth. The church no longer maintain its claim to the allegiance of virtually the entire populace. Change was 'in the air' in any event. The process of parliamentary manoeuvring by which it came is a subject on which Brian had valuable things to say. Most of them are in fact mentioned in the final chapters of this book. The initial strategy – wholesale reform – proved less effective than piecemeal changes. He shows the gradual process by which this lesson became clear to participants. Still, it would have been better to have had Brian's more general reflections on this topic.

No one – least of all Brian Outhwaite – would claim that this book is the final word on the subject. It has little to say, for example, about the careers and works of the English civilians, some of whom are well worth fuller study. It has even less to say about many of the legal technicalities attending, say, the law of last wills and testaments or the working of Lord Hardwicke's Marriage Act. But what it does, it does very well. It presents a clear picture of what happened to the several heads of jurisdiction exercised by the courts of the church from time immemorial as they passed into modern times. Brian's fair-minded examination, found in the first half of the book, of the work by other scholars who have drawn conclusions from the court records is itself a useful advance in scholarship. He brought to his assessment a sophisticated understanding of the economic forces that affected the exercise of eccesiastical jurisdiction. His notes suggest that he meant to go further with the evidence presented in this book, discussing the wider question of whether eighteenth-century England can accurately be described as an *ancien regime*. He thought the history of ecclesiastical jurisdiction in England had a bearing on it. This would have been a worthwhile discussion, I have no doubt. We can now only lament that he did not have time enough to complete it. But we can also be glad that this book exists. It has been an honour for me to have had a hand in securing its completion.

PREFACE

As executor for this book, I wish, on behalf of the Outhwaite family, and on my own account, to express gratitude to Professor Richard Helmholz, Ruth Wyatt Rosensen Distinguished Service Professor of Law at the University of Chicago, for taking editorial charge of Brian Outhwaite's manuscript, and to Cambridge University Press for expediting its publication. My only contribution has been the index.

Brian and I were professional colleagues, relations by marriage, and close friends and travel companions – going back over forty years. I read his splendid *Scandal in the Church* shortly after it came out in 1998, Brian presenting it to me as 'a diversion'. I later heard from him about his more general work on the English ecclesiastical courts. When he was diagnosed with prostate cancer, his labours on the volume, unsurprisingly, faltered; and, with a view to gaining some external encouragement in the new circumstances, he sent the incomplete manuscript to CUP in July 2004. The Press's reaction, based on two readers' reports, was broadly positive, but not conclusive. When Brian received a further, now terminal, prognosis in January 2005, I asked him whether he still had plans for the book. His reaction was entirely dismissive: partly through an urgent reordering of priorities, partly through a genuine modesty concerning the worth of his contribution. It was only in late March that, unprompted, he passed the typescript, with attendant correspondence, into my care. I read it, with a decidedly non-expert eye, and a week or so later discussed with him how we might proceed. He was able, with his wife Christine's help, to convey clear agreement and disagreement with the proposals offered. Brian died the following day.

I communicated immediately with Professor Helmholz in Chicago, as Brian had suggested that he would be the best person to carry the project forward. He replied at once to express, without proviso, his willingness to take charge. It was a fine example of a warm-spirited international academic community at work. Learning that Professor Helmholz would, specifically, be undertaking corrections and elucidations, as well as writing a foreword, CUP – in the persons of Professor Sir John Baker, the Legal History Series Editor, and Finola O'Sullivan, Publisher, Law – declared a ready willingness to proceed.

Brian loved Cambridge and his college, Gonville & Caius. He would have been delighted to know that CUP would be presenting the book to the public. He would also have been gratified to learn of Professor Helmholz's high valuation of his final work and unconditional commitment to its completion.

W. M. Mathew
School of History
University of East Anglia,
Norwich

TABLE OF PARLIAMENTARY STATUTES

ABBREVIATIONS

AJLH	*American Journal of Legal History*
CJ	*The House of Commons Journals*
DRO	Derbyshire Record Office, Matlock
EHR	*English Historical Review*
JEH	*Journal of Ecclesiastical History*
LHR	*Law and History Review*
LJ	*The House of Lords Journals*
LPL	Lambeth Palace Library, London
LRO	Lichfield Record Office, Lichfield
PD	W. Cobbett, *Parliamentary Debates, 1812–20*
PP	*Parliamentary Papers*
SCH	*Studies in Church History*
TRHS	*Transactions of the Royal Historical Society*

1

THE ECCLESIASTICAL COURTS: STRUCTURES
AND PROCEDURES

People's lives are regulated by custom and by law, enlivened by
flashes of wilfulness that might well get them into trouble. Men
and women in the three-and-a-half centuries examined here
functioned within various social units – households, kinship
groups, manors, parishes, villages, towns, gilds – all of which had
formal and informal rules governing behaviour and imposing
sanctions on those who had misbehaved. This book is not concerned, however, with informal rules and informal sanctions,
important though these are, but with those formal rules and formal sanctions that were dispensed by courts of justice, operating
in acknowledged systems of law.

There were two overarching systems of law operating in the
early modern period, one secular or temporal and the other
spiritual. Temporal law was dispensed in manorial, hundred and
borough courts, in petty and quarter sessions, in assizes and in the
royal courts situated in London – the Court of Common Pleas, the
Court of Requests, the King's Bench and so on. Spiritual law –
our concern – was dispensed through hundreds of ecclesiastical
courts scattered the length and breadth of the country. How many
there were is difficult to establish. Hill, reviewing their operations
in the sixteenth and early seventeenth centuries, put their number
at over 250.[1] A parliamentary report of 1832 stated that there were
372 courts, of which 285 were 'peculiars' in ecclesiastical districts
that were exempt from the oversight of the bishops in whose
dioceses they were geographically situated.[2] The principal courts

---

[1] Christopher Hill, *Society and Puritanism in Pre-Revolutionary England* (1966),
299.
[2] *PP*, 1831–2, xxiv, 552. Peculiars were monastic, royal, episcopal or cathedral
properties claiming exemption from the jurisdiction of the bishop in whose

1

were both ubiquitous and active in the sixteenth and early seventeenth centuries. Their activities touched the lives of many people. Sharpe notes that only 71 of the 400–600 people who dwelt in the Essex village of Kelvedon in the first half of the seventeenth century fell foul of quarter sessions, but there were 756 presentments made of the village's inhabitants in the local archdeacon's court.[3] Macfarlane has shown that in the period 1570–1640, the inhabitants of the large Essex village of Earls Colne were involved in about twenty ecclesiastical court cases a year. Most inhabitants could expect to be summoned to appear in one of these tribunals at some point in their lives.[4] 'They formed', writes Marsh, 'a vast web of justice covering the entire country, and extending into a great many spheres of local behaviour'.[5]

The system in which the ecclesiastical courts operated is best envisaged as a graded hierarchy with overlapping functions. At its base were the peculiar courts and the courts of the archdeacons. The latter were officials appointed by a bishop to supervise the clergy within a specified geographical area of jurisdiction – the archdeaconry – and to deal with the complaints of those parishioners who dwelt there. In its simplest form the archdeaconry coincided more or less with the county. This was the case, for example, in Huntingdonshire, Leicestershire, Staffordshire and Surrey. One has to say 'more or less' because most counties contained peculiars, many of which claimed the right of operating their own courts, and some counties, such as Staffordshire, were riddled with them.[6] Many counties, and not just the larger ones, contained several archdeaconries, and not all of them belonged to the same diocese. Cambridgeshire, for example, was subjected to the control of at least four archdeacons – those of Ely, Sudbury, Norfolk and Huntingdon – who were in turn controlled by three bishops – those of Ely, Norwich and Lincoln. At least nine different ecclesiastical courts were at work in Sussex at the end of the

diocese they lay. See *The Oxford Dictionary of the Christian Church*, ed. F. L. Cross and E. A. Livingstone (1983), 1057.

[3] J. A. Sharpe, 'Crime and delinquency in an Essex parish 1600–1640', in *Crime in England 1550–1800*, ed. J. S. Cockburn (1977), 109.

[4] A. Macfarlane, *Reconstructing Historical Communities* (1977), 44, 60, 132.

[5] C. Marsh, *Popular Religion in Sixteenth-Century England* (1998), 108.

[6] See the helpful county maps published in C. Humphery-Smith, *The Phillimore Atlas and Index of Parish Registers* (1984).

fifteenth century.[7] At the county level, therefore, structures could be very complex.

Above this bottom layer there existed various superior diocesan courts. How many there were, what functions they performed and what relationships prevailed with the archdeaconry courts seems to have been dictated primarily, but by no means solely, by the size of the diocese. Episcopal sees varied widely in size. The see of Canterbury was one of the smaller ones. Here, apart from some exempt areas, there were only two ecclesiastical courts: the commissary court and an archdeacon's court.[8] Whereas the diocese of Canterbury covered little more than half of Kent, that of pre-Reformation Lincoln extended over eight and a half counties. It was the largest diocese in the country. As Owen has written, 'The size of the diocese made it difficult, and indeed virtually impossible, for one man to be responsible in one consistory court for all the legal business likely to arise.' By the early sixteenth century, the bishop of Lincoln appears to have had two courts: a court of audience that he presided over personally, which convened wherever he happened to be residing, and a consistory court presided over, principally in Lincoln itself, by his official principal. In addition, the bishop exercised jurisdiction through appointed commissaries in each of the many archdeaconries that made up this huge diocese. Problems of competition with the archdeacons appear to have been solved by agreed compositions defining their respective jurisdictions and by the practice of appointing the archdeacon's official to the post of commissary. In smaller dioceses such arrangements might be unnecessary because the consistory court could be near enough for litigants and others to reach it without great difficulty.[9]

In pre-Reformation England the richest see appears to have been Winchester, and although it stretched over most of Hampshire

---

[7] S. Lander, 'Church courts and the Reformation in the diocese of Chichester, 1500–58', in *Continuity and Change: Personnel and Administration of the Church in England 1500–1642*, ed. R. O'Day and F. Heal (1976), 216.

[8] B. L. Woodcock, *Medieval Ecclesiastical Courts in the Diocese of Canterbury* (1952), 4.

[9] K. Major, 'The Lincoln diocesan records', *TRHS*, 4th series 22 (1940), 39; M. Bowker, *An Episcopal Court Book for the Diocese of Lincoln 1514–1520* (1967), xvi; M. Bowker, *The Secular Clergy in the Diocese of Lincoln 1495–1520* (1968), 7, 19, 26; D. Owen, *The Records of the Established Church in England* (1970), 47; D. Owen, *Church and Society in Medieval Lincolnshire* (1971), 31–2.

and Surrey, it was one of the smaller dioceses in the kingdom.
There, after 1528, the bishop does not seem to have operated a
court of audience, though before this there is evidence of the
periodic functioning of such a court. Instead there was a consistory court presided over by the bishop's official principal, a
man who held this position conjointly with that of vicar general,
and who, confusingly, was often referred to as the chancellor.[10]
The consistory court sat mainly in the cathedral at Winchester,
though occasionally it convened in other places. Consistory courts
could, therefore, be peripatetic.[11] It was more usual, however, for
the peripatetic courts to be commissary ones. In the larger dioceses much consistory business was handled in these commissary
courts, which shifted from one archdeaconry to another in the
course of the year.[12]

Appeals generally lay from lower to higher courts. Thus most
appeals from the archdeacon's court proceeded to the consistory
court. But those stemming from cases in the commissary and
consistory courts would be decided in one of the provincial courts,
depending on whether the initiating courts were situated in the
province of Canterbury or that of York. The appellate court for
the northern province was the archbishop's Court of court at
York; that for the southern province was the court of arches,
which sat not in Canterbury but in the church of St Mary de
Arcubus in London.[13] The court of arches not only heard appeals,
but could also try causes sent to it from lower courts by means of
letters of request. Appeals from the two provincial courts before
the Reformation went to Rome whereas after the Reformation
they went to the high court of delegates, which was an *ad hoc*
tribunal of ecclesiastical and temporal lawyers.[14]

---

[10] R. Houlbrooke, *Church Courts and the People during the English Reformation
1520–1570* (1979), 22–4; F. Heal, *Of Prelates and Princes* (1980), 54.

[11] The Canterbury consistory court also operated a circuit that included Dover,
Hythe and Romney in addition to the cathedral city: Woodcock, *Medieval
Ecclesiastical Courts*, 33.

[12] Houlbrooke, *Church Courts and the People*, 32–3.

[13] 'Until the Great Fire of London, the court sat in the church of St Mary de
Arcubus or Bow Church; after the Great Fire until April 1672 in Exeter House
in the Strand; and afterwards in the great hall of the rebuilt Doctors'
Commons': M. D. Slatter, 'The records of the Court of Arches', *JEH*, 4
(1953), 142.

[14] G. I. O. Duncan, *The High Court of Delegates* (1971).

Although structures varied widely, almost defying general-isation, these courts performed a range of functions, though not all courts offered a complete range. They varied in the powers that they had and in the functions they performed, depending in part on the agreements that had been hammered out between them in the three centuries before 1500. It should also be remembered that court officers conducted some business not only in formal court sittings but also out of session, sometimes even in their own homes. The ecclesiastical courts and their officials had at least four important functions, namely, a corrective function, an adjudicative function, a function of acting as courts of verification and record, and a licensing function. All of these activities were shaped by the requirements of canon law.

The corrective powers of the church naturally embraced purely spiritual matters. They had power to seek out and to punish spiritual nonconformity and religious misbehaviour among both clerics and laymen. The scope of such jurisdiction is well illu-strated by visitation articles – those lists of questions drawn up by the higher clergy to be put to clerics and laymen in parish after parish when particular jurisdictions were visited by archdeacons, bishops or archbishops. The visitation articles drawn up by Archbishop Cranmer in 1547 asked of the clergy whether they had preached against the 'pretensed authority' of the pope and for the power and authority of the king; whether they had taken away and destroyed 'all images, all shrines, coverings of shrines, all tables, trundles, or rolls of wax, pictures, paintings, and all other monuments of feigned miracles, pilgrimages, idolatry and super-stition'; whether the Bible, in English, was publicly available in the church; whether they were keeping a register of weddings, christenings and burials; whether they had provided a poor men's box in which parishioners could bestow what they had formerly spent on 'pardons, pilgrimages, trentals, masses satisfactory, decking of images' and so on. The church's jurisdiction, however, was not confined to matters of doctrine, faith and practice, for it embraced also a wide range of moral offences. In addition to being called on to present any layman performing popish rituals, and any who 'commune, jangle and talk in the church in the time of common prayer', parishes were also to present 'common drun-kards, swearers or blasphemers', any who have 'committed adultery, fornication or incest, or be common bawds', any 'that use charms, sorcery, enchantments, witchcraft, soothsaying, or any like craft invented by the devil', any 'who have made privy contracts of matrimony' and much else besides. This was 1547, and here we have the Edwardian Reformation in full flow.[15] Other, and later, visitation articles would have different obsessions. Most prosecutions derived from presentments made by parish churchwardens at or after such visitations, though offences, or the 'fame' that offences may have been committed, could be reported to the ecclesiastical authorities at any time.

The corrective powers of the church extended, therefore, over a wide range of human behaviour, taking in not only spiritual concerns but also communal discord, marital arrangements and sexual misbehaviour. As canon 109 of the ecclesiastical canons of 1604 put it:

If any offend their brethren, either by adultery, whoredom, incest, or drunkenness, or by swearing, ribaldry, usury, and any other uncleanness, and wickedness of life, the churchwardens, or questmen, and sidemen, in their next presentments to their ordinaries, shall faithfully present all and every of the said offenders to the intent that they, and every of them, may be punished by the severity of the laws, according to their deserts; and such notorious offenders shall not be admitted to the holy communion, till they be reformed.[16]

The courts had, as listed earlier, important adjudicating functions. They were institutions in which private litigants could pursue grievances. The sort of misbehaviour that led people to be punished by these courts could also lead them into personal legal actions against each other, hoping for sentences in their favour or some sort of compromise settlement. So people went to court to prove that they were, or were not, married to some other person. Husbands sought separations from their wives on the grounds of the wife's adultery. Wives sought separations from their husbands on the grounds of the husband's cruelty. People sought to clear themselves of imputations of misbehaviour, contesting an alleged remark made by some individual that they were fornicators, adulterers, usurers or whatever. These defamation suits comprised a large portion of business in the courts that handled such litigation. Other common actions included pew disputes and

---

[15] E. Cardwell, *Documentary Annals of the Reformed Church of England* (1844), i, 49–59.
[16] G. Bray, *The Anglican Canons 1529–1947* (1998), 409.

quarrels over tithes and wills. It is hardly surprising that disputes about church seating should be handled in the ecclesiastical courts, but the other two categories of business are quite surprising and merit a brief explanation.

As tithes were originally grants made by laymen to support the church, jurisdiction relating to tithes lay generally with the church courts, even though by the later sixteenth century many tithe-receivers were laymen. One reason laymen held tithes was that after the dissolution of the monasteries between 1536 and 1540 a great deal of spiritual property passed into lay hands. The monks had earlier been given many rights over parish churches, and laymen eventually succeeded to them.

Disputes between the church and the crown in the early Middle Ages over their respective powers of jurisdiction in relation to wills were usually resolved through compromise. Issues relating to the inheritance of real property – land – fell to the royal courts; those revolving around the disposal at death of personal property – goods and chattels – fell to the church courts. Typical testamentary disputes were those concerned with the non-payment of legacies by executors. But the probate of wills and the administration of the estates of intestates – those who died without making a will – also came into the ecclesiastical courts. This brings us to the third important function of these institutions: they were courts of verification and record.

Wills were 'proved' or authenticated by church court officials and subsequently lodged in their archives for safe keeping. So also were the inventories of goods and chattels compiled by or for executors and the accounts of those called on to administer the estates of intestates. Most wills were proved in local archdeaconry courts, but the will of a person with property in more than one archdeaconry was supposed to go to a diocesan court, whilst the wills of those with assets in more than one diocese were legally subjected to probate in one of the two provincial courts. That for the southern province was the prerogative court of Canterbury, situated in London, whilst that for the northern province was the exchequer court at York. These rules were not strictly adhered to, however; sometimes executors went to the courts that were geographically most convenient for them.

The fourth, and final, function of these courts and their officials is that they were licensing bodies. This naturally embraced the licensing of the clergy themselves, from whom fees were extracted at their ordination and during the periodic visitations when their credentials were inspected. Schoolteachers also were supposed to obtain licences from the ecclesiastical authorities, though the majority of those who taught in schools were probably unlicensed. The same applies to midwives, who were theoretically required to be godly women, if only because they might periodically have to baptise babies on the point of death. They were required to swear oaths in order to obtain their licence to practise, such as this example from 1726:

> You shall swear that you will faithfully and truly execute the office of Midwife in those places where you shall be licenced and authorized, you shall afford your help as well to the Poor as to the Rich for reward, you shall not deliver any privately or clandestinely to conceal the Birth of the Child. If you help to deliver any whom you suspect to be unmaryed you shall acquaint the Ecclesiastical Court of the Jurisdiction therewith and before you yield your assistance or helpe you shall perswade and by all lawful means labour with them to declare who is the father of the said Child ... [17]

There are reminders here not only of how intrusive the powers of the church courts actually were but also of how their various functions interlocked and fed each other. Midwives were obliged to attempt to force an unmarried mother to reveal the name of the father of her child. The mother, and less often the father, might subsequently be prosecuted for fornication. Married women might be cited for prenuptial fornication if the midwife reported that the child was born within nine months of the church ceremony and was not visibly premature. Such prosecutions were all too common in the later sixteenth and early seventeenth centuries. One party might attempt to thwart such a prosecution by beginning an action against a partner to prove a prior clandestine marriage, but this in turn might precipitate a prosecution for irregular marriage.

Court officials derived income from the issue of licences, and after the Reformation a major source of income under this head came to be that derived from the issue of marriage licences. These dispensations avoided the calling of banns in parishes where the couple normally resided, and also avoided the prohibitions on marrying in any one of the closed seasons for matrimony inherited

[17] Hair, *Before the Bawdy Court* (1972), 58.

from the medieval liturgical calendar. They became in time an important source of revenue to all the higher clergy and officials who had a hand in their issue.

These courts had, therefore, at least four important functions. In addition to their corrective, adjudicative, licensing functions, they also served as courts of record and verification. The first two functions require further discussion, if only because they involved different court procedures.

Corrective prosecutions – the so-called office causes – were either initiated by complaints about a particular individual's activities made by churchwardens and clerics, often in the course of routine ecclesiastical visitations, or arose from the 'common fame' of an individual's misbehaviour, brought in other ways to the court's attention, perhaps by the activities of apparitors or summoners. If, after being so alerted, the judge decided to take action, the defendant would be served notice by an apparitor to attend the court at a particular place and time. If the person attended, he or she would be charged either *ex officio mero*, that is, with the judge acting as the prosecuting agent, or *ex officio promoto*, where the cause was promoted by some individual other than the judge. The defendant would then be compelled on oath to make a true answer to the accusations levelled against him or her. If the party admitted the offence, the judge could proceed straight to sentence. If he or she denied it, then two courses of action usually presented themselves. The judge could take evidence to help determine the outcome of the case. Such evidence was usually presented orally, leaving little or no record in the court's registers, though it was possible for the case to proceed via the submission of written 'articles', 'interrogatories' and 'responses'. The alternative was that the defendant could be purged of the charge. 'Compurgation' meant mustering on some future court day a stipulated quota of trustworthy people who would swear to their belief in the defendant's oath. If the compurgators duly appeared to so swear, the charge against the defendant would be dismissed.[18]

---

[18] D. Owen, 'Ecclesiastical jurisdiction in England, 1300–1550: the records and their interpretation', in *Materials, Sources and Methods of Ecclesiastical History*, ed. D. Baker (1975), 206; Houlbrooke, *Church Courts and the People*, 38–40.

These office causes are to be distinguished from instance causes, where the judge adjudicated private disputes between litigants. The procedures involved were different in several ways. Proof in instance causes was made by witnesses and documents, rarely by oaths. Such causes began with a complaint and the consequent summons by an apparitor for the litigants to appear at a specified court. At their first appearance, they would appoint proctors – officials who would conduct the case on their behalf in an elaborate sequence of written complaints – and then articles containing questions which were put to the witnesses and answered by them. Each procedural stage was presented at separate court sessions. Every document drawn up and presented had to be paid for by the parties, and cases could stretch on for months, and sometimes years.[19] Most, however, did not. Indeed only a minority of these instance suits seems to have culminated in a judicial sentence. In the consistory court of Wells in the fifteenth century, only about 10 per cent seemed to have reached this point.[20] Most of them petered out through exhaustion or through compromise, as the litigants began to appreciate the financial implications of continuing the case.

If an instance cause came to sentence, the judge – and the judge alone since there were no juries in these ecclesiastical courts – would find for one party or the other, allocating the payment of costs to be imposed on the loser. In office cases, however, the defendant would be declared guilty of the charges that were levelled or dismissed if he succeeded at compurgation. If guilty, what then happened depended largely on the seriousness of the charge. Lesser offences might simply receive a 'monition' – a judicial warning; greater offences would merit sentences of penance, varying in the severity of their demands. Before the Reformation a penitent might be forced to process around his church, bearing a candle that was subsequently placed before the high altar or on some shrine. The most usual post-Reformation

---

[19] Woodcock, *Medieval Ecclesiastical Courts*, 53, implies that a contested case could not be terminated in less than three months. R. W. Dunning, 'The Wells consistory court in the fifteenth century', *Proceedings of the Somersetshire Archaeological and Natural History Society* 106 (1962), 54–5, agrees with this, if the case was simple; the average duration of a contested instance suit in Wells at this time was six months, 'which amounted to fairly speedy justice'.

[20] Dunning, 'Wells consistory court', 55.

sentence was the imposition of a single act of penance, involving a public confession of one's sin before the congregation in the parish church whilst bare-legged, dressed in nothing more than a white sheet, and carrying a white staff in one's hand. But the court might also insist on multiple penances, involving a succession of such ritual appearances and not always in a single parish church. A Gloucestershire woman convicted of bawdry in the mid-sixteenth century was ordered to perform penitential acts four times in her parish church and once in the market places of Wickwar, Chipping Sodbury and Thornbury. That same consistory court also sentenced a Gloucester man to tour from Gloucester cross to Gloucester cathedral, Tewkesbury, Cirencester and Berkeley, saying at each point, 'This I doo suffer for the kepyng of ii wyffes.'[21]

This highly humiliating procedure was, after the Reformation, the principal punishment inflicted, although it was possible for the affluent guilty to escape by volunteering to make a financial payment in lieu of penance, the proceeds of which were to be passed on to the poor. Reformers carped at these things, arguing, as we shall see, for sterner punishments for sexual and other delinquents, harking back to earlier eras when the ecclesiastical courts could be found inflicting whippings and other bodily punishments on offenders.[22]

In punishing office offenders, therefore, penance prevailed through the period from the Reformation onwards, the courts attempting to bring the sinful to repentance and the community to forgiveness. In instance causes, they also sought to settle personal disputes by reconciling warring parties rather than insisting on cases coming to sentence.

Not all of those cited to appear in the ecclesiastical courts, however, were willing to attend. Many failed to put in an appearance, and not all of them were defendants, for some plaintiffs also failed to materialise. The courts attempted to combat this contumacy by first imposing a sentence of suspension upon them, a

[21] F. D. Price, 'Gloucester diocese under Bishop Hooper, 1551–3', *Transactions of the Bristol and Gloucestershire Archaeological Society*, 60 (1939), 93–4.

[22] For examples see M. Bowker, 'The Commons' supplication against the Ordinaries in the light of some archidiaconal acta', *TRHS*, 5th series 21 (1971), 73. The bishop of Durham's court imposed whippings as late as 1580: see M. K. McIntosh, *Controlling Misbehaviour in England, 1370–1600* (1998), 114.

sentence that forbade their attendance at church. If this failed to
bring them to heel, a further order of excommunication was
available. Greater excommunication not only meant being suspended from church, but also entailed various legal and social
disabilities. Not only was the excommunicate banned from entering the church, but the community was not supposed to have any
dealings with him or her. This might be carried to extreme limits.
Marchant cites the complaint of one parish priest to the archdeacon's registrar at Nottingham about the predicament of his
pregnant parishioner Mary Bell:

I have received a writt of Excommunication against Marie Bell (my
parishioner) and I dare not stay it without warrantie from your Court.
Will you be pleased to be certified, that she waites her every houre, and
not able to travaile halfe a mile out of the towne. Let mee intreat so much
favour of you (if it may bee) as to reverse that which is done, or els to
absolve her againe, that she be not deprived of womens helpe, which now
shee is like to stand in need of. I hope you will pittie a woman in her
case ...[23]

We learn nothing more of Mary Bell. If, however, she died
through neglect of 'women's helpe', the church could have denied
her burial within the churchyard.

The sentence also carried economic penalties. 'The excommunicated person', writes Hill, 'could not buy or sell, could not be
employed, could not sue or give evidence in the courts (and so
could not recover debts), could not give bail, make a will or receive
a legacy, or serve as an administrator or guardian.'[24] In practice,
however, the disabilities of excommunication may have been fewer
than this gloomy catalogue suggests. There were exceptions under
the canon law itself. Moreover, Marchant has pointed to the
comparative rarity of church court prosecutions for consorting
with excommunicates.[25] Some may even have gone about their
everyday lives little disturbed by their technical state. Matters
might have depended on a whole number of factors: the individual's psychological resilience; the nature of the offence that lay
behind the excommunication; how seriously such offences were

[23] R. A. Marchant, *The Church under the Law: Justice, Administration and
Discipline in the Diocese of York 1560–1640* (1969), 221.
[24] C. Hill, *Society and Puritanism*, 355–6; M. Ingram, *Church Courts, Sex and
Marriage in England, 1570–1640* (1987), 52–4.
[25] Marchant, *Church under the Law*, 221.

regarded by the host community; the degrees of tolerance shown by neighbours and last, but by no means least, the number of excommunicates within the locality. If many stood in that state, as was the case in some areas, they could find solace in each other's company.

If, after forty days, the excommunicated person had not submitted and sought absolution, the church, through the bishop, could seek from chancery a writ *de excommunicato capiendo*, asking the sheriff to take the offender into custody until he or she had submitted to the ecclesiastical authorities. This, however, was a time-consuming process and because in office cases the judge effectively bore the costs of obtaining the writ, it was also an expensive one; also it was not always successful in its outcome and, as a result, it was a step not frequently undertaken.

As time went on, large, and perhaps growing, numbers of people refused to appear before the church courts, and many of these were subsequently excommunicated. Some people remained in this state for lengthy periods, thumbing their noses at the ecclesiastical authorities. High-placed offenders and particularly obdurate or sinful individuals could, however, attract the attention of special ecclesiastical commissions. These tribunals, composed of a mixture of authoritative lay and ecclesiastical members, operated in particular dioceses from time to time. Special commissions were sent into the north-west in 1543 and 1550, allegedly to curb the sexual proclivities of licentious Lancastrians, and from 1559 to 1562 permanent 'high commissions', operating as a sort of ecclesiastical court of star chamber, were established in the southern province in London, and also in the north for the dioceses of York, Carlisle, Durham and Chester.[26] Although the prime purpose of these bodies appears to have been to suppress religious unorthodoxy and to implement the Elizabethan religious settlement, they functioned as ecclesiastical courts, albeit ones with additional sanctions at their disposal. The high commissions had powers to pursue offenders who were attempting to evade justice by moving from one diocese to another, a strategy always open to those attempting to evade the clutches of ecclesiastical justice, and

---

[26] Philip Tyler, 'The significance of the ecclesiastical commission at York', *Northern History* 2 (1967), 27–29; C. Haigh, 'Slander and the church courts in the sixteenth century', *Transactions of the Lancashire and Cheshire Antiquarian Society* 78 (1975), 6–7; Ingram, *Church Courts, Sex and Marriage*, 39.

all the special commissions had powers to fine and to imprison offenders as well as to take bonds to ensure fulfilment of their dictates. The commission established in 1574 for the dioceses of Bristol and Gloucester sentenced Thomas Grenewaie of Coles-bourne in December 1575:

> For horrible incest with his owne sister. On which daie yt was ordred by the commissioners that the saide Thomas Grenewaie shalbe relesed out of prison and delivered to the messinger of this courte, and he to bringe him to the sheriffs of the citie of Gloucester, and to be putt in the pillorie with a paper on his hedd written with these wordes, for horrible incest with his owne sister, in great letters, and there to remayne from one till two of the clock this daie in the market place, and then to be taken downe and whipped aboute the citie at a cartes tayle; and on Mondaie next being market daie to be sett in the pillorie at Cirester with the like paper on his hedd the space of two howres from xi till one of the clock; and the saide Marie Grenewaie to be sett at libertie till she be brought a bedd, and then to appere to receve ponishment etc.[27]

The existence of these ecclesiastical commissions not only put teeth into the system, but also alarmed and armed, as we shall see, the opponents of the church courts. That opposition had many roots. Before we explore these, we need to examine further the character and scale of the actual business of these courts in the hundred years after the English Reformation.

---

[27] *The Commission for Ecclesiastical Causes in the Dioceses of Bristol and Gloucester*, ed. F. D. Price (1972), 98.

2

THE BUSINESS OF THE COURTS, 1500–1640

The Reformation brought few changes in structure and administrative procedures to the English ecclesiastical courts. Headship of the church was transferred from pope to king, necessitating new procedures and institutions to deal with appeals; episcopal boundaries were altered as new dioceses were carved out of old ones; special ecclesiastical commissions became more numerous as the crown sought to deal with spiritual and moral radicalism; and the teaching of canon law in the universities was abolished, though its practice in the largely unchanged ecclesiastical courts was continued.[1]

Nevertheless, the effect of the Reformation upon the business and authority of the church courts has been the subject of debate. Some historians have argued that both business and authority peaked even before the Reformation and that the break with Rome led to further decline.[2] The consistory court of Canterbury experienced a sharp fall in levels of instance causes in the 1490s, and levels continued to decline until 1535. No fewer than 693 such causes were introduced into that court in 1486, but only 93 in 1535.[3] This precipitous decline is almost entirely explained, however, by the diminution of *fidei laesio* causes, causes which numerically dominated business in late medieval church courts.[4] These could arise from any situation in which an oath to fulfil an

---

[1] R. H. Helmholz, *Roman Canon Law in Reformation England* (1990) is an authoritative guide to questions of continuity and change in the legal practices of the church courts in this era.

[2] For a summary of such views see C. Haigh, 'Anticlericalism and the English Reformation', in *The English Reformation Revised*, ed. C. Haigh (1987), 67, and his *English Reformation, Religion, Politics and Society under the Tudors* (1993), 73–4.

[3] Woodcock, *Medieval Ecclesiastical Courts*, 84, 89, 125.

[4] Helmholz, *Roman Canon Law*, 25.

obligation had been uttered, but most appear to involve trade debts for relatively small sums, sums perhaps too small or too informal to merit backing with a sealed obligation.[5] Helmholz demonstrated that similar declines in such breach of faith cases occurred in the consistory courts of Hereford, Lichfield, Chichester and Exeter.[6] The late 1490s saw 'a marked drift away from London church courts by London litigants', a process evident in both the consistory and commissary courts, and here also breach of faith suits, which had been prominent only a few years before, virtually vanished.[7] Such suits had disappeared from the Norwich consistory court by 1509, from which time records of that court's activities survive, although they continued in considerable numbers in Durham until the 1530s.[8]

Episcopal courts in the diocese of Chichester, however, appear to have exhibited different tendencies, for here there was no diminution in the overall volume of instance business between 1506–7 and 1520 and a three-fold increase in office cases. This appears to have been the product of energetic attempts to curb abuses under bishop Sherburne (1508–36) and transfer of business from archidiaconal to consistory and commissary courts.[9] There are reminders here that increases in activity in particular courts could be the result of greater zeal and efficiency or the product of diocesan administrative changes in which one court siphoned off the business of another. Although the statistical basis for such assertions is limited, there is little sign of change in the overall volume of office proceedings in the consistory court of Norwich in the first three decades of the sixteenth century.[10] Until more dioceses are investigated, it is difficult to be certain whether there was a secular decline in the business of the church courts from some high point in the later fifteenth century, or whether that decline continued to the 1530s, or whether, if it did

---

[5] An outstanding discussion of the nature of these cases is to be found in R. H. Helmholz, *Canon Law and the Law of England* (1987), 263–90.
[6] Ibid., 283–4.
[7] R. M. Wunderli, *London Church Courts and Society on the Eve of the Reformation* (1981), 23–4, 104–7.
[8] R. Houlbrooke, 'The decline of ecclesiastical jurisdiction under the Tudors', in O'Day and Heal, *Continuity and Change*, 240.
[9] S. Lander, 'Church courts and the Reformation in the diocese of Chichester, 1500–58', in O'Day and Heal, *Continuity and Change*, 222–3.
[10] Houlbrooke, *Church Courts and the People*, 273.

exist, the decline was evident in anything other than causes involving perjury or breach of faith.[11]

The events that followed Henry VIII's break with Rome do appear to have disturbed the flow of cases. Attacks on the church courts began as soon as parliament was assembled in 1529, culminating in the presentation in the Commons in 1532 of the 'Supplication against the Ordinaries'.[12] 'The Reformation', wrote Houlbrooke, 'set in train or accelerated a series of changes which gravely undermined the authority and the efficiency of the church courts.' Parliament proceeded, he argued, to pass statutes that had widespread implications for church court jurisdiction.[13] The impact of these measures will be explored in later chapters that examine in detail particular classes of business. Before this, however, we must attempt to chart the direction of changes in the overall volume and nature of business in the English ecclesiastical courts.

Only 93 instance suits were introduced into the consistory court of Canterbury in 1535, compared with 223 in 1522.[14] Whereas 543 cases had come into the episcopal courts in the archdeaconry of Chichester in 1520–1, only 270 did so in 1533–4, and the figure fell further to 251 in 1537–8, with both office and instance causes sharing this contraction.[15] The average volume of instance causes in the Durham consistory court in 1535 was less than half of that introduced in 1532, while in the Norwich consistory court causes fell by a third when comparing four complete years between 1519 and 1524 with the average of the five years 1534–8.[16]

How widespread this pattern was we do not know, but what is apparent from the studies that we do have is that this decline appears to have been fairly quickly arrested and then, indeed, reversed. Four hundred and eighty-two causes came into the episcopal courts of Chichester in 1556–7 compared with 251 in

---

[11] Contrary opinions are offered by Helmholz, *Roman Canon Law*, 33–4, and Haigh, *English Reformations*, 86–7.

[12] G. R. Elton, 'The Commons' Supplication of 1532: parliamentary manoeuvres in the reign of Henry VIII', *EHR* 66 (1951), 507–34; 'The Supplication against the Ordinaries reconsidered', *EHR* 72 (1957), 616–41; Wunderli, *London Church Courts*, 133–4.

[13] Houlbrooke, 'The decline of ecclesiastical jurisdiction', 244, 250.

[14] Woodcock, *Medieval Ecclesiastical Courts*, 125.

[15] Lander, 'Church courts and the Reformation', 231.

[16] Houlbrooke, *Church Courts and the People*, 37, 273.

1537–8.[17] The five years 1545–9 saw business levels in the consistory court of Norwich nearly fifty per cent up on those of the years 1534–8 and back to pre-Reformation levels. Whereas in the 1520s only three proctors were practising in the courts at Norwich, by the 1560s their number had grown to five.[18] Instance causes in the Winchester consistory court in the 1540s were generally greatly ahead of those recorded in two years in the 1520s.[19] Bowker has drawn attention to the 'dramatic increase in the business of the court' in the archdeaconry of Lincoln between 1536–7 and 1544–5.[20]

Taking a longer-run view we can see that the expansions in activity that appear to have set in by the middle of the sixteenth century continued for the next seventy to eighty years. In 1544, 133 causes entered the consistory court of Chester. Fifty years later this number had more than doubled to 278.[21] Instance business in the Norwich consistory court tripled between 1509–10 and late Elizabethan times.[22] Eighty-one instance causes were heard at the Lichfield consistory court in 1529, but 204 in 1590.[23] In the consistory court at Salisbury there were fewer than 90 instance and promoted office causes pursued in 1566, but by 1615 there were over 150.[24] The number of causes entering the consistory court of York expanded from the mid-sixteenth century to the second decade of the seventeenth century; whereas 213 causes were in process in 1561–2, 379 were under consideration in 1611–12. This appears to have represented a high point in that particular court's activity: numbers thereafter appear to have stagnated at approximately 300 cases a year.[25] The archbishop of York's court of audience – the chancery court – experienced a four- to five-fold expansion in levels of activity from 1571–2 to the end of Elizabeth's reign. Activity thereafter subsided somewhat,

---

[17] The increase was most evident in probate cases, swollen predictably by the demographic crisis of 1556–7, but it also revealed itself in office causes: Lander, 'Church courts and the Reformation', 231.

[18] Houlbrooke, 'The decline of ecclesiastical jurisdiction', 248.

[19] Houlbrooke, *Church Courts and the People*, 273–4.

[20] Bowker, *The Henrician Reformation: The Diocese of Lincoln under John Longland 1521–1547* (1981), 86.

[21] Haigh, 'Slander and the church courts', 2.

[22] Marchant, *The Church under the Law*, 16.

[23] Helmholz, *Roman Canon Law*, 43.

[24] Ingram, *Church Courts, Sex and Marriage*, 69.

[25] Marchant, *The Church under the Law*, 62.

before rising steeply in the reign of Charles I.[26] The exchequer court at York dealt with testamentary business. Here there was a near five-fold rise in the seventy-five years before the period 1612–19, when the court was dealing with an average yearly load of 970 probates and 675 administrations.[27] Marchant, from whom much of this evidence of growth derives, concluded in 1969 that 'the church courts were never busier, nor ecclesiastical discipline more intense, than in the post-Reformation decades', a judgement with which O'Day and Heal concurred when they wrote in 1976 that 'by the end of the sixteenth century the volume of business transacted in most courts was greater than it had been in the lively era before the Reformation'.[28] 'In the seventeenth century', Hill argued, 'the courts remained very active, and their activity even seems to have been on the increase under Laud.'[29] Such views sit at odds with Houlbrooke's judgement that 'the ecclesiastical courts emerged from the Reformation gravely weakened'.[30]

To understand how such conflicting opinions can coexist and why volumes of activity in these courts expanded from the mid-sixteenth century, despite the curbs put on their activities by Parliament and the common law, we must first examine where – in what classes of business – growth was most marked.

Once again attention must be drawn to the diversity that prevails, diversity that was the product not only of chronological shifts in the balance of activities but also of those political and administrative compromises that shared out responsibilities between potentially competing courts in any one diocese. Litigation, or instance causes, dominated the business of the consistory courts.[31] Certain types of litigation shrank, however, as we move from medieval to early modern times. Perjury or breach of faith causes, which had dominated the business of some courts in the mid-fifteenth century, largely disappeared in the early sixteenth century. Defendants had begun to resort to the court of the King's Bench, invoking the medieval statute of *praemunire* to

---

[26] Ibid., 68.   [27] Ibid., 88.

[28] Ibid., 1; O'Day and Heal, *Continuity and Change*, 21.

[29] Hill, *Society and Puritanism*, 307.

[30] Houlbrooke, *Church Courts and the People*, 266.

[31] Woodcock, *Medieval Ecclesiastical Courts*, 31; Dunning, 'The Wells consistory court', 61.

plead that such church court cases offended the rights of the crown and were temporal rather than spiritual matters.[32] Faced with the possibility of stringent punishments under *praemunire*, creditors seeking settlement of trade and other debts resorted increasingly to the common law. Business rose in the central courts of the King's Bench and Common Pleas, and small debts actions expanded also in borough courts throughout the land.[33] Such facilities were not exclusively the right of town dwellers for, as Muldrew has pointed out, 'Very few people in the country lived more than a half-day's horse ride from a court of record in a major market town, and most lived much closer, perhaps even within walking distance.'[34]

Matrimonial suits had also loomed large in many medieval consistory courts. They comprised more than a third of the instance suits heard in the consistory court of Canterbury in 1373 and 1374, more than a quarter of cases before the Ely consistory court in the period 1374–82 and a quarter of the instance business in the consistory court of Wells in the second half of the fifteenth century.[35] By the sixteenth century, for reasons that will later be discussed, such business was playing a much less prominent part in the litigation entering the consistory courts. Matrimonial, testamentary, tithe and defamation suits accounted for more than nine-tenths of the instance business before the consistory courts of Norwich and Winchester in the period 1520–70, but the matrimonial component shrank rapidly thereafter.[36] By the 1620s and 1630s, defamation and tithe causes dominated the consistory court of Norwich's proceedings.[37] The same is true of the consistory court of York: by 1638–9, tithe and defamation cases made up no

---

[32] Helmholz, *Roman Canon Law*, 25–6.
[33] C. Muldrew, *The Economy of Obligation: The Culture of Credit and Social Relations in Early Modern England* (1998), 203–4.
[34] Ibid., 211. Attempts at calculating shifts in rates of litigation per capita (ibid., 236) need to take into account this transference from the ecclesiastical to common law courts and should not be confined to common law actions alone.
[35] Woodcock, *Medieval Ecclesiastical Courts*, 85; M. M. Sheehan, 'The formation and stability of marriage in fourteenth-century England: evidence of an Ely register', *Medieval Studies*, 33 (1971), 234; Dunning, 'The Wells consistory court', 59.
[36] Houlbrooke, *Church Courts and the People*, 39; M. Ingram, 'Spousals litigation in the English ecclesiastical courts, c. 1350–c. 1640', in *Marriage and Society: Studies in the Social History of Marriage*, ed. R. B. Outhwaite (1981), 43.
[37] Marchant, *The Church under the Law*, 20.

less than 83 per cent of all causes.[38] Nottingham had its own consistory court: there, by the 1630s, defamation and tithe causes dominated its instance business, but office prosecutions also loomed large.[39] The latter tended to be more prominent in the lower ecclesiastical courts, justifying the contemporary labelling of the archdeacons' courts as the 'bawdy courts', but office causes generally increased in number, and perhaps in proportion, in many courts in post-Reformation England.[40]

Office prosecutions offered, however, few financial rewards to those officials who administered these courts. Because most were dealt with summarily and few documents were drawn up, they were settled comparatively quickly. Perhaps only the scribes who drew up the citations and the apparitors who delivered them gained rewards. Visitations appear also to have played little part in initiating prosecutions in late medieval times. Woodcock is not alone in arguing that 'one of the great permanent changes in the application of ecclesiastical jurisdiction during the later sixteenth century was the substitution of a regular visitation and present-ment system for the hitherto haphazard process of hauling people into court upon the instigation of the apparitors'.[41]

Nearly 60 per cent of the income that came to the consistory court of Norwich in the year 1635–6 came from two sources – routine probate work and the fees derived from instance business. Court fees from disciplinary business brought in a mere 2.5 per cent of the total. Nearly 30 per cent came from the sale of mar-riage licences, bearing out Marchant's observation that 'in the sixteenth and seventeenth centuries the issuing of marriage licences was a growth industry, and any chancellor who knew his job took care to develop his retail outlets'.[42] Over a half of the income of the commissary court of the archdeaconry of Suffolk in 1610–11 came from probate work and about 13 per cent from the sale of marriage licences.[43] These calculations offer further reminders that the ecclesiastical courts derived much income from

---

[38] Ibid., 62. Testamentary causes were, as we have previously noted, handled in the exchequer court at York.

[39] Ibid., 194.

[40] Woodcock, *Medieval Ecclesiastical Courts*, 79, thought that this began after 1500 as perjury cases declined.

[41] Ibid., 68–9; Houlbrooke, *Church Courts and the People*, 45, 51.

[42] Marchant, *The Church under the Law*, 15–21.

[43] Ibid., 29.

administrative tasks, such as probate and routine inspections of the clergy. Calling in 1604 for the abolition of the ecclesiastical courts, William Stoughton listed the benefits that would ensue for clergymen: they would be

disburdened from all fees ... for letters of orders; letters of institution; letters of inductions; for licences to serve within the diocese; for licences to serve in such a cure; for licences to serve two cures in one day; for licences to preach; for licences of resignation; for testimonials of subscription; for letters of sequestration; for letters of relaxation; for the chancellor's, register's and summoner's dinners; for archidiaconal annual, and for episcopal triennial, procurations.[44]

It is also clear that litigation was far more profitable to them than their criminal jurisdiction.

These findings will help us to put some criticisms of the courts, both contemporary and modern, into perspective. The 'Supplication of the Commons against the Ordinaries' of 1532 was not the first such set of complaints and it was by no means the last.[45] Such grievances were reiterated decade after decade, and century after century, until the courts were eventually stripped of most of their jurisdiction in the mid-nineteenth century. The courts quickly felt the effect of the attacks in the run-up to the 1640s. Office causes in the consistory court of Gloucester, for example, ceased in 1641 and the last suits for tithe and defamation there came in December 1642.[46] Although probate and testamentary causes lingered on in the courts for some time afterwards, divines and parliament had to turn their minds to fashioning replacement systems of discipline, arbitration and probate.

The hundred years from the 1540s to the 1640s saw, therefore, both a remarkable expansion in the activities of the ecclesiastical courts and their sudden death. What lay behind the expansion merits further consideration and this will be undertaken by examining in the chapters that follow some of the most important case categories, beginning with tithe causes.

[44] Hill, *Society and Puritanism*, 327–8.
[45] *English Historical Documents*, v, *1485–1558*, ed. C. H. Williams (1967), 732–6.
[46] F. S. Hockaday, 'The consistory court of the diocese of Gloucester', *Transactions of the Bristol and Gloucestershire Archaeological Society* 46 (1924), 200.

3

TITHE CAUSES

Tithe causes, as we have seen, were one of the three foundations that sustained the great rise in instance business in the ecclesiastical courts from the mid-sixteenth century to the English Revolution, the other two being testamentary causes and defamation suits. But what, in turn, stimulated this increase in tithe causes?

Tithes, originally offerings in kind of a tenth part of agricultural produce, were of ancient origin, one of the means by which our ancestors maintained their priesthood in what were predominantly agricultural societies. The 1763 edition of Burn's *Ecclesiastical Law* tells us that

Tithes, with regard to their several kinds or natures, are divided into praedial, mixt, and personal:

Praedial tithes are such as arise merely and immediately from the ground; as grain of all sorts, hay, wood, fruits, herbs ...

Mixt tithes are those which arise not immediately from the ground, but from things immediately nourished from the ground, as by means of goods depastured thereupon, or otherwise nourished with the fruits thereof; as colts, calves, lambs, chickens, milk, cheese, eggs.

Personal tithes are such profits as do arise by the honest labour and industry of man, employing himself in some personal work, artifice, or negotiation; being the tenth part of the clear gain, after charges deducted.[1]

Predial tithes were thus a tenth part of things growing on the land; mixed tithes derived mainly from animals kept on the land and personal tithes were the tenths paid by those whose incomes derived from their labour, trades or professions.

To whom were they paid? Here there was a further division into great and small tithes. As a general rule, great tithes were those of corn, hay and wood. Small tithes were all the remaining

---

[1] R. Burn, *Ecclesiastical Law* (1763), ii, 374–5.

predial tithes, plus the mixed and personal ones. Great tithes were
paid to the rectors of churches or their impropriators; small tithes
to vicars or impropriators. Impropriators come into the picture
because by the end of the Middle Ages a great many churches had
come to be controlled or owned by cathedral deans and chapters,
monasteries and other spiritual bodies. Approximately one-third
of the livings in the vast diocese of Lincoln had been so appro-
priated by 1535.[2] Opportunities always existed to divert tithes and
other incomes from the pockets of the clerical incumbents to those
bodies who possessed the advowson – the right of presentation to
the living. Tithes could, therefore, be paid to clerical incumbents
or to their patrons, and these patrons could be either institutional
or individual ones.

Tithes and trouble were always potential bedfellows. They
were payments that were always likely to generate occasional
tension and conflict. This was not because people resented supporting their local clergy; there is little evidence of this before the
mid-seventeenth century. Resentment had other causes. It came
from such things as the reluctance of arable farmers to pay what
were in essence taxes and to yield a true tenth of their output,
tendencies that were likely to be particularly marked in years
when their crops were deficient because of harvest failures. Tithe-
receivers must have constantly been alert to the farmer trying to
disguise the true volume of his output, something that was perhaps easier for the open-field farmer to accomplish, because his
holding consisted of a myriad of scattered strips, than it was for
the farmer cultivating fewer but larger enclosed fields. Resentment might also spring from the animal farmer's difficulties of
establishing what should go to the parson when his herd of cows
produced only five cows or his sow a litter of fewer than ten. Local
customs developed to deal with such contingencies; the sixth or
seventh calf might be offered, with the payer receiving a monetary
payment for each animal below ten, or the parson might delay
collection until the animals produced a tenth offspring, perhaps
the following season.[3] Personal tithes must have been particularly

[2] M. Bowker, *The Henrician Reformation: the Diocese of Lincoln under John
Longland 1521–1547* (1981), 111.
[3] C. Hill, *Economic Problems of the Church from Archbishop Whitgift to the Long
Parliament* (1956), 78–9, 94. Chapter 5 of Hill's work contains the best
introduction to the history of this subject in this period.

hard to assess and collect: the tithe-receiver could visually scan crops in a field, but not so a merchant's profits.

Conflict could erupt, therefore, between tithe-receivers and tithe-payers, and also between one tithe-receiver and another. Rectors and vicars might quarrel about the division of spoils, particularly when changes in land use occurred. Such changes were constantly occurring. Routine two-, three- or four-year fallows created no difficulties. Tithe was not collected on the ground that grew no crops in a particular year. But convertible husbandry must have created problems because of the tendency for arable land to be rested under grass for years at a time, without there necessarily being a compensatory ploughing-up of permanent grassland. Land going out of cultivation altogether would obviously hit tithe income, making tithe-receivers more anxious to secure their incomes in other ways. The century and a half after the Black Death may have been a formative period in several of these respects, since this was a period that saw declining population, falling arable prices, shrinking margins of arable cultivation, changes in cropping and extensions of grazing along with land reverting to waste. Although the history of tithes in the later Middle Ages has yet to be written, one can envisage that these developments, along with the inherent tensions generated by tithe collection, might well have encouraged tithe-receivers to settle for fixed valuations and for money payments instead of produce tithes.

Certainly the sixteenth century began with many such agreements – *modi decimandi* – already in place. There were customary *modi* involving individual crops or commodities, usually the small vicarial tithes, and prescriptive *modi* involving all tithes payable by an individual parish or other area of land.[4] Arrangements such as these probably suited both payers and receivers in the conditions that prevailed in the century and a half before 1520. Variations in yields could produce periodic difficulties, but both parties might have felt that they were involved in a swings and roundabouts situation and have been relatively content to have entered into such agreements. Certainly there were few tithe causes in the church courts before the Reformation.[5]

Many reasons have been offered to explain the rise in tithe litigation that got under way in the sixteenth century. Hill has

[4] Ibid., 95–6.   [5] Haigh, 'Anticlericalism', 68–9.

provided a rich compendium of possibilities. He drew attention to
the emergence of new forms of economic enterprise, forms that
presented challenges to the clergy while increasing the potentialities
for tithe evasion. He also noted the harm that the tithe legislation
of the mid-sixteenth century did to tithe-receivers. Inflation
undermined the real value of *modi*, contributing to the gradual
impoverishment of the clergy. The latter are depicted as the chief
aggressors in this battlefield, albeit that they were attempting to
reverse a situation in which tithe was bringing them a diminishing
share of the nation's expanding wealth.[6]

But were clergy the principal plaintiffs in tithe actions in the
ecclesiastical courts? Purvis demonstrated that in the diocese of
York between 1540 and 1560 not only was there a clearly per-
ceptible rise in the volume of tithe causes reaching the courts, but
this rise was entirely due to laymen pressing their tithe claims.
Laymen, not clergymen, were overwhelmingly the chief plaintiffs.[7] Sheils has more recently demonstrated that this rise in tithe
causes in the consistory court of York went on until the second
decade of the seventeenth century: by 1611–12 the number of
such cases was at least seven times greater than in the year 1541–2.
He also demonstrated that amongst plaintiffs 'the laity were
always the majority, and often a substantial one'. Around two-
thirds of plaintiffs appear to have been laymen rather than clerics.[8] This tendency was not confined to York. Tithe causes at
Chester in the 1540s were double those of the 1530s and the
increase was again dominated by lay rather than clerical litigants.[9]

An unknown proportion of these laymen were, however, men
whose rights to collect tithes were dependent on leases they had
purchased from clerical tithe-owners. Leasing rights of collection
to a farmer in the parish who knew what his fellow cultivators
were up to had some real advantages for the tithe-owner. For the
resident cleric, it minimized friction with tithe-payers. It was also
an obvious remedy for absentee clergymen, of whom there were

[6] Ibid., 80–131.
[7] J. S. Purvis, *Select XVI Century Causes in Tithe*, Yorkshire Archaeological
Society, Record Series 114 (1949), vii.
[8] W. J. Sheils, ' "The right of the church": the clergy, tithe and the courts at York,
1540–1640', in *The Church and Wealth*, ed. W. J. Sheils and D. Wood (1987),
234–6.
[9] C. Haigh, *Reformation and Resistance in Tudor Lancashire* (1975), 59.

not a few in a church rife with pluralism. In addition it offered an assured, rather than fluctuating, annual income to the leaseholder, as well as the opportunity for him to raise lump sums via fines given in exchange for beneficial leases. Entering a new living almost invariably involved a cleric in substantial capital outlays.

Some of these laymen were, therefore, lessees rather than proprietors of the claims they were pressing in the courts. The rise in tithe litigation in the dioceses of Norwich and Winchester in the period 1520–70 was not due to lay proprietors pressing their claims, but it seemingly owed much to lay lessees doing so.[10] Although O'Day notes that in diocese of Coventry and Lichfield in the reign of the early Stuarts 'tithe litigation almost monopolised the instance side of the consistory and ... a large number of cases were initiated by clergymen', it also seems to be the case that non-clerical cases comprised just over two-thirds of all tithe cases brought into the consistory court.[11]

These general patterns enable us to offer an explanation of the overall expansion in tithe business in the long sixteenth century. The price rise must have caused many tithe-receivers to question the wisdom of the *modus* that applied to their tithes, leading them into attempts to alter such arrangements or even to set them aside altogether and return to payments in kind. The average level of agricultural prices in the 1520s and 1530s was 50 per cent higher than that of the first two decades of the sixteenth century. Indeed, prices moved to levels generally above those experienced in the previous 120 years. This signified the beginnings of an inflation that became particularly acute in the 1540s and 1550s and was to last until the 1640s.[12] Even before the religious changes of the mid-1530s, therefore, some tithe-owners may have been regretting that they were saddled with an increasingly uneconomic *modus*.

Whilst agricultural producers generally benefited from this inflation, smaller producers would be hit by events such as bad harvests that left them with little or nothing to sell. Larger producers might also resort to cheating tithe-receivers of a proper share of their output in years when yields were hit, resenting lost opportunities for the high profits that came to sellers through

---

[10] Houlbrooke, *Church Courts and the People*, 144.
[11] R. O'Day, *The English Clergy: the Emergence and Consolidation of a Profession 1558–1642* (1979), 191–2.
[12] R. B. Outhwaite, *Inflation in Tudor and Early Stuart England* (1982), 11–17.

scarcity. The 1520s concluded with three poor harvests in succession, events that may well have triggered defaults on tithe payments.[13] Houlbrooke noted the sensitivity of tithe causes to good and bad harvests in the diocese of Norwich in the mid-sixteenth century, as O'Day had done in the diocese of Coventry and Lichfield in the early seventeenth century. 'A deficient or terrible harvest', the latter asserts, 'could bring a flood of clerical and lay suits against impoverished farmers'.[14]

The parliament that assembled in 1529 provided a forum for the articulation of numerous resentments against the clergy, their exactions of tithe and mortuary, and the ecclesiastical courts that upheld their rights.[15] These attacks may also have encouraged some tithe-payers to default or underpay. The preamble to a parliamentary act of 1535, *For tithes to be paid throughout this realm*, complained that

Forasmuch as divers numbers of evil disposed persons inhabited in sundry counties, cities, towns and places of this realm, having no respect to their duties to Almighty God, but against right and good conscience have attempted to subtract and withhold, in some places the whole, and in some places great parts of their tithes and oblations, as well personal as predial, due unto God and holy church; and pursuing such their detestable enormities and injuries, have attempted in late time past to disobey, contemn and despise the process, laws, and decrees of the ecclesiastical courts of this realm, in more timorous and large manner than before this time hath been seen ...

This act went on to insist that tithes should be paid 'after the laudable usages and customs of the parish' and that 'the parson, vicar, curate, or other party in that behalf grieved' could invoke the assistance of Justices of the Peace to uphold the jurisdiction of the ecclesiastical courts for 'any contempt, contumacy, disobedience or other misdemeanor of the party defendant'.[16] There was recognition in this measure of a profound interest in the receipt of tithes, an interest that was about to be dramatically consolidated amongst the laity by the dissolution of the monasteries

---

[13] W. G. Hoskins, 'Harvest fluctuations and English economic history, 1480–1619', *Agricultural History Review* 12 (1964), 44.

[14] Houlbrooke, *Church Courts and the People*, 150; O'Day, *The English Clergy*, 193.

[15] C. Cross, *Church and People, 1450–1660: The Triumph of the Laity in the English Church* (1976), 60–4.

[16] 27 Henry VIII, c. 20.

and the appropriation by the crown of their vast estates, a process that began in 1536 and was more or less complete by 1540. Almost immediately the crown began to dispose of these new acquisitions through gifts, through property exchanges and through periodic land sales to relieve growing pressures on royal finances. The effect of these transfers in the hundred years after 1540 was a dramatic reinforcement of lay ownership of parsonages and tithes. A more immediate consequence was the passage of the act *For the true payment of tithes and offerings of 1540*. This measure argued that the withholding of tithes was being encouraged by the inability of the lay owners of such spiritual properties to sue for their rights in the ecclesiastical courts. It extended such jurisdiction to them, adding the support of the justices of the peace, as in the act of 1535.[17] There is little doubt that litigation was stimulated by these measures.[18] Not all of this litigation found its way to the ecclesiastical courts, for the common law and equity courts claimed a parallel jurisdiction where title to property needed to be established and where contracts such as *modi* were concerned.[19] The church courts tended, however, to favour plaintiffs and to look critically at customs that reduced the real value of tithes. They also allowed tithe-receivers to recover twice or three times the value of tithes withheld.[20]

New lay tithe-owners were probably anxious, in the same way that new clerical ones were, to establish at an early point their legal rights in the community to tithe, a process that might involve questioning the antiquity of customs and the reasons for exemptions. Lay tithe-owners may also have been less accommodating than clerical ones when dealing with those who tried to avoid paying their dues.[21] Assets purchased at or near the market price had to pay a proper economic return: there were financial limits to indulgence, especially given persistent price inflation. Laymen certainly appear to have been more inclined to seek the assistance of the courts when dealing with defaulters, and after 1540 they were encouraged by legislation to do so.

The price rise had numerous consequences, therefore, as did the Henrician and Edwardian Reformations. The beneficed clergy

[17] 32 Henry VIII, c. 7.   [18] Houlbrooke, *Church Courts and the People*, 147.
[19] Hill, *Economic Problems of the Church*, 124–31; W. J. Jones, *The Elizabethan Court of Chancery* (1967), 395–9.
[20] Helmholz, *Roman Canon Law*, 90–9.   [21] Ibid., 145.

began to shoulder a heavier tax burden at a time when inflation was putting their incomes under pressure. It was possible for real incomes to increase, but this meant either that the glebe had to be cultivated directly and produce tithes collected in full or that the rents and fines paid by glebe- and tithe-lessees had periodically to be revised upwards. Though parliament in 1535 had shown concern that tithes were not being paid, subsequent legislation increased the opportunities for evasion. The act of 1539 that dissolved the larger monastic houses took care to continue the exemption from tithe payments that all monastic properties had apparently enjoyed.[22] Subsequent land sales gave opportunities to purchasers to mingle such properties with their own, claiming exemption for the whole.[23]

Further opportunities for evasion were presented in *An act for payment of tithes*, passed in that year of rebellion, 1549, by a parliament anxious to still the disquiet such exactions were arousing. Complaints against tithe had earlier surfaced amongst the northern rebels in 1536.[24] The articles of complaint drawn up by the East Anglian rebels in 1549 laid much emphasis on the burdens imposed by rising rents and fines, and they called for a return to the values 'that wer in the First yere of King Henry the vii'. They also pleaded that 'no lord knight nor gentleman shall have or take in ferme any spirituall promocion'; and the articles seemingly asked for the commutation of tithes, pleading that 'no proporiatie parson or vicar in consideracon of advoyding trobyll and sute between them and ther pore parishners whiche they daly do procede and attempt shall from hensforth take for the full contentacon of all tenths which now they do receive but viii d. of the noble in the full discharge of all other tythes'.[25] This tithe act of 1549 attempted to uphold the rights of tithe-receivers while reconciling them with the grumbles of tithe-payers. Predial tithes had to be rendered, but 'in such manner and form as hath been of right yielded and paid within forty years next before the making of

---

[22] 31 Henry VIII, c. 13, clause 21.
[23] Hill, *Economic Problems of the Church*, 106, also points out that 'endless disputes were possible about the distinction between land formerly owned and farmed by the monastery, and land merely leased by them'.
[24] C. S. L. Davies, 'The Pilgrimage of Grace reconsidered', *Past & Present* 41 (1968), 58, 68; A. Fletcher and D. MacCulloch, *Tudor Rebellions* (1997), 134.
[25] Fletcher and MacCulloch, *Tudor Rebellions*, 146.

this act'. Tithes were not to be paid on any properties 'exempted by the laws and statutes of this realm or by any privilege or prescription', and 'barren heath or waste ground' newly brought into cultivation was given a seven-year exemption from payment of tithe for any corn or hay that might be grown upon it after its reclamation. Those persons 'exercising merchandises, bargaining and selling, clothing, handicraft or other art or faculty' who 'within these forty years have accustommably used to pay such personal tithes' should continue to do so, though 'common day labourers' were excluded, as was the necessity of personal tithe-payers to attest on oath if questioned by a court about their incomes.[26]

With its repeated emphasis on the customs prevailing forty years before, the act made it difficult for tithe-receivers to alter customary arrangements that through inflation or other changed circumstances were now unfavourable to their interests. *Modi* established in the reign of Henry VII would have become unrealistic, especially after the rapid inflation of the 1540s, and new forms of enterprise might well escape tithe payments altogether. With the abolition of the need to swear under oath, the amount of a true tenth of the net incomes of those liable for personal tithe became virtually impossible to establish. Conversion of pasture to arable, encouraged by three successive bad harvests that followed the passage of the act, gave rise to disputes about whether these lands were formerly 'barren heath or waste ground' and consequently whether they were tithable or not.[27] 'Everywhere attempts to levy tithe from new industries and new agricultural processes', Hill wrote, 'gave occasion for squabbles and bickering.'[28]

Most tithe causes, however, concerned older agricultural lands and arrangements, and either they were about default of payment or they were disputes about the prevalence or mutability of customs. Before the mid-sixteenth century the withholding of payment was treated in some dioceses as an office cause; later, following the acts of 1535 and 1540, default gave rise to an instance cause.[29] Increasing lay involvement in the collection of

[26] 2 and 3 Edward VI, c. 13.
[27] Hoskins, 'Harvest fluctuations ... 1480–1619', 45; Houlbrooke, *Church Courts and the People*, 127.
[28] Hill, *Economic Problems of the Church*, 84.
[29] Houlbrooke, *Church Courts and the People*, 137–8.

tithes was probably a more important source of litigation than
changes in the character of tithable property or administrative
procedures. It was the massive transfer of spiritual property into
the hands of the laity in the hundred years after 1540, and the
tendency for these properties to change hands in a mobile land
market, that underlay this rise in litigation.[30] In 1969, Marchant
drew attention to the similarities in the behaviour of the volume
of tithe litigation and Stone's indexes of land sales: the latter more
than doubled between 1560 and the second decade of the seventeenth century, subsiding a little in the two decades before 1640.[31]
The dissolution of the monasteries and royal indebtedness that
necessitated periodic land sales combined to stimulate the land
market. This, along with inflation, produced tithe-receivers
anxious to secure adequate returns on their investments. We
should also not be surprised that when presented with the
opportunity not to pay tithe, or to pay less than was really due,
people took it. This did not represent hostility to the church; it
betokened the reluctance of people to give away part of their hard-
won surpluses and to pay what were in effect taxes. The legislation of the mid-sixteenth century and economic change gave many
people opportunities for evasion, and it was evasion that occasioned dispute.

[30] Sheils, 'The right of the church', 252, argues that the rise in such cases resulted
mainly from the 'greater involvement of the laity as tithe-holders, for they could
pursue their legal dues in this area without the constraints of pastoral care or
good neighbourliness which must have acted upon many of the clergy'.
[31] Marchant, *The Church under the Law*, 63.

4

WILLS AND TESTAMENTARY CAUSES

The second plank sustaining the instance side of the business of the ecclesiastical courts was the testamentary cause, most often a wrangle between individuals over the details of wills and testaments. The will was the document by which people disposed of their assets at their death. In the Middle Ages the will and the testament were assumed to be separate instruments – a fact that finds recognition in later writings. 'Testament and will', wrote Burn in the eighteenth century, 'strictly speaking, are not synonymous.' 'A will', he continued, 'is properly limited to land; and a testament only to chattels.' The will, therefore, dealt with the disposal of real property – land; the testament with the disposal of chattels or personal property – household effects, working tools and equipment, livestock, cash and credits. By the mid-sixteenth century the two instruments are usually conjoined in one – the last will and testament. Burn recognised this, writing that usually 'the words will and testament are used indiscriminately'.[1]

Although, as Helmholz has demonstrated,[2] the church courts lost litigation over debts owed by and due to the deceased early in the sixteenth century, other testamentary causes rose in marked fashion in many ecclesiastical courts in the later sixteenth and early seventeenth centuries, despite the fact that, as with tithe cases, the common law and equity courts were also dealing with such matters. Chancery, for example, encroached on the spiritual courts in respect of trusts, legacies and debts in wills.[3] Nevertheless, in the consistory court of Chester there was a five-fold increase in testamentary causes in fifty years, with such suits

[1] Burn, *Ecclesiastical Law*, 504.
[2] R. H. Helmholz, 'Debt claims and probate jurisdiction in historical perspective', *AJLH*, 23 (1979), 76–80.
[3] Jones, *The Elizabethan Court of Chancery*, 400–17.

rising from 11 per cent of identifiable causes in 1544 to 25 per cent in 1594.[4] There was also a 'striking increase' in the consistory courts of Norwich and Winchester in the sixty years before 1580.[5] Testamentary litigation, along with the normal courses by which people secured probate of wills and letters of administration for those dying intestate, brought valuable income into the pockets of those who officiated in the courts. 'Probates and administrations' brought in over one-quarter of the income of the registrar of the Norwich consistory court in 1635–6 and over a half of the income of the registrar of the archdeaconry court of Suffolk in 1610–11.[6]

Wills were challenged in the courts for many reasons, many of them due to the dashed expectations of family and friends. Some plaintiffs pleaded that the testator was not of sound mind when the document was signed or that it had been signed under duress. Both things were possible when crucial decisions were made on a deathbed or in an old and enfeebled state. Some claimed that the will was a forgery or that a later will had been suppressed in favour of an earlier one. There were complaints that people had seized and disposed of goods before probate had been secured and consequently that the missing items were not inventoried as they should have been. Inventories were often the subject of complaint. Goods, it was claimed, were undervalued and subsequently sold at higher prices, with executors or administrators illegally pocketing the difference. Some people challenged the appointment of particular executors or administrators, arguing, for example, that the latter were not the deceased's next of kin. There were frequent complaints that legacies had not been paid by executors, with legatees being put off time and again with excuses. Executors often excused themselves with the argument that the property was not worth as much as the testator thought or that debts had subsequently come to light, debts that drained off the disposable residue of the estate.[7]

In some courts the increase in testamentary litigation was partly the product of changes in court procedure. At Winchester, for example, cases that had formerly been dealt with as office

---

[4] Haigh, 'Slander and the church courts', 2.
[5] Houlbrooke, *Church Courts and the People*, 108, 276.
[6] Marchant, *The Church under the Law*, 15, 29–30.
[7] J. Addy, *Death, Money and the Vultures: Inheritance and Avarice, 1660–1750* (1992), supplies copious examples of such complaints, albeit for a later period.

prosecutions came, by the later 1560s, to be proceeded with as instance causes, and a similar change appears to have occurred in Norwich by the later 1620s.[8] The scale and ubiquity of the increase in testamentary litigation suggests, however, the existence of more important underlying causes. Similarly, while Houlbrooke has argued that the increase in such business in the period from 1540 to 1640 owed something to declining standards in the administration of probate, it is difficult to believe that this generalised rise was entirely the product of increasing levels of corruption or malpractice on the part either of ecclesiastical court officials or of executors and administrators.[9] It seems far more likely that, in an age of expanding population and of inflation, it was the product of increasing numbers of people making wills.

With a doubling of population between the early sixteenth century and the middle of the seventeenth, and with a seven-fold increase in agricultural prices that boosted the incomes of agricultural producers and rent-receivers, it would not be surprising to find an increase in the number of individuals who felt obliged to make a will. The 'Ordre for the Visitacion of the Sicke' in the second Edwardian prayer book of 1552 instructed the priest to enquire of the ailing man:

And yf he have not afore disposed hys goodes, let him then make hys wyl. But men must be ofte admonished that they sette an ordre for theyr temporall goodes and landes whan they be in health. And also declare his debtes, what he oweth, and what is owing unto him, for discharging of his conscience, and quietnesse of hys executours.[10]

Divines and moralists in the sixteenth and seventeenth centuries urged people to make a will. For some, such as William Perkins, it was the Christian duty of the dying man to dispose of his property in ways that promoted peace and harmony amongst family, friends and neighbours. A will, said Perkins, 'cuts off much hatred and contention in families and it staies many suits in law'. Not making a will, according to William Gouge, brought 'discredit to the partie deceased' and 'contentions among his surviving

---

[8] Marchant, *The Church under the Law*, 23; Houlbrooke, *Church Courts and the People*, 111.

[9] Houlbrooke, *Church Courts and the People*, 109–10.

[10] *The First and Second Prayer Books of Edward VI*, ed. E. C. S. Gibson (1910), 417–19.

children'; it led to the 'wasting a great part, if not his whole estate, in suits of law', as well as 'defeating many creditors of their due debt'.[11] Edward Leach of Milton, Cambridgeshire, was clearly heeding such messages when he made his will 'because there should be no controversy after my death for my goods and possessions and for the maintenance of love and peace in the world'.[12] Love and peace were not, however, the inevitable consequences of willing one's possessions, as the rising volume of testamentary litigation attests. Most of these legal battles were over wills that had been drawn up, not wills that had never existed.

Who made wills and how many were made? The first question is easier to answer than the second. Wills were supposedly made by people of 'sound mind'; by those who had reached the age of majority; and mostly by adult males. Wives needed their husband's permission to make a will, and because a wife's goods became her husband's at marriage, most wills made by females were made by widows and ageing spinsters.[13] Existing studies of sixteenth- and seventeenth-century communities suggest, however, that perhaps only about 20–25 per cent of adult males left wills that have survived.[14]

The majority of the population, therefore, died without making a will. They died intestate. Most wills in the sixteenth and early seventeenth centuries appear to have been made within days or weeks of the testator's death. Many people made wills only when faced with the distinct possibility that they were about to meet their maker.[15] This close association of the will with dying may have persuaded some people not to make their last will and

---

[11] C. Marsh, 'In the name of God? Will-making and faith in early modern England', in *The Records of the Nation*, ed. G. H. Martin and P. Spufford (1990), 220; S. Coppel, 'Willmaking on the deathbed', *Local Population Studies* 40 (1988), 39.

[12] Marsh, 'In the name of God?', 248.

[13] N. Goose and N. Evans, 'Wills as an historical source', in *When Death Do Us Part*, ed. T. Arkell, N. Evans and N. Goose (2000), 45–7.

[14] S. Coppel, 'Wills and the community: a case study of Tudor Grantham', in *Probate Records and the Local Community*, ed. Riden (1985); N. Evans, 'Inheritance, women, religion and education in early modern society as revealed by wills', in *Probate Records*, ed. Riden, 54–5.

[15] Coppel, 'Willmaking on the deathbed', 38; D. Beaver, ' "Sown in dishonour, raised in glory": death, ritual and social organization in northern Gloucestershire, 1590–1690', *Social History* (1992), 394–5.

testament. It seemed like tempting fate. Henry Swinburne, the Elizabethan author of an important treatise on wills, noted:

It is received for an opinion amongst the ruder and more ignorant people, that if a man should chance to be so wise, as not to make his will in his good health, when hee is strong and of good memorie, having time and leasure, and might ask counsel (if any doubt were) of the learned; that then surely he should not live long after.[16]

William Gouge could complain that men deferred making wills 'on vaine hope that they may live longer, and when they are sicke, upon conceit that they may recover'.[17]

There were other, perhaps more pertinent, reasons why people failed to make wills. Many people probably had little or nothing to bequeath and the costs of making a will and of securing probate could be a considerable disincentive in the light of this. It was those who had something to bequeath and who had potentially competing claims on their property who felt most compelled to make wills. Some may not have had surviving children and only a wife to worry about. Some, who had children, may have already set them up in life with *inter vivos* transfers of property.[18] Others may have felt that local customs of inheritance served their own particular purposes. A decline in the importance of manorial and village customs may have been one underlying reason for the growth in will-making that appears to have occurred in the century and a half before 1640.

Wills begin to survive in significant numbers only from the later fifteenth and early sixteenth centuries. Some have argued that this reflected a real growth in the practice of will-making, but Takahashi has argued convincingly that the pattern owed more to processes of recording and preservation than to actual testamentary behaviour. Examination of the records of the consistory court of Ely and the archdeaconry court of Leicester reveals a tendency for wills to survive in significant quantities from 1515 onwards, while in the consistory court of Worcester a similar pattern is observable from 1527. Graphs of will numbers also show marked annual fluctuations, with sharp upward leaps in years of epidemic

---

[16] H. Swinburne, *A Briefe Treatise of Testaments and Last Willes* (1590), fol. 24v.
[17] W. Gouge, *Of Domesticall Duties* (1622), 571.
[18] L. Bonfield, 'Normative rules and property transmission: reflections on the link between marriage and inheritance in early modern England', in *The World We Have Gained*, ed. L. Bonfield et al. (1986), 155–76.

disease outbreaks such as the years 1557–9. Once this multiple
crisis had passed, however, all three series reveal an upward
buoyancy. Between the 1560s and the 1620s the total number of
wills in all three series expanded by 32 per cent, perhaps half the
rate at which England's population expanded in the same period.
A more spectacular 72 per cent rise took place in the numbers of
wills proved in the same period in the prerogative court of Canterbury.[19] The latter expansion may have been fuelled by
increases in the numbers of wealthy gentry and merchants
residing in London and the home counties.[20] Periodic royal land
sales, all of which were organised and took place in London,
helped to create situations in which wealthy individuals found
themselves with substantial property in more than one diocese and
were thus legally obliged to secure probate in one of the two
provincial probate courts. Developments in will-making may also
have influenced this tendency for executors to drift towards the
two highest probate courts, the prerogative court of Canterbury
and its counterpart at York. At the beginning of the sixteenth
century wills were strongly spiritual in tone, drawn up as many of
them were by priests. But as we move towards the later sixteenth
and early seventeenth centuries they became more secular in tone
and content, as more and more came to be composed by common
lawyers and literate laymen, aided by published will formularies.
Lawyers must have been particularly aware of the many pitfalls
posed by the laws relating to *bona notabilia*. A critic of the courts
in the mid-nineteenth century, anxious to suppress the 372
ecclesiastical courts that he said then existed, pointed to some of
these problems. A will was provable in the district in which a
testator dwelt at the time of his death. But if he had goods to the
value of £5 out of that district, then the grant of probate was
invalid and he would have to secure probate all over again in one
of the two provincial courts.[21]

[19] M. Takahashi, 'The number of wills proved in the sixteenth and seventeenth
centuries', in *The Records of the Nation*, ed. Martin and Spufford (1990),
187–213.

[20] Goose has noted that a higher proportion of Reading will-makers secured
probate in the prerogative court of Canterbury than will-makers in Cambridge
and Colchester: N. Goose, 'Fertility and mortality in pre-industrial English
towns from probate and parish register evidence', in *When Death Do Us
Part*, 194.

[21] See below, pp. 168–72.

An expanding population, rising prices that inflated nominal incomes and an active land market combined to increase in absolute, though probably not relative, terms the number of wills that were drawn up in the sixteenth and first half of the seventeenth centuries. Increased will-making and a social climate that encouraged litigation in general combined to raise the number of testamentary disputes in the church courts. The cost of pursuing such causes in the courts may not have risen to the extent that prices and the incomes of the better-off rose, reducing the real costs of litigation for many.[22] Such developments offer a more plausible explanation of this increased litigation in the church courts than the growing inefficiency of probate officials or the rising cupidity of executors.

---

[22] T. Arkell, 'The probate process', in *When Death Do Us Part*, ed. Arkell et al. (2000), 20: 'The fees for probate that were established from 1530 onwards by the Act of 1529 were based solely on the value of the deceased's personal estate. They appear to have been respected widely for at least a century, certainly at York and Norwich, but were increased eventually because of inflation.'

DEFAMATION SUITS

'The amount of litigation aroused by slander', wrote Marchant referring to the long sixteenth century, 'was a phenomenon of the age.'[1] Slander could be prosecuted in both secular and spiritual courts. By 1550, where one pursued the case depended, in theory at least, on the nature of the accusation embodied in the slander. If someone was the subject of a malicious accusation alleging the perpetration of an offence punishable at common law, then the case should have been pursued in a secular court; if, however, the accusation was one punishable by the ecclesiastical law, then the complaint should have been pressed in the church courts. Thus a remark that someone was a thief should have gone to a secular tribunal, whilst a remark that someone was a whore should have gone to the church courts. In practice, the distinctions were not as clear cut as legal theory suggested, particularly in the case of mixed or multiple slanders, and one can find secular allegations being pursued in spiritual courts and spiritual allegations being actioned in secular tribunals.[2] Both judicial systems, however, witnessed a remarkable growth in slander litigation in the sixteenth and early seventeenth centuries.

Even before the Reformation, defamation causes were prominent amongst instance litigation in the ecclesiastical courts. In the later fifteenth century they comprised a third of church court business in London, and by the 1520s they became the most numerous type of case in the Canterbury consistory court.[3] Despite this early prominence, however, historians talk accurately

---

[1] Marchant, *The Church under the Law*, 61.
[2] J. A. Sharpe, *Defamation and Sexual Slander in Early Modern England: The Church Courts at York* (1980).
[3] Wunderli, *London Church Courts*, 63; Woodcock, *Medieval Ecclesiastical Courts*, 88.

of an 'explosion in litigation over defamation which occurred from the mid sixteenth century'.[4] The number of such suits in the consistory court of Chester quadrupled in the fifty years after 1544; in the consistory court of York they doubled between the 1570s and the 1630s, despite the fact that such cases were also being heard in growing numbers in the chancery court there by the early seventeenth century, and in the London consistory court the numbers rose by 129 per cent between 1572 and 1633, by which time they comprised nearly three-quarters of all the litigation pursued in that tribunal.[5] It seems very likely that in all courts where instance business was heard slander cases rose to occupy a prominent position by the early seventeenth century.

McIntosh has drawn attention to rising levels of concern with scolding and malicious use of the tongue in manorial, hundred and borough courts in the later fifteenth and early sixteenth centuries, and she has also demonstrated how, especially in the more economically advanced regions of England, these courts declined in the course of the sixteenth century, becoming virtually moribund by 1600.[6] Both developments may have pushed business into the church courts. The beginnings of the rise in defamation causes in the church courts may also owe something to changes in some areas in court procedure – to switches from office prosecution for malicious gossip to allowing or encouraging private instance suits. In the archdeaconry court of Buckingham in 1521, for example, Agnes Yve was prosecuted for 'being a common slanderer of her neighbours by calling divers rightly living women loose women and many other scandalous names and sowing discords amongst the aforesaid parishioners', was found guilty and was sentenced to undergo penance.[7] Houlbrooke relates how, in the diocese of Norwich in the mid-sixteenth century, 'very large numbers of "common defamers" and "sowers of discord" were presented in disciplinary sessions' and how later in Elizabeth's reign 'defamation became an instance matter'.[8] Some

---

[4] Sharpe, *Defamation and Sexual Slander*, 3.
[5] Haigh, 'Slander and the church courts', 2; Marchant, *The Church under the Law*, 62, 68; L. Gowing, *Domestic Dangers: Women, Words, and Sex in Early Modern London* (1996), 33–5.
[6] McIntosh, *Controlling Misbehaviour*, 43, 58.
[7] F. W. Ragg, 'A record of the archdeaconry courts of Buckinghamshire during part of 1521', *Records of Buckinghamshire* 10 (1916), 313.
[8] Houlbrooke, 'The decline of ecclesiastical jurisdiction', 247.

of the rise was also the direct product of demographic expansion. With England's population doubling between the 1530s and the 1630s some increase might be expected irrespective of changes in social behaviour, but the examples of growth offered above suggest that the magnitude of the increase in litigation outran those to be expected from a larger population. What, then, lay behind this advancing tide of slander litigation, a development that powerfully sustained levels of activity in the church courts in the post-Reformation century?

Examination of the nature of both the slanderers and those who were slandered offers possible clues. Those who were slandered suffered a wide range of assertions – wider perhaps in the common law courts than the church courts. Whereas in the common law courts, the plaintiffs, who were overwhelmingly male, complained that their honesty – their business probity – was undermined by assertions that they were thieves, fraudsters and rogues, in the church courts the slanders complained of were overwhelmingly sexual in nature and the plaintiffs were always preponderantly female.[9] Men complained of being labelled as sexually active deviants – seducers, adulterers, fornicators, bastard-begetters, whore-masters and carriers of venereal disease – or of being the victims of the sexual deviance of others – so becoming cuckolds. Women were similarly, though obviously not identically, labelled, but their overwhelming complaint was that they had been called a whore. Many and colourful are the adjectival variants that were attached. Laura Gowing provides a rich list – 'maggotie whore', 'shitten whore', 'scurvie fatt arst quean', 'gouty legged whore', 'daggletail quean', being only a few amongst very many.[10] Sometimes these outbursts fused into lengthy tirades. One woman's deposition in 1597 complained that she had been called 'Tinker whore, tinker's bitch, whore, quean, drab and scold, dronkard, drunken whore, drunken quean, drunken harlot, drunken drab, and drunken scold' and that her antagonist had 'said she was a noughtie, an evell and a badd and lewd woman'.[11]

Such remarks were levelled at women, more often than not at married women, and frequently by members of their own sex,

[9] Ingram, *Church Courts, Sex and Marriage*, 14–17, 27–9.
[10] Gowing, *Domestic Dangers*, 66–7.
[11] Sharpe, *Defamation and Sexual Slander*, 9.

although the proportion of women defendants was usually lower than the proportion of female plaintiffs. A number of historians, moreover, have drawn attention to the tendency for such cases increasingly to involve women as the seventeenth century approached and lengthened.[12]

'Slander suits in the church courts', Ingram writes, 'sprang from a society in which sexual reputation, "credit" or "honesty" was of considerable and probably growing practical importance and a major touchstone of respectability.'[13] This is a view with which many other historians have concurred. Gowing's examination of defamation suits in the consistory court of London and Foyster's study of such cases in both Durham and the Restoration court of arches provide the fullest discussions of what sexual insult involved for both men and women in Tudor and Stuart England, and why women in particular were prepared to go to law to clear their reputations of sexual slurs. Such actions hinged upon their not being the subject of gossip and on their maintenance of an unblemished sexual reputation. Not only did their own reputations depend on it, so also did those of their husbands. Men, Foyster tells us, 'were very sensitive to gossip about their wives' misbehaviour', since it implied a loss of male sexual control.[14]

Between them Ingram, Gowing and Foyster have provided a lengthy and plausible list of reasons to explain why people, and women in particular, were prepared to fight slanders and to defend their reputations in the church courts. Rumours had a way of sticking, even if they turned out to be untrue: servants might lose their places and find it difficult to obtain a new one; rumours of wanton behaviour might harm the marriage chances of the unmarried, including widows; discord might grow between husbands and wives; all might suffer 'shame and humiliation' from being the subject of gossip, and sexual delinquency was always open to the possibility of formal punishment or informal sanctions such as *charivaris*.

---

[12] Ibid., 27–8; Ingram, *Church Courts, Sex and Marriage*, 302–4; Gowing, *Domestic Dangers*, 12, 34, 37, 61; S. D. Amussen, *An Ordered Society: Gender and Class in Early Modern England* (1988), 101; E. A. Foyster, *Manhood in Early Modern England: Honour, Sex and Marriage* (1999), passim.

[13] Ingram, *Church Courts, Sex and Marriage*, 292.

[14] Gowing, *Domestic dangers*, 2, 101, 107, 128–9; Foyster, *Manhood*, 151.

But why should there apparently be increasing propensities for people to attempt to counter slanderous gossip by means of litigation? What lay behind this tendency has been the subject of some dispute. Some have seen it as a means whereby people protected themselves against the possibility of being prosecuted for sexual delinquencies such as adultery or fornication. Woodcock thought that the majority of plaintiffs in the consistory court of Canterbury before the Reformation were 'trying to clear themselves of charges which might lead to action being brought against them'.[15] Haigh's analysis of defamation suits in the consistory court of Chester supported this view. Although he was prepared to argue that illegitimacy, for example, was so common in sixteenth- and early seventeenth-century Lancashire and Cheshire that it incurred no local social stigma, the campaigns against sexual deviancy waged by the several ecclesiastical commissions that were imposed on the region led innocent inhabitants to seek to protect themselves against the risks of being cited in the courts by attempting through litigation to quash malicious rumours of sexual wrongdoing. Office prosecutions, Haigh argued, 'were nipped in the bud'.[16]

Not all historians have, however, accepted such arguments. Sharpe, for example, found the thesis 'unconvincing'. Why, he argued, should plaintiffs prefer the certain costs and trouble of litigation to the uncertain risks of being prosecuted? He also pointed out that the offending words were often the result of angry spontaneous outbursts rather than the sustained gossip that might do much more damage to a person's reputation.[17] Others, however, have found the argument more convincing. In truth, slanderous words probably derived from both types of situation – from sudden flare-ups between individuals and from longer-standing feuds and quarrels accompanied by whispering campaigns. What may appear to be a spontaneous quarrel resulting in intemperate words may actually have longer and more tangled roots. Ingram insists that by the early seventeenth century 'many defamation suits were paralleled by disciplinary proceedings for the offence specified in the slander, or were commenced when

---

[15] Woodcock, *Medieval Ecclesiastical Courts*, 88.
[16] Haigh, 'Slander and the church courts', 1–13.
[17] Sharpe, *Defamation and Sexual Slander*, 25–6.

such proceedings were under serious discussion'. Some plaintiffs, he insists also, feared that slander would lower their chances of success in other court or arbitration proceedings in which they were involved. About 30 per cent of the better-documented Wiltshire cases in the years 1615–29 revealed evidence of 'actual or seriously projected legal proceedings'.[18] Gowing has also noted the tendency for one set of legal proceedings to precipitate another: '30 per cent of defamation cases were connected to others at the same court, often involving both the same parties'.[19] Such findings suggest that defamation litigation mostly grew out of neighbourly disputes. Gowing argues that 'the kind of disputes that ended up in court ... arose initially over issues particular to crowded urban life'.[20] This, given that she examined London cases, is obviously true, but it gives insufficient recognition to the rise in defamation causes in jurisdictions other than the metropolitan ones.

The rise in numbers of disputes over defamation in diocese after diocese had several causes. In some instances the increase was kick-started by switches in court procedure, less profitable office prosecutions giving way to more profitable instance ones. Everywhere the rise was also underpinned by demographic expansion. Even without an increasing propensity either to slander or to litigate in response, this could be expected to double volumes between the 1530s and the 1630s. Demographic expansion, however, created its own tensions and strains that were likely to engender communal conflict. One example of this is that the population rise appears to have been accompanied by decreasing nuptiality and by rising bastardy levels, making extra-marital sex even more of a social issue than it already was. This era was also characterised by increasing rates of prosecution and of litigation in both spiritual and secular courts, and especially in the royal courts in London. 'On the eve of the civil wars', Brooks writes, 'there was twice as much litigation in King's Bench and Common Pleas as there had been in 1580, perhaps fourteen times more than in the 1490s.'[21] Increases in litigation in one tribunal were likely, as we have noted, to spark off cases elsewhere. Neighbourhood quarrels,

---

[18] Ingram, *Church Courts, Sex and Marriage*, 307–8.
[19] Gowing, *Domestic Dangers*, 133.   [20] Ibid., 22.
[21] C. W. Brooks, *Pettyfoggers and Vipers of the Commonwealth* (1986), 54.

whether ephemeral or long-standing, were likely to produce abusive outbursts. Disputes over relatively trivial matters could easily lead to intemperate accusations being flung between angry men and women. Slanderous words were often couched in sexual terms because sexual abuse was the language most likely to cause offence.[22] A dispute over church seating in an Oxford church led to a freeman's wife, Barbara Nicholles, jostling with Margery Hopkins, warning her that she would sit upon her lap if she didn't move, and 'thereupon grewe Further woordes of inconvenience bewtene theime, as whore and basterd and such lyke'.[23] A witness in an early seventeenth-century London case attested that she did not think 'that Phebe Cartwright by calleing Margerie Hipwell queane did meane that she had committed fornicacon or adultery or plaied the whore with any man but only spake the same wordes in her anger'.[24] Protestantism's stern stance against sexual deviancy must have made terms such as 'whore', 'queane' and 'jade' even more potent weapons of personal abuse than they had been previously among many people who were perhaps increasingly putting a premium upon respectability. Taking the abuser to court was not only a way of demonstrating that respectability; it was also a way of exacting recantation and retribution. The abuser, if found guilty, had to bear legal costs and undergo a humiliating penance. Even though only a minority of cases got as far as this, there was satisfaction to be derived from citing an abuser to appear before a court, making him or her incur some costs as a consequence, before perhaps accepting arbitration and a peaceful settlement.[25]

[22] The 'language of whoredom was a powerful weapon of insult': Foyster, *Manhood*, 154.
[23] E. R. Brinkworth, *The Archdeacon's Court: Liber Actorum 1584*, ii, 171.
[24] Gowing, *Domestic Dangers*, 59.
[25] J. A. Sharpe, '"Such disagreement betwyx neighbours": litigation and human relations in early modern England', in *Disputes and Settlements: Law and Human Relations in the West*, ed. J. Bossy (1983), 175–87.

6

MARITAL SUITS AND MARRIAGE LICENCES

If the officials who administered the law in the English church courts in the sixteenth and early seventeenth centuries had had to rely on marital causes to maintain their incomes, they would quickly have become eligible for poor relief. Such causes, as we shall see, were rare at the outset and became rarer still as the period progressed. They merit discussion, however, because of this increasing rarity and because issues relating to both marriage and divorce played important strategic parts later in the drama relating to the dismemberment of church court jurisdiction in the eighteenth and nineteenth centuries.

Before the Reformation the law relating to the making of marriages and their dissolution was Roman canon law, and after the Reformation it was continued as the 'King's ecclesiastical law of England', the old canon law modified to a certain extent by statutes passed from 1534 onwards to the calling of the Long Parliament and the beginnings of the Revolution of the 1640s. In both eras – pre- and post-Reformation – that law was administered by the ecclesiastical and not the temporal courts. The latter had from the mid-twelfth century onwards, in Pollock and Maitland's words, 'no doctrine of marriage'. If, as was sometimes the case in property suits, the temporal courts were asked questions in which the validity of a marriage was an issue, they would refer the matter to an ecclesiastical court.[1] Questions relating to the validity of marriages were not always easy to answer because of the nature of the law relating to the making of marriage. Although the church preferred eligible couples to be married before a priest, in church, in parishes where they dwelt, and at prescribed

---

[1] F. Pollock and F. W. Maitland, *The History of English Law*, 2nd edn (1898), ii, 374.

times and seasons, many couples obstinately refused to obey these rules, coupling themselves in private in irregular ways. When one party or the other subsequently backed out of the agreement, it was the church courts that had to decide whether the agreement they had made was a marriage or not, the acid tests being whether consent had been rendered in words of the present tense and whether it could be proved by two reliable witnesses to the event.[2] Similarly, while there are occasional examples before the Restoration era of parliament overriding the ecclesiastical law and allowing a second marriage to take place whilst a first spouse was still alive, it was the ecclesiastical courts that dissolved marriages through annulling them or effectively dissolved them by granting legal separations. Both processes were often confusingly termed divorces, though divorce as we now know it did not exist.[3]

Although marital suits were generally reserved to the higher ecclesiastical courts, the consistory rather than the archdeaconry courts, one can find a full range of suits being entertained wherever such causes were contested. Espousals were adjudged to be valid or not, individuals sought to compel their spouses to live with them or not to do so, and marriages were annulled on the grounds of consanguinity, affinity, prior marriage and non-consummation. In the central Middle Ages, moreover, marital suits appear to have occupied a prominent part in the business of the ecclesiastical courts. Approximately one-third of the suits heard in the consistory court of Canterbury in the two years 1373 and 1374 were matrimonial ones, and approximately one-quarter of the instance business before the Ely consistory court in the years 1374–82 revolved around real or alleged marriages, 89 of these 122 cases arising from clandestine contracts.[4]

Divorces – annulments and separations – were comparatively rare, being greatly outnumbered by cases revolving around real or alleged marital contracts. 'By far the most common matrimonial cause in the medieval church courts', Helmholz writes in his

---

[2] Much of the subject matter in this chapter is discussed more fully in my *Clandestine Marriage in England 1500–1850* (1995).
[3] The best introduction to the early history of such actions is L. Stone, *Road to Divorce: England 1530–1837* (1990).
[4] Woodcock, *Medieval Ecclesiastical Courts*, 85; M. M. Sheehan, 'The formation and stability of marriage in fourteenth-century England: evidence of an Ely register', *Mediaeval Studies* 33 (1971), 234.

authoritative account of this subject, 'was the suit brought to enforce a marriage contract.' Ninety-eight cases relating to marriage were brought into the consistory court of Canterbury from 1372–5, and seventy-eight of these were petitions to establish and enforce alleged marriage contracts. The same pattern, though not identical proportions, was to be found not only in Ely in 1374–82 but also in Lichfield in 1465–8 and at Rochester in 1437–40.[5] The prominence of such cases is not surprising, given that consent was often rendered in private rather than in public. As Helmholz pointed out: 'Of the forty-one marriages contracted by words of present consent and found in the Canterbury deposition book of 1411–20, fully thirty-eight took place at home or in some other private place. Only three were made in church.'[6] The fact that in these court cases clandestine marriages appeared to outnumber regular unions does not necessarily show that in medieval England irregular marriages greatly outnumbered regular unions. What it does show is that these private unions were more likely to give rise to subsequent dispute and thus end in litigation.

From perhaps the fourteenth century onwards a decline appears to have taken place in the number of marital causes coming into the ecclesiastical courts. Discussing developments in the later Middle Ages, Helmholz drew attention to the fact that 'both absolutely and comparatively, matrimonial suits occupied a smaller place in the Church courts as time went on.' This opinion was based on what was happening in the later Middle Ages in the consistory courts of Canterbury, Rochester and Lichfield.[7] This tendency for the volume of marital causes to decrease continued into the sixteenth and early seventeenth centuries. By this later date they represented in many dioceses a tiny proportion of consistory court business. Marchant, for example, found thirty to forty cases a year being heard in the consistory court of York in three sample years between 1571 and 1592, but this fell to four to seven cases a year in three sample years between 1626 and 1639. In the diocese of Norwich he found nine matrimonial cases in the period 1509–10, but only one in 1623–4, and none at all in 1636–7.[8] Similar trends have been recorded in London: about thirty

---

[5] R. H. Helmholz, *Marriage Litigation in Medieval England* (1974), 25.
[6] Ibid., 28. [7] Ibid., 166–7.
[8] Marchant, *The Church under the Law*, 16, 20, 62.

marriage contract cases a year entered the London consistory
court in the 1570s, but only about nine such cases a year by the
1620s; about eight to ten 'separation and bigamy' cases a year were
to be found there in the late sixteenth century, but by the 1630s
there was often no more than one a year.[9]

As these examples suggest, the decline in marriage business was
most marked in spousal or contract causes: annulment and
separation causes appeared to have suffered much less of a contraction. Bigamy cases may have disappeared from the ecclesiastical courts after bigamy was made a felony in 1604, but why
spousal cases experienced this long-run contraction is more pro-
blematic. Helmholz thought that the decline experienced during
the Middle Ages was due to the success that the church enjoyed in
imposing its own vision of how marriage should ideally be entered
into – publicly, before witnesses, in church and with the ceremony
being conducted by a priest. This left, he argued, less ambiguity,
'less need for marriage litigation to sort out ensuing tangles'.[10]
Others, such as Houlbrooke and Ingram, have taken the same
line, lengthening its influence to take in the subsequent, post-
medieval decline. 'Over the centuries', wrote Ingram, 'there was a
growing acceptance of the principle that solemnization in church
was the only satisfactory mode of entry into marriage.'[11]

A number of developments may indeed have persuaded some
couples that fully regular ceremonies were to be preferred to folk
or customary ones. One was the attitude of the common law,
which from the time of Bracton in the thirteenth century had
come to insist that no widow could claim her dower or jointure –
the husband's provision for her widowhood – unless she had been
endowed 'at the church door'.[12] The institution, under Thomas
Cromwell in 1538, of parochial registration of baptisms, marriages
and burials may have given a further boost to such tendencies.
Also, encouraged by the Statute of Frauds of 1677, common and
equity lawyers came to insist on 'some Memorandum or Note ...
in writing' as proof that contracts had in fact been agreed.[13] But
one must not overstress the influence of such developments.

---

[9] Gowing, *Domestic Dangers*, 142, 183.
[10] Helmholz, *Marriage Litigation*, 167.
[11] Ingram, *Church Courts, Sex and Marriage*, 193.
[12] Pollock and Maitland, *History of English Law*, ii, 374.
[13] 29 Charles II, c. 3.

Parochial registration was far from universal, especially in its first half-century, and it became noticeably deficient again in Restoration England. Such legalities were anyway always more likely to influence far-seeing, property-owning parents than love-struck young people eager to taste the delights of wedlock.

It has also been argued that pressure to marry in a regular fashion was encouraged in the sixteenth and early seventeenth centuries by the church court authorities pursuing aggressive office prosecutions against sexual incontinence in all its forms and clandestine marriages, in the latter case prosecuting not only the couples concerned but also those who witnessed such events.[14] The problem here is that such prosecuting zeal may have been a late development, intensifying particularly from the late sixteenth century onwards, well after the decline in spousal cases had announced itself. Also this rise in office causes varied in its intensity from area to area, depending on the attitudes of local communities, local churchmen, and also on actual levels of sexual incontinence and bastardy.[15] Although there was no uniformity in these respects, levels of pre-nuptial pregnancy were high in the second half of the sixteenth century. Many couples were clearly coming together sexually after the exchange of informal promises to marry, indicating that the moral dictates of the church were not being obeyed by a substantial proportion of newly married couples. The best that can be said for this explanatory factor is that office prosecutions may have driven home a lesson that informal matches carried dangers and that church marriages were more secure. These prosecuting tendencies did not survive into the Restoration era with anything like the same force, however, and once again clandestine marriages became a noticeable problem, though by this stage most were at least being conducted by priests.[16]

Other reasons have been put forward to account for this decline in spousal cases. It has been argued that such disputes were related to female age at marriage: the older the woman, the more courtships she was likely to have experienced, and the more courtships, the greater the likelihood of disputable contracts. Female age at

[14] Helmholz, *Roman Canon Law*, 71–2, provides Elizabethan and Jacobean examples of such prosecutions.
[15] These matters are further examined in chapter 7 below.
[16] Outhwaite, *Clandestine Marriage*, 19–26, 44–5.

marriage, in turn, was shaped by the opportunities open to women in the labour market: the better their economic prospects, the later they married.[17] But can an argument of this sort explain why fewer disputes took place in the hundred and fifty years after the Black Death of 1348, when opportunities for women to enter the labour market probably improved, and go on to explain the further decline in spousal disputes through the following 150 years to the mid-seventeenth century? Demographic trends probably did turn the balance of economic advantage against females in the later fifteenth century, and continued to do so in the Tudor and early Stuart eras. There is some evidence of a marked decline in nuptiality in the hundred years before 1650.[18] It would be unusual for a decline in nuptiality to coexist with a falling trend in marriage ages, and the latter would be required to corroborate this sort of explanation. The long-run decline in spousal cases seen in many different ecclesiastical jurisdictions appears to have coexisted with divergent demographic and economic trends. The century or so before 1520 was very different from the 120 years that followed.

Another suggestion that has been made is that this sort of business was squeezed out of the ecclesiastical courts by the expansion of other, more profitable categories of cases. Houlbrooke argued that 'matrimonial suits as a class were considerably less profitable to the men who ran them than were other types of cause', such as tithe and testamentary ones, both of which grew remarkably in the sixteenth and early seventeenth centuries. Ingram has supported this, arguing that 'defamation causes and many matrimonial suits were often straightforward and therefore speedy, while tithe actions dragged on'.[19] Apart from doubts as to whether this sort of explanation can be pushed back into the later medieval past to explain the fall in spousals cases that occurred then, one must also point out that those supposedly unprofitable defamation causes rose remarkably in volume from the mid-sixteenth century onwards. Moreover, no direct evidence is forthcoming to support the notion that potential plaintiffs were

[17] J. P. Goldberg, *Women, Work, and Life Cycle in a Medieval Economy* (1992), 203–79.

[18] E. A. Wrigley and R. Schofield, *The Population History of England 1541–1871* (1981), 421–30.

[19] Houlbrooke, *Church Courts and the People*, 65; Ingram, *Church Courts, Sex and Marriage*, 50.

turned away by court officials for mercenary motives. Plaintiffs may have been discouraged from bringing spousal complaints to court, but not because officials were turning away unprofitable business.

Two developments take on significance in this respect. Whilst the abandonment of suits had always been a prominent feature of instance litigation, it has been suggested, first, that abandonment of marriage suits became ever more common in the course of the sixteenth and early seventeenth centuries, and, second, that in that decreasing proportion of cases where judicial sentences were given, they tended increasingly to go against plaintiffs. Ingram argues that this reflected growing judicial impatience with the law relating to the formation of marriage, with the judges demanding ever-higher standards of proof that marriage promises had indeed been made: 'ecclesiastical lawyers', he writes, 'were, in practice, gradually turning their backs on the ancient law of spousals and coming to regard unsolemnised contracts as well-nigh unenforceable'.[20] Whatever the reasons for this development, the fact of its occurrence must have made disgruntled suitors reluctant to press their point at law. The increasing unwillingness of judges to give decisions in favour of ill-witnessed and unsolemnised unions meant that such suits were not worth the trouble and expense involved. Suitors not only brought in fewer suits, but also increasingly abandoned those few that they did bring.

While spousals causes shrank, there was no compensating expansion in other types of matrimonial business. Divorce actions – those for separation and annulment – were never very common, despite the claims of an earlier generation of scholars who argued that the canon law provided abundant opportunities for couples to part from one another. It was not until serious work on ecclesiastical court records began that historians realised the error of their ways. It is hard now to disagree with Helmholz's judgement that 'the most striking fact about divorce litigation in medieval England is how little of it there was'.[21] Starting from a low point in the later middle ages, such actions appear to have become even rarer in many consistory courts by the later sixteenth and early

---

[20] Ingram, 'Spousals litigation in England, 1350–1640', 51–3; Ingram, *Church Courts, Sex and Marriage*, 206–9.
[21] Helmholz, *Marriage Litigation*, 74.

seventeenth centuries.[22] Those consistory courts which were geographically not too distant from the metropolis may have lost some of this profitable business to the ecclesiastical lawyers in Doctors' Commons who operated in the London church courts.[23] Thus we find the archdeacon of St Albans complaining in the early seventeenth century that much of the instance business in his court had been drawn to London, where cases could be concluded more rapidly, if only because there were more sittings there per year.[24] Gowing argues, however, that far from there being a rise in such litigation in the London consistory court, the number of divorce actions actually fell, although this judgement sits at odds with an earlier graph showing a level fluctuating between three and five cases a year from 1570 to 1639.[25] In the light of what happened in the later seventeenth century, however, this question of the degree to which business before 1640 was being siphoned off to the proctors and advocates in Doctors' Commons merits further investigation.

Marriage litigation thus fell to insignificant levels by the 1630s. The licensing activities of the ecclesiastical authorities, however, expanded considerably at the same time. This was especially true in relation to marriage licences, the issue of which greatly exceeded other types of dispensation. An extant licence book for the chancery court at York, covering a period of twenty-one months in the years 1618–20, reveals that thirty-nine curates' licences were issued, as were fifty-two schoolmasters' licences, but these numbers were dwarfed by the 746 marriage licences issued in the same period.[26] By 1635–6 nearly £80 or 28 per cent of the income of the registrar of the consistory court of Norwich was derived from the sale of marriage licences, exceeding the income he derived from probates and administrations.[27] By this time the chancellor and registrar at York were each receiving an estimated £140 a year from the sale of marriage licences, and even in a small jurisdiction, such as the archdeaconry of Suffolk, the registrar was

---

[22] Ingram, *Church Courts, Sex and Marriage*, 172–3.

[23] Doctors' Commons housed the London civilians, the lawyers who practised in the court of arches, the consistory court of the Bishop of London, the Prerogative Court of Canterbury and the High Court of Admiralty.

[24] R. Peters, 'The administration of the archdeaconry of St Albans, 1580–1625', *JEH* 13 (1962), 66.

[25] Gowing, *Domestic Dangers*, 29–30, 81.

[26] Marchant, *The Church under the Law*, 81–2.   [27] Ibid., 15.

earning an estimated £45 a year.[28] The rewards at York pale into insignificance when compared with the estimated £450 a year that the bishop of London's chancellor was netting from such sales by 1640.[29]

Marriage licences took two forms. The first, and most important, was the ordinary ecclesiastical licence dispensing with the calling of banns, which, if an additional fee was paid, also allowed couples to be married during the prohibited seasons. The canons of 1604 insisted, however, that couples should marry in the parish where one or the other party to the match normally resided. The second type of licence was the archbishop of Canterbury's special licence, permitting a couple to be married at any convenient time and place. This was an expensive dispensation, issued in very small numbers and supposedly only to the 'quality'. The figures of sales and profits that we have noted derive from the first type of licence, issued by the chancellors and registrars of those who had powers of ecclesiastical jurisdiction within particular districts.

The sale of marriage licences was clearly a growth industry, though over the country as a whole it is one that is still remarkably uncharted. An exception has to be made for London, where Boulton has revealed something of the astonishing surge taking place in marriage by licence in the early seventeenth century. Whereas an average of 82 licences a year were purchased from the bishop of London's officers in the 1560s and 157 a year in the 1570s, this had climbed to 925 a year by the 1630s. But, because of peculiar and overlapping jurisdictions, Londoners bought licences from many different authorities, such as the archbishop of Canterbury's faculty office as well as the office of the dean and chapter of Westminster. We know this because the register of the parish of St Dunstan Stepney records the origins of the licences and the numbers of such weddings in that parish. Whereas there were 423 marriages by licence in the years 1621–5, 745 took place in the years 1636–40. Similarly, the number of marriages by licence in the parish of St Gregory by St Paul grew from 138 in the period 1601–5 to 1207 in the years 1631–5.[30] Although the rush to marry in this fashion was perhaps most powerfully felt in

---

[28] Ibid., 29–30, 81.

[29] J. Boulton, 'Itching after private marryings? Marriage customs in seventeenth-century London', *London Journal* 16 (1991), 28.

[30] Ibid., 15–34.

London, it was not a trend confined to the metropolis. If surviving marriage bonds and allegations are any guide, then at least sixteen licences of the archdeacon of Nottingham were issued in 1590, and thirty-six in 1600. By 1640, however, the number had grown to 218.[31] The number of licences issued in the archdeaconry of Suffolk in 1616–17 was 137; by 1636–7 the number had expanded to 264.[32]

The reasons behind this extraordinary growth have been explored elsewhere.[33] One important one was that the stipulation that such couples should marry in a parish where one or the other party to the union normally resided was widely flouted. Couples used these licences to marry in fashionable churches or in places where they were not known. It was for this reason that the practice can legitimately be called 'licensed clandestinity'. Another reason was that the cost of licences probably lagged behind the growth of nominal incomes, especially in places where there was competition between licence providers for what was clearly profitable custom. The ecclesiastical authorities faced a considerable dilemma. If they were to obey the canons about residence, then the trade in licences and their own profits would diminish. There was also the danger that if 'licensed clandestinity' had been curbed, unlicensed clandestinity would flourish and people would marry without either banns or licences in even greater numbers. As it was, little or nothing was done before the 1640s to curb this practice. The trade, to the consternation of parents and the disgust of Puritans, continued to flourish.

---

[31] R. B. Outhwaite, 'Sweetapple of Fledborough and clandestine marriage in eighteenth-century Nottinghamshire', *Transactions of the Thoroton Society of Nottinghamshire for 1990* 94 (1991), 43–4.

[32] Marchant, *The Church under the Law*, 29–30.

[33] In Boulton, 'Itching' and Outhwaite, *Clandestine Marriage*.

7

OFFICE CAUSES

The width of the church's jurisdiction with respect to discipline has already been noted. It was empowered to correct the behaviour of both clerics and laymen, not only to impose spiritual orthodoxy amongst them but also to regulate their morals and attempt to ensure social harmony in the communities in which they lived. Visitation articles reminded clergymen and churchwardens of their responsibilities in these respects and urged them to present for correction those whose behaviour fell short of acceptable standards. Most, but not all, of this correction was undertaken in the lower courts, the archdeaconry and commissary ones, during their periodic visitations of particular circuits. Offenders were named, mostly by churchwardens or by apparitors, and were summoned to appear at a particular time and place, where their cases were usually, but not invariably, dealt with summarily by the presiding judge.

The corrective work of the church courts increased after the Reformation, partly to impose new religious orthodoxies and partly to fill the regulatory vacuum that was created by both the ending of auricular confession and the decline in levels of activity in manorial, hundred and borough courts.[1] Hill noted that in this period 'visitations became more frequent and more thorough', precipitating parliamentary complaints against them at the end of the sixteenth century and the beginning of the seventeenth century.[2] Churchwardens became legally obliged to present written 'bills of detections' to ecclesiastical visitors and were sometimes prosecuted for their failure to do so.[3] Between 1573 and 1603, the

---

[1] Houlbrooke, 'The decline of ecclesiastical jurisdiction', 247; Helmholz, *Roman Canon Law*, 113; McIntosh, *Controlling Misbehaviour*, 134.
[2] Hill, *Society and Puritanism*, 300.   [3] Helmholz, *Roman Canon Law*, 106–7.

number of office cases before the archdeaconry court of Salisbury nearly doubled.[4] Whereas Archbishop Grindal's visitation of the diocese of York in 1575 produced charges against 1,200 individuals, Archbishop Neile's in 1636 led to accusations being levelled against over 5,000 people.[5] Certainly in many jurisdictions the volume of corrective activity seems to have increased between 1530 and 1640, perhaps reaching its apogee in the later 1630s, when the see of Canterbury was occupied by William Laud.[6]

The pattern of offences brought to the attention of the correction courts varied from district to district and from one court to the next, but some consistent features emerge. The range of offences punished was invariably wide: churchwardens were presented for neglecting their responsibilities; clergymen for improper performance of their duties; laymen for failing to attend church, working or playing games on holy days, or for blatant recusancy; couples for clandestine marriages or for not cohabitating; men and women for remaining obstinately excommunicate, a state usually occasioned by their failure to obey earlier court dictates. In the deanery of Doncaster, 416 presentments were made in 1619, a number embracing all these offences. Ninety-three of these were presentments of laymen for playing games or drinking instead of attending church services; some of them were for outright recusancy. No fewer than 206 of this total, however, were presented for sexual offences. There were 407 presentments in the same deanery in 1633, when a drive appears to have been in operation against religious nonconformity and a perceived neglect of duty by clerics and churchwardens. But 90 of these 407 presentments – still the largest single number – were for sexual immorality.[7] It was the prominence of this category of business in the lower courts that gave them the popular titles of the 'bawdy courts' or 'bum courts'.[8] This concentration on sexual offences was an enduring feature of these bodies, as readers of *The Canterbury Tales* will recall. It was said of Chaucer's archdeacon that he 'could boast; that lechery was what he punished most'. Out of 158 charges brought at the London consistory court in 1474,

---

[4] Ingram, *Church Courts, Sex and Marriage*, 69.   [5] Ibid., 13.
[6] Marchant, *The Church under the Law*, 219, 230; Houlbrooke, *Church Courts and the People*, 27; Ingram, *Church Courts, Sex and Marriage*, 69.
[7] Marchant, *The Church under the Law*, 219.
[8] Ingram, *Church Courts, Sex and Marriage*, 17–8.

110 were 'sexual in character'. In the four years from Christmas 1496 to Christmas 1500, 1,854 persons were cited before the commissary court of London, one half of whom, archdeacon Hale told us, 'were charged with the crimes of adultery and others of like nature'. 'The correction of sexual lapses', says Houlbrooke, 'took up more of the time of the church courts in these dioceses [Norwich and Winchester] in the period of the Reformation than any other branch of their *ex officio* activities.' Forty-three per cent of the office causes pursued in the Peterborough consistory court in 1630 and 1632 were for 'lapses in moral behaviour', as were over a third of those in the Northampton archdeaconry court.[9]

The range of sexual lapses that were punished was extraordinarily wide, though some categories were distinguished by their extreme rarity. Not many men, for example, were brought into court for sodomy or bestiality, perhaps only partly because such practices became felonies triable at common law after 1534.[10] But even before this, active homosexuality was rarely punished: only one among over 21,000 defendants was tried for sodomy in the London courts between 1470 and 1516.[11] Similarly, very few women were charged with abortion, which was a sin but not a temporal crime in this period.[12] Infanticide brought about by 'overlaying' of babies was also rarely encountered, even before infanticide became a statutory crime in 1624.[13] Incest cases were more common, but still not very common. The twenty-eight prosecutions for incest that were launched in Wiltshire between 1615 and 1629 were dwarfed by the hundreds involving other sexual offences. Only four of these twenty-eight cases were for marrying proscribed kin, a figure that is perhaps explained by the fact that the prohibited relationships were by this time well established and involved relatively close kin, most of whom would be known to each other, as well as to the wider communities in

---

[9] Woodcock, *Medieval Ecclesiastical Courts*, 79; W. Hale, *A Series of Precedents and Proceedings in Criminal Causes* (1847), liii; Houlbrooke, *Church Courts and the People*, 75; M. D. W. Jones, 'The ecclesiastical courts before and after the Civil War: the office jurisdiction in the dioceses of Oxford and Peterborough, 1630–1675', unpublished Oxford B Litt, 1977, 17.

[10] Ingram, *Church Courts, Sex and Marriage*, 152.

[11] Wunderli, *London Church Courts*, 83.

[12] Houlbrooke, *Church Courts and the People*, 78.

[13] K. Wrightson, 'Infanticide in European history', *Criminal Justice History* 3 (1982), 5–6.

which they dwelt. Most cases of incest involved sexual activity within the prohibited relationships, though some were presented on the 'fame' of such activity, simply because in the cramped dwellings in which the bulk of the population lived, kin of the opposite sex sometimes shared their bed space.[14]

Far more men and women were charged with adultery – sexual activity between a man and a woman, one or both of whom was already married to someone else. This may have been the most commonly cited sexual offence in late fifteenth-century London.[15] By the middle of the sixteenth century, however, we find this offence greatly overtaken in its incidence by that of fornication – the offence of sexual activity with an unmarried person. Given that one party could be married and the other not, it is hardly surprising that the terms 'adultery' and 'fornication' were sometimes used interchangeably and imprecisely.[16] Fornication was itself divisible, depending seemingly on whether it was consequent on betrothal and followed by marriage to the sexual partner. Most cases of pre-nuptial fornication appear to have been the product of that well-established English custom of couples 'jumping the gun', a practice that was given additional force by the ambiguities that were inherent in the English law of marriage.[17] This state of affairs did nothing to discourage couples wishing to begin a physical relationship after promises to wed had been privately exchanged between them. Early in the period, pre-nuptial incontinence seems to have been variably treated in the courts. It was more often punished in Winchester than it was, for example, in Norwich, where the commissary frequently dismissed couples who had been cited for this offence.[18] The most authoritative discussion that we have of this subject insists, however, that 'the policy of the church courts became increasingly rigorous towards the end of the sixteenth and in the early seventeenth century'.[19]

---

[14] Ingram, *Church Courts, Sex and Marriage*, 222, 238, 246–9.
[15] Wunderli, *London Church Courts*, 85.
[16] C. Haigh, *Reformation and Resistance in Tudor Lancashire* (1975), 49–50; Ingram, *Church Courts, Sex and Marriage*, 239.
[17] See above pp. 47–50.
[18] Houlbrooke, *Church Courts and the People*, 78.
[19] Ingram, *Church Courts, Sex and Marriage*, 221.

This increasing rigour may have had ideological origins. There undoubtedly was a growing volume of condemnation of sex outside of marriage, stemming particularly from Protestant moralists and divines.[20] Nothing was better calculated to raise the temperature of the 'hotter sort' of Protestants than other people's sexual misdemeanours. But it is more likely that this condemnation was a product of social and economic forces, rather than purely ideological ones. Demographers have established that bridal pregnancy rates rose gradually from the mid-sixteenth century, peaking at around 25 per cent between 1580 and 1620. This rate measures the proportion of all fertile brides who baptised a live child within eight months of a church wedding.[21] The number of women who were sexually active before marriage must have been greater than this figure suggests, however, given that sexual activity often began with betrothal, that not all couples were fertile, that not all coition results in pregnancy, that not all pregnancies come to term and that not all babies were baptised, or, if they were, were not baptised promptly. Pre-nuptial pregnancy might have been forgiven, despite the increasingly strident strictures of moralists, if all of these women had gone on to marry, but not all managed to get a man to the altar. The result was bastardy and the possibility that the parish might have to support both mother and child.

Recent work on baptism registers has established what must be seen as the minimum scale of bastardy in early modern England. From a level of 2.3 per cent in the decade 1551–60, the bastardy ratio[22] gradually rose to a peak level of 4.3 per cent in the years 1601–10, before falling back to 2.5 per cent in the 1640s. Some regions, such as the north-west of England, had distinctly higher levels than these national average figures: there the bastardy ratio reached 8.4 per cent in the years 1601–10.[23] Some regions, conversely, had low levels, though the direction of trends tended to be similar in most of them. Rising rates of fornication and bastardy

---

[20] K. Thomas, 'The Puritans and adultery: the Act of 1650 reconsidered', in *Puritans and Revolutionaries*, ed. D. Pennington and K. Thomas (1978), 99–111.

[21] Wrigley and Schofield, *Population History of England*, 254; R. Adair, *Courtship, Illegitimacy and Marriage in Early Modern England* (1996), 100.

[22] The ratio expresses the baptism of illegitimate children as a percentage of all baptisms.

[23] Adair, *Courtship*, 48–63.

may well have been linked with declining rates of nuptiality – increasing proportions of those eligible to marry were not doing so in the later sixteenth and early seventeenth centuries.[24] Behind this trend lurked powerful economic forces: declining real wages, perhaps growing underemployment, a labour market tilting against women, and increasing difficulties in amassing dowries. With a larger number and proportion of sexually capable but unmarried adults around, it would not be surprising to find some increase in extra-marital sexual activity. For women especially, such activity was generally a prelude to marriage – a sign that something akin to a promise of marriage had been exchanged. Some women, desperate to find partners, may have used their sexuality, and resultant pregnancy, as a gambit in the marriage game. It was not, of course, a risk-free strategy. Men were not always willing or able, in what were increasingly difficult times, to uphold such promises, leaving their partners holding (quite literally) the baby.

It is hard to resist the argument that the rise in office cases in the hundred years after 1540 largely reflected an increasing number of presentments for sexual offences and that the latter were tied to rising tides of fornication, adultery and bastardy. Because these were not solitary pursuits and because couples were often presented, there was no very marked imbalance in the male–female ratio of presentments.[25] The slight preponderance of women presented for fornication is to be explained by the fact that it was usually pregnancy that precipitated their citation and that pregnancy was frequently visible. Maternity, it has often been said, is a matter of fact; paternity, a matter of repute. Because the social costs of bastardy could be high, pressures were imposed on unmarried women to reveal the names of the fathers of their babies. Midwives, as we have noted, were instructed to press such questions during childbirth, the point at which a woman was most likely to yield up such an answer. Some midwives threatened to leave the woman in childbed unattended unless she offered up the name of the father.[26] The Sussex woman who after giving birth to twins told the court that 'Henry Smith now of Horsham and

[24] Wrigley and Schofield, *Population History of England*, 421–30.
[25] Jones, 'Ecclesiastical courts', 185.
[26] For an example, see Houlbrooke, *Church Courts and the People*, 261.

William Walter late of Rusper are fathers, and that they lay with her, one one night and the other the next' was obviously diversifying her paternity portfolio.[27] The magistrates, when faced with differentiating between several possible putative fathers, sometimes forced all the suspects to pay their share of maintenance costs.[28] Bastardy was the offence least likely to be overlooked and most likely to lead to a court presentment.[29] It could also reduce the levels of tolerance exhibited in communities and could lead consequently to other sexual delinquencies being sought out and punished. Here, however, it was the most blatant offences and offenders who were likely to be cited to appear before the courts.

Sudden surges in prosecutions, and communal disparities in numbers of presentments, could be due to the enthusiasm of ecclesiastical judges, apparitors and local churchwardens for policies of sexual 'zero tolerance', but behind many of these differences, and behind the upward drift of numbers, lurks the increasing incidence of bastardy. 'Economics, not morality', the historian of bastardy in early seventeenth-century Somerset insists, 'was the prime consideration of the parish', and in that county, the county magistrates began to whip those bastard-bearers who were brought before them 'as a matter of course'.[30] 'In large measure', Ingram has concluded, 'the parish-by-parish distribution of cases simply reflected the actual incidence of illegitimacy, which in turn was a function of a complex set of variables of which population size and density and the scale of local poverty were probably the most important.'[31] Here also, it seems, we have a facet of court business that was profoundly affected by demographic expansion in the sixteenth and early seventeenth centuries.

[27] Hair, *Before the Bawdy Court*, 94.
[28] G. R. Quaife, *Wanton Wenches and Wayward Wives* (1979), 234.
[29] Ingram, *Church Courts, Sex and Marriage*, 261.
[30] Quaife, *Wanton Wenches*, 218, 245.
[31] Ingram, *Church Courts, Sex and Marriage*, 275.

8

THE ROOTS OF EXPANSION AND CRITICAL VOICES

The discussion in the previous chapters has revealed a number of important characteristics of the business of the ecclesiastical courts in the hundred years after the 1530s. One is that the instance side of their business, especially in the higher courts, was much more important than the office side. Litigation, in other words, was more important than prosecution. This is true in relation both to the numerical incidence of cases and to the profits that the courts and their officials derived from the system. Private litigation lasted longer than office prosecutions. It often spawned large quantities of paper and parchment, every piece of which had to be paid for by the parties engaged in the suit. It is abundantly clear, moreover, that the instance side was dominated by tithe, testamentary and defamation litigation. Without these three classes of action there would have been little instance business to discuss, because some formerly prominent classes, such as matrimonial litigation, had shrunk to insignificant proportions. But the rise in the business of the courts was not totally dependent on these three classes. Office prosecutions also expanded, albeit spasmodically, and apparitors and court scribes received some financial benefit from this, through the production and service of citations and absolutions. Chancellors and registrars, on the other hand, stumbled into an increasingly profitable trade in marriage licences, the sale of which, as we have seen, was burgeoning from the later sixteenth century onwards. All of these things contributed to that 'rise of the ecclesiastical courts' delineated in earlier chapters.

In exploring why this expansion occurred, explanations have been offered for the growth of particular classes of business. It is now time to consider some of the common elements in this experience and to assess some general explanations of this rise, particularly as offered by specialists in the field.

Even before the Reformation move towards professionalisation and laicisation of the administration of these courts was under way, the judges, proctors and registrars were not always clerics. The majority of the judges and advocates practising in the church courts of the diocese of Canterbury in the later Middle Ages were the products of the universities, trained in canon law. Later, as part of the attack on Rome, Thomas Cromwell suppressed the teaching of canon law in the universities. Canon law, the law that guided the ecclesiastical courts, was not itself abolished. It remained in existence, confirming those laws which, as the 1534 Act for the Submission of the Clergy stated, 'be not contrarient or repugnant to law, statutes and customs of this realm'. Hencefor-ward those who practised in these courts had either to learn their canon law on the job and by private study or by studying canon law in some foreign university. They could not graduate in canon law in England. But graduates from Oxford and Cambridge continued to infiltrate these courts, taking over many of the highest and most profitable positions.[1] They were, however, graduates in civil law – effectively Roman law. An Act of 1545 made laymen and doctors of civil law eligible for appointment as ecclesiastical judges, speeding up these tendencies for laicisation and professionalisa-tion. The civilians, as they were known, organised themselves into a gild or college – Doctors' Commons in London, a body that dominated the important ecclesiastical and civil law courts in the metropolis – and the clergy came to be excluded from membership of that body.[2] Although men in holy orders continued as bishops' chancellors, their deputies and others who operated as judges in the courts tended increasingly to be lay lawyers. If they were laymen, holding no benefices or other ecclesiastical preferments, they might be anxious to secure financial rewards, particularly if they had purchased their offices, and to secure these rewards in this life rather than the next.[3]

---

[1] Woodcock, *Medieval Ecclesiastical Courts*, 42–3; 25 Henry VIII, c. 19; B.P. Levack, *The Civil Lawyers in England, 1603–1641: A Political Study* (1973), 161–4; Marchant, *The Church under the Law*, 49, 238; Ingram, *Church Courts, Sex and Marriage*, 59–60.

[2] 37 Henry VIII, c. 17; Levack, *Civil Lawyers*, 18–21, 161–2.

[3] Hill, *Society and Puritanism*, 238, writes, 'Finally, until Dr Trevor's case (8 Jac 1), officers of the courts, from the bishop's Chancellor downwards, purchased their places and expected returns on their investment.'

However, one must not overemphasise the influence of such developments. Most of the causes brought before these lay judges and registrars were instance causes brought to them by aggrieved suitors, and not causes that these officials in any way solicited. This, along with routine non-contentious administrative activities connected with the institution of clergymen, with probate and with the issue of various licences, brought in most of their income. At this elevated administrative level the most that those who were anxious to secure an increasing income could legitimately do was perhaps to prolong cases, not encouraging litigants to settle matters between themselves and to abandon the case, as perhaps ideally they should have done. Lower down the administrative ladder, at the level of the apparitor, it is possible that there was some aggressive seeking out of business. There certainly were complaints to this effect in Parliament and elsewhere in the later years of Elizabeth's reign, forcing the bishops to make a show of curtailing the activities of their subordinates. In 1597 Bishop Bancroft, for example, directed that legal proceedings in the diocese of London were not to be initiated on the complaints of apparitors, but only on the presentments made by churchwardens. Complaints and reactions of this sort were a prelude to canon 138 of the 1604 canons, which ordered that apparitors 'shall not take upon them the office of promoters or informers for the court, neither shall they exact more or greater fees than are in these our constitutions formerly prescribed'.[4] But one should remember that apparitors had long been laymen, that the majority of prosecutions had always derived from churchwardens' presentments and that in the court system as a whole, office business took a decided second place to those instance suits where apparitors were mere citation servers.

Those, such as Hill, who stress the avaricious nature of the ecclesiastical courts and their officers draw attention to rising fees, a development that Marchant also thought was partly a product of laymen taking over control.[5] In truth, it is difficult to get a clear picture of what was happening in this respect. An Act of 1529 laid down a graduated scale of fees to be charged for probate and administrations, and in 1585, in response to complaints in

---

[4] R. Peters, *Oculus Episcopi: Administration in the Archdeaconry of St Albans* (1963), 21; Houlbrooke, *Church Courts and the People*, 28; Bray, *The Anglican Canons*, 443.

[5] Hill, *Society and Puritanism*, 307–9; Marchant, *The Church under the Law*, 238.

Parliament about excessive fees, Archbishop Whitgift ordered that court fees should not exceed those operating at the beginning of Elizabeth's reign. The fees charged for probates and administrations at York in mid-Elizabethan times were those laid down in 1529.[6] This instruction was reiterated in Whitgift's 1597 standard scale for fees to be levied throughout the southern province, a scale that was eventually embodied in the canons of 1604.[7] These developments, it has been argued, probably stabilised individual fees for the next four decades.[8] Similarly the fees charged at the Norwich consistory court in the 1630s were those operating at the beginning of Elizabeth's reign.[9] Although the cost of actions in the church courts rose in terms of current prices, something that was perhaps inevitable given the increases in the cost of living that took place in the sixteenth and early seventeenth centuries, the restraints laid upon the courts almost certainly meant that costs in real terms fell. The fact that this happened in the case of marriage licences has been plausibly demonstrated by Boulton, and it was undoubtedly one of the reasons for their burgeoning popularity. As he pointed out, between the 1530s and 1600, because wages rose more rapidly than the cost of licences, the number of days work that a London building craftsman needed to do to purchase a licence fell from about fifteen to seven.[10] Marchant argued that this reduction in real costs applied to most of the services rendered by the ecclesiastical courts, a finding supported by others.[11] Nor was the influence of this factor confined to the church courts. The period from 1560 to 1640 has been characterised as 'one of the most litigious periods in English history', and one of the many reasons for this is that 'by 1560 litigation at common law was not prohibitively expensive, and that the cost of litigation actually declined steadily relative to prices over the next eighty years'. By 1640, Brooks has argued, 'litigation had perhaps risen fifteen-fold above the levels of the 1490s'.[12]

---

[6] Marchant, *The Church under the Law*, 111.
[7] Burn, *Ecclesiastical Law*, i, 560; J. E. Neale, *Elizabeth I and Her Parliaments, 1584–1601* (1957), 77; Marchant, *The Church under the Law*, 24, 142.
[8] Levack, *Civil Lawyers*, 71.   [9] Marchant, *The Church under the Law*, 19.
[10] Boulton, 'Itching', 17.
[11] Marchant, *The Church under the Law*, 19; Foyster, *Manhood*, 158.
[12] Brooks, *Pettyfoggers and Vipers*, 79, 101; C. W. Brooks, *Lawyers, Litigation and English Society since 1450* (1998), 11.

Behind this price inflation there lurked the population increase of the sixteenth and early seventeenth centuries, and we have seen how the inflation and demographic expansion combined to bring more business to the church courts. Inflation put pressure on tithe-receivers to insist on their rights or to attempt to revise *modi* that had decreased in real terms. It also stimulated the land market, transferring properties from less efficient to more efficient asset managers. Demographic expansion increased the number of deaths taking place, while income inflation increased the number of people who felt obliged to make a will. The population rise put pressure on employment, on earning opportunities and real wages, contributing to poverty and that decline in nuptiality that may have been a contributory factor in the increase in bastardy experienced in many communities in and after the later sixteenth century. The growing cost of supporting the poor that was thrust onto individual parishes by the Tudor poor laws appears to have hardened attitudes towards bastard bearing, increasing the propensity for churchwardens to present people for sexual offences and sensitising the population to allegations of whoredom. It is impossible to ignore the influence of demographic expansion and inflation: they combined to stimulate much of the increased activity within the ecclesiastical courts in the hundred years before 1640.

The 1640s, however, witnessed not only the reversal of this expansion but also the dismantling of the ecclesiastical courts, and it is arguable that the seeds of this destruction lay in the expansion that preceded it. Opposition to church courts existed at the start of the sixteenth century, and little that happened thereafter was sufficient to quieten the criticism to which they were subjected. Not all of the reasons offered by scholars for opposition and decline have real substance. Hill, for example, argued that 'what made the Church courts peculiarly obnoxious was their attempt to enforce standards of conduct, which had been appropriate enough to an unequal agrarian society, long after large areas of England had left such a society behind'. What people objected to, he argued, was that these courts 'persisted in interfering with matters of trade and credit', interfering 'with the free workings of the market'. The criticism represented 'a revolt of the industrious sort of people against the institutions and standards of the old regime'. The examples offered by Hill relate largely to the office prose-cutions launched against those who persisted in working and playing on Sundays and feast days.[13] There is no denying the existence of such prosecutions, but the argument overlooks several incontrovertible facts: instance suits outnumbered office prosecutions in the regular business of the church courts, and, among the office cases, prosecutions for sexual offences dominated their proceedings. There is little evidence, moreover, that prosecutions of the latter sort were unpopular, except among those unfortunates who were cited to appear before the courts to answer for their real or alleged sexual lapses.

One must also have some doubts that the church courts were fundamentally weakened by the effects of the Reformation. The greater frequency of parliamentary sittings after 1529 and the decline in spiritual representation in the Lords seem to have led to more vociferous and sustained attacks on the courts in Parliament. These attacks, along with changes in personnel and religious policies, may have disrupted administrative procedures for several decades. There is some evidence, as we have previously noted, of short-term decline in some courts. But Houlbrooke was not thinking of the short-run effects of the Reformation on the courts when he argued that 'there can be little doubt that in the long run it weakened them'. Part of his argument is that 'statutes were passed affecting almost every area of [their] jurisdiction'.[14] It is true that a few of these statutes effectively removed jurisdiction from the spiritual to the temporal courts, examples of this being the more serious forms of witchcraft, usury, buggery and bigamy. However, none of these, with the possible exception of witchcraft, ever accounted for large numbers of cases coming into the church courts and the numbers of usury, buggery and bigamy cases in the common law courts was always minuscule.

Other statutes effectively gave the temporal courts concurrent jurisdiction in certain areas of church court business: examples here include aspects of tithe business, and probate where legacies were involved.[15] These measures undoubtedly increased the opportunities for the temporal courts to interfere in the workings of the ecclesiastical courts through the issue of prohibitions.[16] But change was slow and it must not be forgotten that it was in such

---

[13] Hill, *Society and Puritanism*, 309–14.
[14] Houlbrooke, *Church Courts and the People*, 1.   [15] Ibid., 18.
[16] Levack, *Civil Lawyers*, 76, points out that 75 per cent of all prohibitions issued against proceedings in the church courts involved tithe causes.

areas that church court business actually expanded during these years. Presumably, in the absence of such limitations, activity in these areas would have been even greater. Before the Civil War these diversions were mere leaks rather than great flows, despite Jones's view that 'over the Elizabethan decades one cannot escape the inevitable conclusion that Chancery, perhaps more than any other single court, was slowly robbing the spiritual courts of their instance jurisdiction'.[17] Perhaps a more serious consequence was that these statutes gave the temporal courts a greater foothold, one that they were subsequently able to enlarge through the continual citing of legal precedents.

The limitations on the fees that could be levied also had important consequences. Inflation and laicisation created strong pressures to increase fees, pressures that some ecclesiastical courts were unable to resist. Whilst the general level of official fees lagged behind the rising price level, opportunities were presented to impose higher charges for things unspecified in fee tables, to multiply bureaucratic processes or to insist on 'unofficial fees' – bribes – to speed up or shape the outcome of cases. At their worst, these temptations lapsed into blatant corruption, as was the case in Gloucestershire in the 1560s and 1570s when Thomas Powell was the bishop's chancellor, despite a 'life of amazing corruption and immorality'. When eventually, in 1579, he was arraigned before the High Commission, he faced no fewer than thirteen charges. These began with the accusation that he was 'a fornicator, and adulterer ... and a committer of rape', a bastard-begetter, and 'a common haunter of taverns, a drunkard, a blasphemous swearer' and continued with a succession of charges relating to corruption. Within the previous two or three years, it was alleged, three or four hundred people found guilty of various crimes had had their sentences of penance commuted for money payments, and others, presented for serious offences, had been 'dismissed without correction' on payment of bribes.[18] Incidents such as these fed the stream of criticism that was directed at the church courts and their officials.

Perhaps the most serious consequence of the Reformation was the failure to endow the church courts with greater powers to

---

[17] Jones, *Elizabethan Court of Chancery*, 393.
[18] F. D. Price, 'An Elizabethan church official – Thomas Powell, chancellor of Gloucester diocese', *Church Quarterly Review* 128 (1939), 94–112.

enforce obedience to their demands. Although medieval courts did on occasions impose corporal punishments upon offenders, such sanctions had all but disappeared by the start of the sixteenth century.[19] Those that remained were suspension, excommunication and penance. In an age when there was perhaps greater uniformity of belief than prevailed a century later, both suspension and excommunication were threats that the population took seriously. Nor should the shaming nature of public penance be underestimated. Disinclination to obey the courts grew, however, during the unsettled decades that accompanied the Reformation. Those cited to appear sometimes fled across diocesan boundaries to escape the jurisdictions of local courts, but more and more simply refused to obey citations or sentences of penance. The numbers of those excommunicated grew to sizeable proportions in some dioceses. By the 1570s, ecclesiastical discipline in the diocese of Gloucester, Price relates, had virtually collapsed, due to the lax oversight of bishop Richard Cheyney (1562–79) and the corruption of his chancellor Thomas Powell. Under bishop Hooper, only about one in ten defendants failed to appear before the consistory court, but by 1569–70 two out of three failed to do so.[20] This may have been an extreme case, for after all it led to the setting up in 1574 of a special ecclesiastical commission for the diocese, but there is some evidence to suggest that in the early seventeenth century contumacy grew to sizeable proportions. In two out of four archdeaconries in the diocese of York and three out of four in the diocese of Norwich, only 42–46 per cent of those presented actually appeared before the visitation courts in the 1620s. About 2,100 people were officially excommunicated in the diocese of York in 1623, about the same number in the diocese of Chester, and about 1,600 in each of the years 1627 and 1633 in the diocese of Norwich. Perhaps 5 per cent of all adults dwelling in these dioceses might have been living in a state of excommunication.[21] Other jurisdictions experienced similar problems: 40 per cent of

---

[19] Major, 'Lincoln diocesan records', 64; Woodcock, *Medieval Ecclesiastical Courts*, 98; Houlbrooke, 'The decline of ecclesiastical jurisdiction', 245. For some late examples see Bowker, 'The Commons' supplication against the Ordinaries', 73.

[20] Price, 'Gloucester diocese under bishop Hooper', 150; Price, *The Commission for Ecclesiastical Causes*, 3.

[21] Marchant, *The Church under the Law*, 206, 227.

offenders in the diocese of Oxford in the early 1630s were excommunicated, a third of those in the diocese of Peterborough were in the same state, and about three-quarters of these people remained in that state for at least a year.[22]

It was partly to deal with notorious and blatant offences and offenders that special ecclesiastical commissions were created, though some were set up, as we have seen in the case of the Gloucester commission, to compensate for the inadequacies of the consistory courts at particular times. The High Commissions created early in Elizabeth's reign in the two ecclesiastical provinces of Canterbury and York could deal with blatant offenders who crossed diocesan boundaries. They appear to have dedicated themselves particularly to reinforcing the religious settlement through the pursuit of nonconformity. Their methods, especially the use of the *ex officio* oath, their punishments, which included fines and imprisonment, and what became eventually their principal objectives – the hounding of puritans – aroused vociferous complaints. Puritans objected strongly to being put on oath to answer charges before they knew precisely what these charges actually were. They became, Levack has argued, 'the most successful opponents of the English civil lawyers'.[23]

Even the licensing activities of church court officials fuelled criticism. The spectacular growth in the popularity of marriage licences owed much to attempts by the church courts to curb clandestine marriages, but the popularity of these dispensations depended largely on the relaxed attitude that the issuers took to the canonical restrictions on couples marrying in parishes where at least one of the pair was known. This practice provided minors with opportunities to marry without the knowledge and consent of their parents or guardians and, critics averred, encouraged bigamous, incestuous and generally disordered matches.[24]

---

[22] Jones, 'The ecclesiastical courts before and after the Civil War', 118.

[23] M. H. Maguire, 'Attack of the common lawyers on the oath *ex officio* as administered in the ecclesiastical courts in England', in *Essays in History and Political Theory* (1936), 199–229; Levack, *Civil Lawyers*, 158. M. Ingram, 'Puritans and the church courts, 1560–1640', in *The Culture of English Puritanism, 1560–1700*, ed. C. Durston and J. Eales (1996), 58–91, provides an informed and subtle discussion of the shifting relationships between the church courts and puritans in southern England.

[24] Outhwaite, *Clandestine Marriage*, 8–10.

The expansion of the ecclesiastical courts, along with the nature of their activities, provided critics with ammunition. The complaints emanated from several groups, amongst whom we must number common lawyers jealous of the jurisdiction exercised by the spiritual courts and, from the time of the Elizabethan religious settlement, puritans who experienced or feared persecution for their religious practices. Critical assaults came in various forms: scholarly tracts, polemical pamphlets, parliamentary bills and speeches, and petitions addressed to Parliament or the monarch. They were of long standing. One such petition was a document presented to Parliament in 1532, called *The Supplication of the Commons against the Ordinaries*, which has occasioned dispute amongst Tudor historians. Elton began the controversy with his assertion in 1951 that this petition against ecclesiastical justice was being worked on by the government long before 1532; that it was perhaps precipitated by Wolsey's fall in 1529, but it was later turned into a full-blown assault on the church by Thomas Cromwell in 1532, determined to bring the English clergy to heel. Elton was later taken to task by Cooper, who argued that the document was a more spontaneous, less conspiratorial affair, framed and presented in parliament during the course of the year 1532 itself.[25] The chronological and other origins of the petition matter less to us, however, than the nature of the criticisms that it made.

The petition began with complaints about the 'uncharitable behaviour of divers Ordinaries, their commissaries and substitutes'. It complained that prelates and others were making 'laws and ordinances concerning temporal things', perhaps a response to the canons that convocation was then producing and the campaign that the courts were then conducting against heresy.[26] It asserted that people were being hauled before the ecclesiastical courts without proper cause, and charged *ex officio*, 'sometimes at the only promotion and suggestion of their summoners and apparitors'. It argued that some defendants were being committed

[25] Elton, 'The Commons' supplication of 1532', 507–34; J. P. Cooper, 'The supplication against the Ordinaries reconsidered', *EHR* 72 (1957), 616–41. See also M. Kelly, 'The submission of the clergy', *TRHS*, 5th series 15 (1965), 97–119; J. A. Guy, *The Public Career of Sir Thomas More* (1980), 186–92; C. Haigh, *The English Reformation Revised* (1987), 62–6.
[26] Haigh, *English Reformation Revised*, 64–5; Bray, *The Anglican Canons*, xxxix.

to prison. And all this could happen on flimsy charges or indeed their own admissions while being questioned under oath. There were objections also to being cited for causes being pursued in dioceses other than the ones in which complainants lived. Excommunication for 'small and light causes' aroused complaint, as did the need to pay fees for absolution. 'Great and excessive fees' came in for particular attention. Fees were mentioned in relation to the seeking of probate, as also were long delays and, on occasions, considerable journeys.[27] Defenders of the courts have protested the injustice of many of these complaints, most of which were directed at prosecutions rather than those instance causes that made up a large part of their business.[28]

Many of these complaints emerge again in the *Admonition to the Parliament* of 1572, a puritan tract that was stronger on invective than on specifics. The archbishop's court was condemned as 'the filthy quauemire, and poisoned plashe of all the abhominations that doe infect the whole realme', and the courts of the commissaries as 'but a pettie little stinking ditche'. Complaints were made about the misuse of excommunication:

In the primative church it was in many mennes handes: now one alone excommunicateth. In those days it was the last censure of the church, and never went forth but for notorious crimes: Now it is pronounced for every light trifle. Then excommunication was greatly regarded and feared. Now because it is a money matter, no whit at al esteemed. Then for great sinnes, severe punishment, and for small offences, little censures. Now great sinnes eyther not at al punished, as blasphemy, usury, etc, or else sleightly passed over with pricking in a blanket, or pinning in a sheet, as adulterie, whoredome, drunkenness, etc.[29]

Complaints about the use and misuse of excommunication continued, as did diatribes against the commissary court:

This courte poulleth parishes, scourgeth the poore hedge priestes, ladeth Churchwardens with manifest perjuries, punisheth whoredoms and adulteryes with toyishe censures, remitteth without satisfying the congregation, and that in secrete places, giveth out dispensations for unlawfull marriages, and committeth a thousand such like abhominations.[30]

---

[27] *English Historical Documents*, v, *1485–1558*, ed. C. H. Williams (1967), 732–6.
[28] Bowker, 'The Commons' Supplication against the Ordinaries', 61–77.
[29] W. H. Frere and C. E. Douglas eds., *Puritan Manifestoes* (1954), 17, 32.
[30] Ibid., 34.

Complaints about the church courts re-emerged in the parliament of 1584–5, with separate bills being floated to reform appeal procedures, to curb the taking of excessive fees and against prohibited seasons for marriage.[31] Although nothing was achieved, critics returned to the issue of reform in 1593 when James Morice, a common lawyer, made an impassioned speech against the *ex officio* oath. Not for the first time, however, reform proposals ran up against the queen's interdict that Parliament should not proceed with bills 'touching the said matters of State or reformation in Causes Ecclesiastical', and Morice was duly arrested. Criticism of the courts could not be suppressed, however, and a bill against excessive fees was introduced in the parliament of 1597–8, while the subject of 'sundry great abuses by Licences for Mariages' was much discussed. Elizabeth's final parliament in 1601 witnessed an abortive attempt to suppress 'certaine idle Courtes kept every three weekes by Archdeacons and their Officialls and Commissaryes and theire Registers'.[32]

Many of these complaints surfaced again in the so-called *Millenary Petition* presented in 1603 to James I by critics of the established church, anxious for a new broom to sweep away what they regarded as relics of popery. James, who had arrived from Presbyterian Scotland and who had Calvinist leanings, was thought likely to be sympathetic to the cause of reform. Section 4 of this petition ran:

For Church discipline: that the discipline and excommunication may be administered according to Christ's own institution, or, at the least, that enormities may be redressed, as namely, that excommunication come not forth under the name of lay persons, chancellors, officials, etc.; that men be not excommunicated for trifles and twelve-penny matters; that none be excommunicated without consent of his pastor; that the officers be not suffered to extort unreasonable fees; that none having jurisdiction or registers' places, put out the same to farm; that divers popish canons (as for restraint of marriage at certain times) be reversed; that the longsomeness of suits in ecclesiastical courts (which hang sometimes two, three, four, five, six, or seven years) may be restrained; that the oath *Ex Officio*, whereby men are forced to accuse themselves, be more sparingly used; that licences for marriages without banns asked, be more cautiously granted.[33]

---

[31] Neale, *Elizabeth I and Her Parliaments*, 77, 82–3; D. Dean, *Law-Making and Society in Late Elizabethan England* (1996), 116–7.

[32] Dean, *Law-Making and Society*, 117–20, 185.

[33] H. Gee and W. J. Hardy, *Documents Illustrative of English Church History* (1910), 508–11.

The petitioners were soon disappointed: little change was forth-coming, though the church did clarify its beliefs and institutions through the issue of 141 canons, some of which were attempts to regularise proceedings in the courts and silence the sort of criti-cism that had been directed against them and their officials in previous decades.[34]

Silence was not forthcoming, however, particularly after Laud became archbishop of Canterbury in 1633. Increased activity against puritans by the High Commission, the intensification of prosecutions in visitation courts, attempts to restore to the church the income derived from tithes and a surge in the numbers of those being excommunicated all provided critics of the eccle-siastical courts with ammunition. The issuance in 1640 by Con-vocation of a set of seventeen new canons after Parliament had been dissolved, canons that upheld the divine right of kings and required the clergy to accept the existence and authority of the established church hierarchy, set Parliament and the episcopal bench on a collision course. Puritan criticism erupted again in the so-called *Root and Branch* petition presented to the Commons by London protestants in 1640.[35] It began by inveighing against 'the government of archbishops and lord bishops, deans and arch-deacons, etc., with their courts and ministrations in them', which have 'proved prejudicial and very dangerous both to the Church and Commonwealth'. Their government, it continued, 'is found by woeful experience to be a main cause and occasion of many foul evils, pressures and grievances of a very high nature unto his majesty's subjects in their own consciences, liberties and estates'. It pleaded for the abolition 'root and branch' of episcopal gov-ernment and went on to particularise grievances. It inveighed against the 'prohibiting of marriages without their licence, at certain times, almost half the year, and licensing of marriages without banns asking'; 'The pressing of the strict observation of the saints' days, whereby great sums of money are drawn out of men's purses for working on them' and 'The great increase and frequency of whoredoms and adulteries, occasioned by the

---

[34] See canons 92–8, 101–38, in Bray, *The Anglican Canons*.

[35] I have used the customary 'Root and Branch' label rather than the 'roots and branches' term that the petition itself employs: see R. Strier, 'From diagnosis to operation', in *The Theatrical City: Culture, Theatre and Politics in London, 1576–1649*, ed. D. L. Smith et al. (1995), 224–33.

prelates' corrupt administration of justice in such cases, who taking upon them the punishment of it, do turn all into moneys for the filling of their purses'. 'The general abuse of that great ordinance of excommunication' came in for lengthy comment, especially as it was pronounced 'for vain, idle and trivial matters', so that it became 'a hook or instrument wherewith to empty men's purses'. Finally, there was the customary diatribe against the oath *ex officio* as employed by the High Commission: 'reaching even to men's thoughts', leading to 'fining and imprisoning', and the 'breaking up of men's houses'. Only 'papists, Jesuits, priests, and such others as propagate popery or Arminianism, are countenanced, spared, and have much liberty', it argued, in what was clearly a broadside fired at the policies pursued under Laud. It was no surprise that soon after this the newly assembled Long Parliament began to receive petitions for the abolition of episcopacy, and when the bishops disappeared so did the church courts.[36]

---

[36] D. L. Smith, 'The Root and Branch petition and the Grand Remonstrance', ibid., 209–17.

9

CHARTING DECLINE 1640–1830

The opening of the Long Parliament in November 1640 witnessed
considerable hostility directed at Archbishop Laud and the
Arminian policies associated with him. Five weeks later, in mid-
December, the *Root and Branch* petition was presented to the
Commons and this helped to focus hostility towards the structure
of the English church and the role of bishops within it, a redir-
ection that was encouraged by a welter of county petitions calling
for the abolition of episcopacy.[1] In 1641 the High Commission
was abolished and the ecclesiastical courts were stripped of their
corrective powers; in 1642 bishops were excluded from the House
of Lords; in 1643 episcopacy was abolished altogether, along with
cathedral deans and chapters. In 1645 Archbishop Laud was
executed, and in the following year episcopal estates were put up
for sale along with the estates that had belonged to deans and
chapters.

It is hardly surprising to find that the business of the church
courts withered in the face of these repeated assaults. The church
courts effectively fell with the bishops. Office causes in the consistory court of Gloucester ended in 1641, and the last tithe and
defamation suits were heard there in December 1642.[2] Probate
and testamentary business appears, however, to have continued
there for some years thereafter, even surviving the formal abolition of the courts by the Long Parliament in October 1646.[3]
Similar patterns have been found in other ecclesiastical jurisdictions, such as those of the courts of Canterbury.[4] In some areas

[1] Smith, 'The Root and Branch petition', 209–14.
[2] Hockaday, 'The consistory court of the diocese of Gloucester', 200.
[3] Jones, 'The ecclesiastical courts before and after the Civil War', 29–30.
[4] J. M. Potter, 'The ecclesiastical courts in the diocese of Canterbury, 1603–1665',
unpublished MPhil thesis, University of London (1973), 26–7, 175–80.

marriage licences continued to be issued, though in diminishing numbers. Issuance probably ceased altogether, however, before the Civil Marriage Act of 1653 rendered such marriage instruments invalid.[5] For nearly twenty years, until the Restoration, English men and women went unpoliced by the ecclesiastical courts, and for over a decade they had to find other ways of resolving their tithe, testamentary, matrimonial and slander conflicts.

The underlying disputes did not themselves disappear. It is far from surprising that the courts had no shortage of cases with which to resume their activities when monarchy, episcopacy and ecclesiastical jurisdictions were restored in and after 1660. The courts were restored, moreover, with their jurisdictions and functions virtually unchanged from pre-Civil War days. The only major exceptions were that the courts of High Commission were not reintroduced and the compulsory *ex officio* oath was abolished.[6]

Even before the powers of the church courts to impose punishments were restored in July 1661, some were at work with probate and, to a lesser extent, with instance causes. The Canterbury diocesan court was dealing with requests for probate within ten days of the day when its officials were appointed in July 1660.[7] By 1661 a backlog of complaints about non-payment of tithes began to reach it; these causes would dominate the business of that court between 1661 and 1663. Similar experiences in these years occurred at the consistory courts of Winchester and York.[8]

Describing what happened in the decades thereafter, however, presents major problems. As Spurr has written, 'although shafts of scholarly light have illuminated the workings of some courts in a few dioceses, most of the church courts of Restoration England remain unstudied, and consequently all generalisations about

---

[5] Jones, 'The ecclesiastical courts before and after the Civil War', 39; Boulton, 'Itching after private marryings?', 26; Outhwaite, *Clandestine Marriage*, 11–12.

[6] A. Whiteman, 'The re-establishment of the Church of England, 1660–1663', *TRHS*, 5th series, 5 (1955), 117–18. These changes were made by statute in 1661 (12 Charles II, c. 12).

[7] I. M. Green, *The Re-establishment of the Church of England, 1660–1663* (1978), 132–3.

[8] Ibid., 134–5; B. D. Till, 'The administrative system of the ecclesiastical courts in the diocese and province of York', unpublished typescript, Borthwick Institute, York (1963), 10.

them remain fragile'. What is more, few of these studies directly compare Restoration experiences with pre-1640 realities. They also have different preoccupations and sometimes cover very different time periods. These few 'shafts of scholarly light' led Spurr, however, to the view that their 'subsequent history seems to be a story of shrinking business and declining authority', a view with which it is difficult to argue, although the periodisation and character of this decline remain to be explored.[9] Given the large number of courts in existence, it would not be surprising to find a wide variety of experiences. The Peterborough courts were apparently as active in 1662–3 as in 1630–1. Instance business in the consistory courts of Canterbury and of Oxford revived after 1660, but at levels below those characteristic of the 1620s and 1630s.[10] The same appears to be true of the consistory court of York: in the years 1664–7, fewer than a hundred new causes a year were begun there, well below the levels of 300 plus a year that seem to have characterised that court's business in the sixty years before 1640.[11] Although business at the York consistory court gradually expanded from the 1660s to the 1690s, it never regained pre-1640 levels. In the early eighteenth century an absolute decline in numbers of causes took place in both of the major York courts, the consistory court and the chancery court.[12] A similar experience seems to have occurred at the consistory court of Coventry and Lichfield.[13] Some of these causes would be office prosecutions, however, and their inclusion complicates the picture, because new prosecuting tendencies exhibited themselves in the years after the restoration of Charles II.

Although office causes were heavily dependent on the willingness of local churchwardens and others to present offenders to the church courts, the volume of presentations tended to rise and fall in line with the frequency of official visitations and the prosecuting zeal of individual bishops and their officials. There was change. As we have seen, a wide range of offences was prosecuted in the

---

[9] J. Spurr, *The Restoration Church of England, 1646–1689* (1991), 209.

[10] Potter, 'The ecclesiastical courts in the diocese of Canterbury', 22; Jones, 'The ecclesiastical courts before and after the Civil War', 49.

[11] Marchant, *The Church under the Law*, 62; Till, 'The administrative system', 61.

[12] Till, 'The administrative system', 61–3.

[13] A. Tarver, 'The consistory court of the diocese of Coventry and Lichfield and its work, 1680–1830', Unpublished PhD Thesis, University of Warwick (1998), 11.

pre-1640 courts, but this category of business was overwhelmingly dominated by the prosecution of sexual lapses, principally fornication and adultery. Although such offenders continued to be pursued by the Restoration courts for several decades after 1661, sexual delinquents were now often outnumbered by other categories of offender. The focus of prosecutions shifted strongly to breaches of the religious code. Some men and women were presented for attending conventicles, failing to receive the sacrament, and neglecting baptism and other religious rites, but the overwhelming majority were cited for their failure to attend church at all.[14] Almost a half of those cited to appear at the Peterborough court from 1662 to 1664, for example, were presented for religious offences.[15] Although at Peterborough and at Oxford the drive against such offenders lost momentum by 1670 and faltered further with Charles II's Declaration of Indulgence of 1672, it appears to have been maintained or to have recovered elsewhere: in the consistory court of Chichester, religious offences comprised 45 per cent of office prosecutions in 1675, whilst at Worcester in the same year, they made up some 55 per cent of office business.[16] The numbers prosecuted for religious offences thus rose and fell. However, they virtually ceased with James II's Declaration of Indulgence of April 1687, which declared that 'from henceforth the execution of all and all manner of penal laws in matters ecclesiastical, for not coming to church, or not receiving the sacrament, or for any other nonconformity to the religion established ... be immediately suspended'.[17] The Toleration Act of 1689 confirmed the freedom of individuals to worship in their own fashion, and thereafter prosecutions for nonconformity virtually ceased.

Whilst these periodic drives against religious dissent touched only a minority of the nation's population, they could be locally intensive. They also had one predictable response: increasing proportions of those cited to appear before the courts refused to make an appearance.[18] Some added insult to their refusal. Richard Heptenstall admitted that he took the citation served on him in 1679 for non-attendance at church and 'did dropp the same into my breeches and did then affirme that I would wipe my arse with

---

[14] Spurr, *The Restoration Church*, 211.
[15] Jones, 'The ecclesiastical courts before and after the Civil War', 50.
[16] Ibid., 53: Spurr, *The Restoration Church*, 211.
[17] Gee and Hardy, *Documents*, 642.   [18] Spurr, *The Restoration Church*, 213.

the same and did refuse to rediliver'.[19] Another apparitor was
derided as but 'a cuntsomoner of the bawdy court'.[20] An inevitable consequence of continued failure to appear was that
increasing numbers of individuals were excommunicated. The
proportion of cases of all kinds that ended in excommunication
rose from around a quarter in the 1630s in the dioceses of both
Oxford and Peterborough to a third in Oxford in the early 1660s,
rising further to well over a third in both dioceses a decade later.[21]
Of the 144 persons cited for nonconformity in the Exeter consistory court in 1663, 85 were excommunicated.[22] There was
nothing new in large numbers of people being in this state; what
was new was that the numbers grew to even greater proportions.
It was not just the laity that was refusing to appear before the
church courts, for some clerics also behaved in this way.

Clearly the church courts had few teeth. What teeth they did
have were drawn in 1641, with the abolition of the High Commission and the failure to restore it, and the other special ecclesiastical commissions, at the Restoration. James II's attempts to
restore the institution in 1686–7 produced a political storm that
led to his downfall. Without such bodies the ultimate sanction that
the church courts were left with was excommunication and the
possibility of subsequent arrest on a writ *de excommunicato
capiendo* if the offender remained obdurate, a state of affairs that
many were clearly prepared to accept, often for lengthy periods.[23]
When the rector of Clayworth in Nottinghamshire threatened some
servants with citations to appear in court, their masters 'told them
that all I could do at them, was to excommunicate them, which was
only their not going to Church.'[24] The threat of excommunication
obviously diminished also with the growth of alternative churches.
Its over-employment drove some excommunicates into the ranks of
the nonconformists, a fact that intelligent clerics noted. Eventually,
of course, policies of official toleration, as articulated in the
Declarations of Indulgence of 1672 and 1687 and in the Toleration
Act of 1689, removed altogether the threat of citation for non-
compliance with the church's rituals. This quickly led in turn to the
drying up presentments of offenders by churchwardens, the

[19] J. Addy, *Sin and Society in the Seventeenth Century* (1989), 205.   [20] Ibid., 128.
[21] Jones, 'The ecclesiastical courts before and after the Civil War', 118.
[22] Green, *The Re-establishment of the Church of England*, 140.
[23] Ibid., 119.   [24] N. Sykes, *From Sheldon to Secker* (1959), 22.

initiators of most office prosecutions, and it is from this time that churchwardens' presentments began to make the routine return *omnia bene* – all is well in the parish: there is nothing untoward to report.[25]

Office prosecutions thereafter came once again to be dominated by sexual delinquency though, as we shall see, the numbers of those cited were noticeably lower than they had been in the later sixteenth and early seventeenth centuries. Some of the lesser courts found their office business shrinking to negligible proportions. 'If the court of the archdeacon of Barnstaple had had to depend on its *ex officio* business after 1688', Smith has written, 'it would soon have ceased to exist.'[26] Whereas in 1665, 165 people were presented to the archdeacon's court in the Yorkshire deanery of Holderness, and 124 in 1674, by 1691 the number presented had fallen to a mere twenty-nine. The decline in Buckrose deanery, which embraced Hull, was even more marked: as late as 1670, 317 people had been presented, but in 1691 the total was a mere 12.[27] By the eighteenth century, archdeaconry courts in some areas may have ceased to function. This appears to have been the case in the diocese of Coventry and Lichfield.[28] In Lancashire, sexual presentments were heard mainly in the deanery courts and such cases appear to have risen from the late seventeenth to the mid-eighteenth century, declining somewhat thereafter only in the southern parts of the county. Increasingly, however, those cited to appear failed to make an appearance in court, and the church and its local representatives appeared increasingly reluctant from the 1770s to press ahead with prosecutions for antenuptial fornication and bastardy against local inhabitants.[29] Sexual transgressions decreasingly figured from the mid-eighteenth century in the office prosecutions pursued in the consistory courts of Norwich, Carlisle and Lichfield.[30] The town of

---

[25] Whiteman, 'The re-establishment of the Church', 125; Smith, 'Study of the administration of the diocese of Exeter', 89.

[26] Smith, 'Study of the administration of the diocese of Exeter', 75.

[27] Till, 'The administrative system', 103.

[28] Tarver, 'The consistory court of the diocese', 12.

[29] J. M. Albers, 'Seeds of contention: society, politics and the Church of England in Lancashire, 1689–1790', unpublished PhD thesis, Yale University (1998), 226–48.

[30] W. M. Jacob, *Lay People and Religion in the Early Eighteenth Century* (1996), 153; M. Kinnear, 'The correction court in the diocese of Carlisle, 1704–1756', *Church History* 59 (1990), 196; Tarver, 'The consistory court of the diocese', 131.

Nottingham doubled in population in the second half of the eighteenth century and bastardy levels there increased, but despite these tendencies prosecutions in the archdeaconry court of its inhabitants for pre-nuptial fornication disappeared after 1765, leaving bastardy as the principal target. Out of 184 immorality prosecutions between 1760 and 1795, 154 were for bastardy. But even this had virtually ceased by the early 1770s, with only two cases being prosecuted after 1774.[31] Prosecutions for pre-nuptial fornication were clearly in marked decline in several places before that Act of 1787 which forbade any suit for fornication or incontinence to be started eight months after the offence was committed. The same statute also forbade any suit for pre-marital fornication after the parties concerned had married each other.[32]

By 1830 the policing functions of the English ecclesiastical courts against the laity had virtually disappeared. The returns made in each diocese to the Royal Commission on the Ecclesiastical Courts of 1830 show a total of fewer than fifty correction causes for all the English and Welsh diocesan courts combined for the three years 1827–29. Many diocesan courts reported no correction causes at all in these three years. Nil returns came in from the consistory courts of Canterbury, Bath and Wells, Bristol, Chester, Chichester, Ely, London, Oxford, Peterborough, Salisbury, Winchester, Worcester, St Asaph and Bangor. Indeed many of them reported that they tried no causes of any description – either office or instance ones – during these three years.[33]

By 1830, therefore, the criminal side of the system was not simply in decline but had virtually collapsed. In many jurisdictions, this state of affairs had existed for fifty years.[34] How did this happen? Impressed by the post-1660 high rates of contumacy and the growing numbers being excommunicated, historians searching for reasons for this lengthy and prolonged decline in levels of

---

[31] R. P. Ruddock, '"The eye of the bishop": Nottingham causes in the archdeacon's court, 1760–1795, a study in decline', unpublished MS thesis, University of Nottingham (1997), 44, and Appendix 1 (n.p.).

[32] 'An Act to prevent frivolous and vexatious suits in Ecclesiastical Courts' (27 George III, c. 44).

[33] *Report of the Commissioners appointed to inquire into the Practice and Jurisdiction of the Ecclesiastical Courts, PP, 1831–2*, xxiv, 554–67.

[34] This appears to be true of the consistory court of Norwich: see W. M. Jacob, 'Clergy and society in Norfolk, 1707–1806', unpublished PhD thesis, University of Exeter (1982), 246–7.

activity have dwelt on the failure at the Restoration to effect reforms in the procedure used in the ecclesiastical courts. As one notable authority has argued, 'in no sphere was the failure to effect reforms more unfortunate and far-reaching in its effects'.[35] It has been argued that the break in the revolutionary period was not long enough to shatter old administrative habits or to break old claims on office. Many former office-holders had been appointed for life, and those who survived the period were anxious to resume both their offices and their old ways of conducting the courts – which had, of course, been profitable ways. The piecemeal nature of the Restoration encouraged these desires.[36] Reforms, therefore, were unlikely to come from those closely associated with the system, from the courts themselves and their officials.

Neither did reform come from above, from the higher clergy, or from those outside the system. Some historians have blamed this inertia on the characters of successive heads of the church, not on the whole an imaginative group of men. Convocation might perhaps have given a lead, but when in 1664 Convocation gave up its right to assess the clergy for taxation, it gave up the opportunities that were presented for frequent sittings of that body. 'An unintended consequence of this financial transaction', Sykes has written, 'was that sitting Convocations ceased from 1664 to the Revolution twenty-five years later.'[37] The Convocation of 1689 failed to address the issues it was called upon to address, including reform of the ecclesiastical courts, and the policy of suspending sitting Convocations continued. Internal quarrels and divisions between the upper and lower houses of that body marred the few sittings that took place between 1701 and 1717, and in 1741 a further internal dispute ended Convocations for more than a century.[38] The end result was that the canons remained unrevised and the church courts unreformed, despite numerous pleas for positive changes, such as that a sentence of contumacy should replace excommunication for all save spiritual offences, and that the sentence should carry with it a real threat of imprisonment.[39]

---

[35] Sykes, *From Sheldon to Secker*, 19.

[36] Whiteman, 'The re-establishment of the Church', 120; Potter, 'The ecclesiastical courts in the diocese of Canterbury', 182; Green, *The Re-establishment of the Church of England*, 132–3.

[37] Sykes, *From Sheldon to Secker*, 41–3.   [38] Ibid., 45–67.   [39] Ibid., 40.

Historians have depicted the decline of the ecclesiastical courts in terms of this erosion of their prosecuting functions, arguing that the decline in office prosecutions led to the decline of the system as a whole. This does not necessarily follow. In the same way that the rise of business before 1640 cannot be ascribed only to a growth in office prosecutions, the decline in business cannot be laid wholly at the door of an increasing disinclination to prosecute their neighbours among local officials, along with an unwillingness among those cited to obey the citations that came their way. Reform in court procedures, especially that substitution of the writ *de contumace capiendo* for the writ *de excommunicato capiendo* that some defenders of the courts called for, might have led to lower rates of contumacy, but they would not necessarily have led to increasing numbers being cited.

In fact, the expansion of the system before 1640, and its fundamental prosperity, rested on its instance side: on probate and the burgeoning state of the marriage licence trade. It was instance business, as we have pointed out, that generated paper and profits, especially when cases were prolonged. Office cases tended to be dealt with summarily, generating little income inside the system. Tithe, testamentary and defamation suits comprised the great bulk of the instance business of the church courts both before 1640 and after 1660. But whereas before the English revolution such business grew noticeably in volume, after 1660 the boom ended.

The attack on the established church in the 1640s also raised a vigorous debate about tithes.[40] Many took the opportunity to campaign for their abolition. Some thought the institution of tithing 'contrary to sound doctrine', arguing that tithes should be swept away with 'episcopacy, prelacy and common prayer'. Others resented paying tithes to the clerics newly installed in sequestered livings. The abolition of the church courts during the Interregnum only increased the propensity of some to refuse these payments, since it was more difficult for tithe-receivers to take action against those who defaulted. The institution was not abolished, however, in parliaments that defended stoutly the

---

[40] E. J. Evans, 'Tithes', in *The Agrarian History of England and Wales, 1640–1750*, vii, ed. J. Thirsk (1985), 389–405, offers a succinct summary of tithe battles and developments in this era.

rights of lay property owners. The fear of the propertied classes was clearly that if tithes were abolished, rents might follow.[41]

By 1660, there was no shortage of complaints about unpaid tithe and these complaints filled the church courts almost as soon as they resumed their activities. Before the end of 1662 the consistory court of Canterbury heard no fewer than 125 tithe causes and the archdeacon's court there a further 119. Business was also brisk in the consistory court of Winchester.[42] Sixty-four of the one hundred instance causes that came into the York consistory court in the Michaelmas term of 1661 were tithe causes.[43] Tithe litigation continued to be brisk in York until 1696: whereas in three years from 1664–7 an average of forty-seven tithe causes a year were heard there, this average had risen to fifty-three causes a year for a three-year period following 1692. These levels, however, were distinctly lower than those achieved before 1640. In six years between 1601 and 1639 the numbers of tithe causes entering the York consistory court had ranged between 101 and 143 cases a year.[44]

In 1696 a parliamentary statute gave jurisdiction to JPs to deal summarily with claims for tithes of the value of forty shillings or less. The JPs were also given powers of distraint against the possession of those refusing to pay after judgments had been found against them.[45] This change was quickly felt in the ecclesiastical courts. Between 1692 and 1695 the consistory court of York heard an average of fourteen new tithe causes per term; by 1700–1 this had halved to seven per term.[46] Similar tendencies were experienced elsewhere. The consistory court of Exeter was hearing an average of forty tithe causes a year in the early 1690s; but in the twelve months after the act came into force in October 1696, it heard only twenty-six causes.[47] The numbers of tithe causes heard in York and at Lichfield continued to fall through the eighteenth century and into the nineteenth century. The York

---

[41] M. James, 'The political importance of the tithes controversy in the English Revolution, 1640–60', *History* **26** (1941), 1–17.

[42] Potter, 'The ecclesiastical courts in the diocese of Canterbury', 188; Green, *The Re-establishment of the Church of England*, 134–5.

[43] Till, 'The administrative system', 10.

[44] Ibid., 67; Marchant, *The Church under the Law*, 62.

[45] 7 and 8 William III, c. 6 'An act for the more easy recovery of small tithes'.

[46] Till, 'The administrative system', 71.

[47] Smith, 'A study of the administration of the diocese of Exeter', 69.

consistory court heard only thirty-six causes in 1700–1 and twenty-nine in 1727–8. By 1827–29 the total for the entire three years was a mere four causes.[48] The Lichfield court was dealing with an average of twenty-two causes a year in the period 1700–19, twelve a year from 1770–89, and fewer than eight a year from 1810–29. By 1827–9, its total for the entire three years was seven tithe causes.[49]

Tithe causes continued to enter the ecclesiastical courts for the same reasons they had before 1640. New tithe owners and lessees grumbled about the erosion of values of previous compositions and felt obliged to establish their rights at the outset of their ownership or tenancy, often by setting aside previous monetary settlements and demanding payment in kind. Tithe-payers disliked having to pay any higher sum, and they sometimes found themselves unable to do so when harvests were poor and marketable surpluses diminished. To these enduring causes new ones were added. Agricultural innovation became more prominent after 1650, taking the form of new field crops, inviting new tithe claims, and also of convertible husbandry, offering new opportunities for tithe evasion. Nonconformity increased in incidence after 1640, with the Quakers often refusing on grounds of principle to make such payments. The Society of Friends claimed in 1736 that since 1696 over 1,180 prosecutions had been launched against its members, with one-third of them being heard in the ecclesiastical courts and two-thirds in secular courts.[50] An act of 1696 permitted plaintiffs to pursue tithe claims of up to £10 against non-paying Quakers before a JP, and cases involving a *modus* were theoretically only resolvable in secular courts.[51]

Despite these new boosts to tithe business, however, levels of activity in the church courts were clearly below those experienced before 1640 and also showed a longer-term tendency to decline. Whilst the acts of 1696 undoubtedly attracted business away from the church courts, the declining levels of business experienced before this date suggest that other and deeper causes were at work. These will be examined in the next chapter.

The disintegration of the business of the church courts that began in the 1640s proceeded at an uneven pace. One of the last

[48] Till, 'The administrative system', 67; *PP*, 1831–2, xxiv, 567.
[49] Tarver, 'The consistory court of the diocese', 184; *PP*, 1831–2, xxiv, 567.
[50] E. J. Evans, *The Contentious Tithe* (1976), 58.   [51] Ibid., 44.

roles to be lost was the provision of probate and administration, largely because parliament failed initially to provide alternative facilities for such a vital need. Eventually, however, this *lacuna* was acknowledged and filled.

The urgency of some provision for probate was apparent from the start. In November 1644, recognising 'the necessity of that service', Parliament appointed Sir Nathanael Brent to continue the service provided by the Prerogative Court of Canterbury (PCC).[52] This failed to relieve poorer successors who were anxious to avoid lengthy journeys. Their predicament was not relieved by an act of 1653, which, consequent upon the death of Brent, set up a centralised probate court in London for 'all and every the Counties and Cities of England and Wales'.[53] One probable consequence of this was that more and more probate business was attracted to London, especially from those counties that were nearest to the metropolis. Whereas fewer than 17 percent of Colchester wills in the years 1660–99 were proved in the PCC and 20 per cent of Cambridge ones, 51 per cent of Reading wills were proved in that London court.[54] There is little evidence to suggest that probate rose substantially in volume in many of the local diocesan and peculiar courts in the later seventeenth century, but it certainly did so in the PCC. Whereas in the 1620s it was proving on average some 1,500 wills per year, by the 1660s this average had risen to over 1,900 a year, by the later 1690s to some 3,000 a year, and by the years 1827–9 this annual average had more than doubled to 6,600.[55]

This growth in PCC activity may, indeed, have leached some of the vitality of the local probate courts. The number of male will-makers in the diocese of Ely peaked in the early seventeenth century and showed no tendency to grow thereafter. It declined drastically after 1750.[56] Whereas in the 1620s the consistory court of Ely was dealing with an average of 152 probates a year, by 1827–9 it dealt with only 94. The Worcester consistory court dealt with an average of 181 probates a year in the 1620s, but by 1827–9

---

[52] C. H. Firth and R. S. Rait, eds., *Acts and Ordinances of the Interregnum, 1642–1660* (1911), 564–66.

[53] Ibid., 702.

[54] Goose, 'Fertility and mortality in pre-industrial English towns', 194.

[55] Takahashi, 'The number of wills proved', 198; *PP*, 1831–2, xxiv, 553.

[56] N. Evans, 'The occupations and status of male testators in Cambridgeshire, 1551–1800', in *When Death Do Us Part*, ed. Arkell et al. (2000), 180.

this had shrunk slightly to 173.[57] Given that local populations grew substantially between the 1620s and the 1820s, there must be some support here for Houlbrooke's view that 'the proportion of the population making wills fell during and after the seventeenth century'.[58] As most testamentary litigation revolved around the validity of wills and of debts payable by executors and administrators, the decline in will making must have affected the volume of testamentary causes entering the church courts.

Legislation also played a part in the decline in the volume of testamentary legislation. An act of 1670 laid down clear rules for the division of the estates of those dying intestate.[59] *An act for the prevention of frauds and perjuries* of 1676 stipulated that nuncupative wills bequeathing estates of more than £30 had to be proved by three witnesses, who not only had been present when the testator made his declaration but also had to have rendered their testimonies in writing within six days of the will being made.[60] Finally, in 1692, an Act was passed that brought the province of York into line with the rest of England, ending the custom whereby wives and children could claim part of the estate of husbands and fathers irrespective of other dispositions having been made in the deceased's will. From March 1693, testators were given freedom to dispose of their estates however they wished, as was true in the province of Canterbury. By providing clearer definitions of what was legally acceptable in wills, these measures defused potential litigation. A measure of this success can be derived from the returns made to the Ecclesiastical Courts Commission of 1830. The annual average of all the probates and administrations granted in the three years was just over 20,000, while the average number of testamentary causes begun in all the ecclesiastical courts in both provinces barely exceeded 300. Comparatively few will disputes, therefore, found their way to court. By the late 1820s, moreover, 61 per cent of all probates and administrations in England and Wales were being granted in the two provincial probate courts of Canterbury and York. It is hardly surprising, therefore, that nearly 40 per cent of all testamentary causes were also being brought before the two provincial courts.

---

[57] Takahashi, 'The number of wills proved', 196; *PP*, 1831–2, xxiv, 553.
[58] R. Houlbrooke, *Death, Religion and the Family in England, 1480–1750* (1998), 85.
[59] 22 and 23 Charles II, c. 10.   [60] 29 Charles II, c. 3.

The other diocesan courts had only about 150 cases a year to share between them. Only Gloucester, Lichfield, St David's and Carlisle managed an annual average that scraped into double figures.[61]

The third great plank of business on the instance side was defamation, though as comparatively few of these suits were pursued through to sentence, there was less profit in them for the lawyers involved. Of the 292 causes entering the York consistory court between 1664 and 1667, 106 revolved around defamatory words, as did 132 of the 393 causes heard there between 1692 and 1695. Thereafter, the number of such causes heard in that forum declined steeply – in part, however, because more and more were being pursued in York's chancery court. Between 1665 and 1705 the number of such causes entering both courts doubled in volume.[62] Despite this, it seems that levels of defamation business in the York courts did not reach those characteristic of the half-century before 1640.[63] Similar tendencies were experienced elsewhere. In 1624, 187 defamation causes were begun in the consistory court of London, and 198 in 1633.[64] By 1700–10, however, the annual rate had dropped to some thirty-five causes a year, declining to an average of twenty-four between 1735–45 and then to only one a year by the years 1827–9.[65] The volume of defamation causes in the Lichfield consistory court remained 'substantial' – around thirty or more causes a year – until the later eighteenth century, but fell away sharply in the early decades of the following century.[66] Morris's investigation of these causes in the consistory court of Bath and Wells between 1733 and 1850 uncovered similar trends.[67] The decline had become marked even before the Act of 1787 that imposed a six months' limitation on the commencement of defamation suits, an event that speeded up the process. In the eight years 1788–95, twelve defamation causes involving Nottingham inhabitants were begun in the archdeaconry court of that town, no fewer than seven of them in 1791, but twenty-one such cases were begun in the eight years 1780–7.[68]

---

[61] *PP*, 1831–2, xxiv, 553, 566–7.   [62] Till, 'The administrative system', 66–7.

[63] Sharpe, *Defamation and Sexual Slander*, 8.   [64] Gowing, *Domestic Dangers*, 33.

[65] T. Meldrum, 'A women's court in London: defamation at the Bishop of London's consistory court, 1700–1745', *London Journal* 19 (1994), 2; *PP*, 1831–2, xxiv, 567.

[66] Tarver, 'The consistory court of the diocese', 300–20.

[67] P. Morris, 'Defamation and sexual reputation in Somerset, 1733–1850', unpublished PhD thesis, University of Warwick (1985), 222–25.

[68] Ruddock, 'The eye of the bishop', appendix 2 (n.p).

Matrimonial causes, a minor component of the activity before the courts, revealed varying patterns. Spousal cases continued their downward drift and ended in 1753 when the Marriage Act of that year abolished enforceable pre-contracts.[69] On average, fewer than two matrimonial causes of any kind reached the Exeter consistory court before the 1720s; after that date the numbers dwindled to negligible levels. Lichfield maintained similar levels until the 1740s, after which its business declined similarly. The Chester consistory court was busier than either of these, though here too matrimonial causes virtually vanished after the 1720s.[70] One reason for this tendency for causes to vanish from country diocesan courts was that more and more separation and nullity causes were being handled by practitioners in Doctors' Commons and were consequently pursued in the London consistory court and the court of arches.[71] During the period 1670–99, 137 separation and nullity causes were apparently begun at the London consistory court, an average of about 7 per year. By 1770–99, however, that average had grown to more than 10 a year, and by 1827–30 to 14 a year, with the court of arches hearing annually a further 5. Of 101 matrimonial causes begun in all the church courts in the three years 1827–9, no fewer than 58 were heard in these two courts held at Doctors' Commons. Most diocesan courts had virtually no matrimonial litigation. Only Gloucester, with 10 causes in these three years, got into double figures.[72] By 1840–3 London's dominance had increased with the courts at Doctors' Commons handling nearly 77 per cent of all matrimonial suits in England and Wales.[73]

One area of ecclesiastical jurisdiction that did grow was the issue of marriage licences, though this growth has yet to be adequately charted for the years after 1660. In the archdeaconry of Nottingham, the numbers of licences issued appeared to continue that upward climb begun before 1640, and by the second quarter of the eighteenth century more than 200 licences a year were being

---

[69] Outhwaite, *Clandestine Marriage*, 167.

[70] Stone, *Road to Divorce*, table 1.7, 427.

[71] It is perhaps going too far to argue that the 'London Consistory Court had, by the second half of the seventeenth century, become the "divorce court" for the whole country' and that London had 'a virtual monopoly': J. Cox, *Hatred Pursued beyond the Grave* (1993), 16, 25. It is true, however, that causes from all over the country were being pursued there.

[72] Stone, *Road to Divorce*, table 1.8, 428; *PP*, 1831–2, xxiv, 567.

[73] A. Horstman, *Victorian Divorce* (1985), 34.

issued.[74] By this stage, Stone has argued, the sale of marriage licences was responsible for about half of the income of those ecclesiastical court officials – the chancellors and registrars – who were responsible for issuing them.[75] The principal attraction of the licence derived from the permission it gave for couples to skirt the canonical rule that they marry in the parish where one or the other resided. This profitable form of licensed clandestinity received a major setback with the passage of Lord Hardwicke's Marriage Act. In the Nottingham archdeaconry the number of surviving licences fell from 286 in 1753 to 161 in 1755, the first full year after the statute came into force in March 1754. Those licence-issuing surrogates, such as William Sweetapple of Fledborough, who boosted their incomes by marrying 'foreign' couples had their wings clipped. Evidence that Lord Hardwicke's Act hit the sale of marriage licences hard can be found in the drop in government tax revenues from sales of licences and the suggestion made that the Act should be repealed to allow the revenue to recover.[76] In the longer run, however, the passage of the 1753 Act may have stimulated demands for marriage licences. It increased the premium on privacy and this, along with the growth of religious dissent and an increase in the numbers of those who could afford to pay for the dispensations, probably helped to swell the demand for ecclesiastical marriage licences from the late eighteenth century.

By 1830, when the ecclesiastical courts were exposed to the scrutiny of a royal commission, the system was a shadow of the healthy self it had been two hundred years earlier. The enquiries undertaken by the commissioners had elicited that in the three years from 1827 to 1829, a total of 1,903 causes were begun in the English and Welsh church courts. These broke down as follows:

Testamentary	947
Matrimonial	101
Tithes	184
Church rates	58
Church seat, faculty, etc.	190
Brawling	22

---

[74] Outhwaite, 'Sweetapple of Fledborough', 44.   [75] Ibid., 43.
[76] E. Hughes, 'The English stamp duties, 1664–1764', *The English Historical Review* 56 (1941), 251.

Defamation	331
Miscellaneous, including correction	49
Appeals	21

Instance causes still dominated the business of the courts, the system's corrective functions having decreased to negligible proportions. Testamentary business dominated litigation in the courts, accounting as it did for nearly 50 per cent of all causes. Tithe and defamation causes still occupied prominent positions, though levels were minute compared with earlier centuries. This shrinkage inflated the proportion of business classified as matrimonial: previously insignificant in percentage terms, it now constituted 5 per cent of all business in the nation's courts. In London its position was even more dominant: forty-two of the fifty-two causes in the London consistory court were matrimonial ones, as were sixteen of the thirty-one non-appealed causes heard in the court of arches.

What this table does not adequately show, of course, are the still rich pickings that came to the courts through the proof of wills and the sale of licences. But if we disregard these profitable 'extras', it is difficult to understand fully the powerful attacks launched against the courts in Parliament, attacks to be explored more fully in the following chapters. Before coming to this, however, we must probe further the reasons for this dramatic decline in the business and authority of the courts.

10

EXPLAINING DECLINE

It seems clear that once the backlog of causes built up in the 1640s and 1650s was reduced, levels of activity in the ecclesiastical courts settled generally at levels below those that prevailed in the years before 1640. This occurred despite the fact that some special ecclesiastical commissions – the High Commission being the most conspicuous – were not restored in the 1660s, and that these courts must previously have siphoned off some considerable number of cases from the ordinary church courts. Subsequent decline in levels of activity appears to have come in stages, stages that may well have been different from court to court and for different classes of litigation. Prosecution of religious dissent collapsed after 1687 and with this collapse came an increasing reluctance on the part of churchwardens, now the principal instigators of such actions, to charge parishioners with sexual immorality. Such actions did not disappear at once; they were still to be found in the eighteenth century and frequently dominated office prosecutions, though they did so at far lower levels than had prevailed before 1640. They appear to have survived longest, and in greatest number, in jurisdictions where economic change was least evident, where small village and modest urban communities prevailed, in those 'face to face' communities where reputation clearly mattered. They disappeared earliest in the large and expanding towns, and in those rural industrialising areas where a high proportion of the population consisted of young immigrants flocking in to take advantage of expanding economic opportunities and where greater degrees of anonymity probably prevailed. So, for example, in eighteenth-century Lancashire such prosecutions declined first in the economically advanced south of the county, and only after 1770 in the more economically static north.[1] Nottingham typified the expanding urban world of the second half of the eighteenth century. The growth of the framework-knitting industry in and around Nottingham resulted in the town's population doubling between 1750 and 1800. The archdeaconry court ceased to prosecute the town's inhabitants for sexual offences by the early 1770s though office cases against county dwellers continued for another twenty years.[2] In many places prosecutions of moral miscreants appear to have virtually ceased before that act of 1787 that imposed eight-month time limits for the commencement of fornication and incontinence causes.

As we have previously argued, the prosperity of the ecclesiastical court system rested not on its office business, which generated comparatively little income, but on instance causes, litigation that was dominated by tithe, testamentary and defamation. To say, as Hill does, that 'after 1660, with no High Commission to enforce their authority, church courts lost most of their functions except disciplining the lower orders' fails completely to recognise the important roles of instance litigation and probate.[3] Tithe causes, as we have seen, came before the courts at lower levels in the Restoration era than in the pre-1640 decades and fell away further after an Act of 1696 permitted plaintiffs to pursue claims for tithes of a value not exceeding forty shillings before two JPs. In the hundred years after 1540, the amount of tithe litigation had undoubtedly been boosted by two influences. One was that there were unprecedented changes in land ownership consequent on the dissolution of the monasteries and on periodic royal indebtedness that necessitated the sale of crown lands. Levels of activity in the land market clearly showed a long-term tendency to rise. The other boost to tithe litigation came from the marked inflation of agricultural prices. This created situations in which tithe-owners became discontented with former agreements that had substituted cash payments for payment of tithes in kind and attempted to wring from tithe-payers a fairer share of surpluses that were rising in nominal value. Even before the middle of the seventeenth century, however, one of these two underlying influences was changing. Activity in the land market may have peaked in the

[1] Albers, 'Seeds of contention', 226–29.
[2] Ruddock, 'The eye of the bishop', 95.
[3] C. Hill, *Liberty Against the Law: Some Seventeenth-Century Controversies* (1996), 199.

second decade of the seventeenth century and by the end of that century seems to have subsided to levels well below those that were characteristic of the early years of Elizabeth's reign. The inflation of agricultural prices continued a little longer, coming to an end around 1650.[4] From then until the middle of the eighteenth century, average levels of agricultural prices remained relatively constant, though annual yield variations continued to produce marked swings around this constant trend, creating from time to time situations in which tithe-payers were unable to meet their obligations. But a more static land market meant that from 1660, new tithe-owners and new tithe-lessees were not as frequently encountered as they had been before 1640 and the constant price trend produced fewer grievances about inappropriate values.

In the same way that the price inflation of the period 1520–1650 was an outcome of the population expansion of those years, the price constancy of the hundred years that followed mirrored the demographic developments of that period: in 1650 the population of England has been estimated at 5.2 million people and by 1750 it had grown only slightly to 5.7 million, with most of this small increase coming in the decade and a half before 1750.[5] Rising death rates before the mid-eighteenth century, however, produced a 20 per cent higher total number of deaths in 1750 than in 1650.[6] Although most of this rising death rate is attributable to the deaths of infants and children, it is likely that there were more adult deaths at the end of the period than at its beginning. Will-making, however, did not keep pace with the rising number of deaths. Legislation between 1670 and 1692 both tightened and clarified the rules relating to wills. More and more of these were also probably being drafted by lawyers rather than by laymen. The combination of all these developments must have led to fewer disputable wills being drawn up. Trends in probate, as we have previously noted, negatively affected the prosperity of the diocesan courts. By the late 1820s, over 60 per cent of all probates and administrations were being granted in the two major provincial courts. People resorted to them for a variety of reasons, the most

---

[4] L. Stone, *The Crisis of the Aristocracy 1558–1641* (1965), 37; Outhwaite, *Inflation in Tudor and Early Stuart England*, 12–16.
[5] Wrigley and Schofield, The *Population History of England*, 532–3.
[6] Ibid., 498–9.

important being the laws relating to *bona notabilia*, the growing ubiquity and value of personal property (which came to include things like bank and company stocks) and the increasing sensitivity of those lawyers who drafted wills to problems that could arise if wills were proved in the wrong place. It is hardly surprising, therefore, that nearly 40 per cent of all the 316 testamentary causes pursued annually between 1827 and 1829 took place in the two prerogative courts. They were the courts with greatest expertise. What this domination meant, however, was that very little testamentary business was left for the great mass of consistory, archidiaconal and peculiar courts in the rest of the country. Many handled only one or two causes a year: not enough to keep their proctors employed.[7]

These courts were hardly likely, moreover, to be rescued financially by the defamation causes that came their way, even though such litigation retained its popularity longer than other types of instance suits, maintaining in the process the appellation of these institutions as 'bawdy courts'. Such suits outlived the propensity of the church courts to prosecute sexual offenders, a propensity that appears to have been in decline almost everywhere by the third quarter of the eighteenth century, undermining the argument that people embarked on such actions in order to forestall prosecution by the ecclesiastical authorities.[8] The volume of defamation litigation was cut back by the Act of 1787; it required that plaintiffs begin such a suit within six months of the date the offending words had been spoken.[9] Certainly by the time of the Royal Commission investigation of the 1830s the number of suits being pursued was a tiny fraction of former levels: between 1827 and 1829 an annual average of 110 causes were begun in all the English and Welsh courts, a figure lower than the 198 cases pursued in the consistory court of London alone in the year of 1635.[10]

Defamation suits may not have declined because the prosecution of sexual delinquents declined, but both developments may have been affected by that decreased proportion of the population living in 'face to face' communities, a development to which attention has already been drawn. Sexual reputation may have

---

[7] *PP*, 1831–2, xxiv, 564–7.
[8] Morris, 'Defamation and sexual reputation', 236. [9] 27 Geo. III, c. 44.
[10] Gowing, *Domestic Dangers*, 33.

been more esteemed in those villages and small towns where inhabitants expected to pass their whole lives than in those industrial areas and towns that burgeoned in the course of the eighteenth and early nineteenth centuries, creating restless communities with a high proportion of immigrants and societal cultures that were less sensitive to reputation.

Other reasons have also been offered to explain this decline in defamation suits. Some have argued that the men who ran the church courts became disinclined to permit such cases, finding the evidence related in court too distasteful for their increasingly refined tastes.[11] There is certainly evidence that by the early nineteenth century judges were attempting to discourage such suits. A York proctor stated that 'cases of defamation are very little encouraged or countenanced by the judge of our court', a remark corroborated by the judge himself who admitted that 'he would gladly be relieved of [defamation cases] altogether'. Such views were not confined to York: the deputy registrar of Chester said that his court 'discourages [defamation suits] as much as possible' and the chancellor of Salisbury admitted that he had stopped the worst of them by awarding only nominal sums for costs.[12] Awarding only nominal costs, or no costs at all, to plaintiffs must have been a severe discouragement to such actions, particularly as contested cases were unlikely to be resolved in less than six months.[13] The judges may have been reacting also to the changing nature of the parties to such litigation. Members of the more respectable middling groups in society became less and less inclined to initiate such suits, preferring where they could to pursue actions for slander in the common law courts.

This left the church courts as a forum for poor women.[14] There was, of course, no shortage of poor women in eighteenth- and early-nineteenth-century England. No doubt they also continued to hurl sexual insults at each other. However, decreasing proportions of them were inclined to begin actions in the church courts in consequence. Changes in environment and in cultures

---

[11] Morris, 'Defamation and sexual reputation', 17–18; R. Trumbach, *Sex and the Gender Revolution* (1998), 24.
[12] S. M. Waddams, *Sexual Slander in Nineteenth-Century England: Defamation in the Ecclesiastical Courts* (2000), 56–7.
[13] Ibid., 71, 103–6.
[14] Morris, 'Defamation and sexual reputation', 8, 20, 232, 349.

may account for some of this reluctance, but it was influenced also by two further changes that increased the costs of litigation for poorer litigants, dissuading them from beginning such suits or continuing with them if already begun. One was the beginning in the Restoration era of the imposition of stamp duties on legal paper. An Act of 1671 laid down duties of four pence on every citation, monition and deposition of a witness, six pence for every answer, sentence or final decree, one shilling for every libel or allegation, two shillings for every commission issued by an ecclesiastical court, three shillings and four pence for every appeal made from an inferior to a superior court, and ten shillings for every appeal to the delegates. Although this measure lapsed in 1680, even heavier duties were imposed from 1694 onwards.[15] This was an important additional cost in a legal system where parties and witnesses were summoned on paper and parchment, and evidence and rebuttals were written rather than oral interchanges. The other influence derived from the gradual cessation of the lesser church courts, those of the archdeacons and rural deans, leaving would-be litigants with longer distances to travel in order to lodge their complaints and pursue their grievances. Apparitors would also have to travel greater distances, and they tended to be paid by the mileages they covered. In the diocese of Lichfield and Coventry, for example, the archdeaconry courts no longer sat in the eighteenth century.[16] By the 1830s this situation prevailed in a great number of English dioceses, including Chichester, Gloucester, Hereford, Worcester, Carlisle and Durham.[17]

The decline in both correction causes, especially the correction of sexual behaviour, and of defamation causes raises the question of whether other agencies stepped in to attempt to fill a potential vacuum. That there was such a vacuum and response is suggested by the establishment and brief efflorescence of those private Societies for the Reformation of Manners that were established in the reigns of William and Mary and their successors, societies that employed the magistrates and not the church courts to punish those who were reported.[18] These societies, it has been said,

---

[15] Hughes, 'The English stamp duties', 234–64.
[16] Tarver, 'The consistory court of the diocese', 12.
[17] *PP*, 1831–2, xxiv, 552.
[18] M. Ingram, 'Reformation of manners in early modern England', in *The Experience of Authority in Early Modern England*, ed. P. Griffiths, A. Fox and

'flourished between 1690 and 1710, began to decline after 1725, and were moribund by 1738'.[19] Thereafter it seems possible that people turned more and more, especially but not exclusively in urban environments, to the JPs to resolve conflicts and regulate behaviour. This, of course, had long been a role the magistrates played, but they now found themselves dealing, formally and informally, with offences that in the past had been more or less the exclusive province of the church courts. In addition, the process was encouraged by the encroachment of statute law into the field of moral behaviour. Bishop Edmund Gibson, noting this tendency, warned of its consequences, arguing that 'the Clergy as well as people, slide into a general opinion that this or that crime is punishable nowhere but inn the temporal courts ... and the punishment of Vice and care of Spiritual Matters are by degrees transferred to the Laity, who have neither at heart'.[20]

Various sanctions were available to the JPs, ranging from the warrants or summons for individuals to appear before them, to arbitrating between parties, to delivering summary justice, to binding people by recognizances to maintain good behaviour or to appear at future sessions and risk the process of trial. These devices were used to control a wide range of offences, including defamation and sexual misbehaviour.[21] As the lesser church courts ceased to meet so frequently, people resorted more and more to their local magistrates to settle their disputes. The latter lay more thickly on the ground than did the ecclesiastical courts, especially in urban communities, and were consequently more accessible. Distance and accessibility were important determinants of the patterning of legal processes[22] and the magistrates were also 'open all hours', conducting most business informally in their own homes, in contrast to the church courts, which met at strict times and mostly only once a month. Moreover, the

S. Hindle (1996), 47–8, supplies a perceptive commentary on this 'reformation' and those that preceded and followed it. A recent detailed account of the late-seventeenth- and early-eighteenth-century societies is in Jacob, *Lay People and Religion*, chapter 5.

[19] Trumbach, *Sex and the Gender Revolution*, 91.

[20] Cited in M. G. Smith, *Pastoral Discipline and the Church Courts: The Hexham Court 1680–1730* (1982), 10.

[21] R. S. Shoemaker, *Prosecution and Punishment: Petty Crime and the Law in London and Rural Middlesex, c. 1660–1725* (1991), passim.

[22] Ibid., 279.

numbers of magistrates in most areas tended upwards from the late seventeenth century onwards. Whereas in 1680 there were at least 2,219 justices on the commissions of the peace in England's counties, by 1702 there were at least 3,286, a number that more than doubled to 7,334 by 1761.[23]

The church's interests were not necessarily lacking in this altered forum. Thereafter overall growth may have ceased but the proportion of justices who were also clergymen did not. In 1761 some 11 per cent of JPs were clergymen, but by 1831 the proportion was nearly 22 per cent.[24] It would seem natural that disputes and offences that came previously to the vicar's attention, and thence perhaps were sent on to the church courts, were now more easily and promptly dispatched by the vicar in his own home, acting in his capacity as magistrate. The notebook of one such clerical magistrate, Edmund Tew, the rector of Boldon, county Durham, reveals that he dealt regularly with sexual offences, examining women to establish putative fathers, binding over the men to indemnify the parish and dealing with cases of defamation, many of which were those classic disputes between women that had previously been fodder for the ecclesiastical courts.[25] Tew's notebook also reveals that there was a vast discrepancy between the number of cases that came to his attention and the number that eventually ended in court.[26] Arbitration and summary justice, processes that leave no mark in formal records, were far more common than trials, and this was something that was not likely to have been peculiar to Edmund Tew.

Decline in the business of the church courts thus bred further decline. Smith noted: 'Fewer causes meant less business: less business meant less income for those who practised in the courts; less income forced advocates and proctors to take on more causes than they could handle or to find a second job; a greater work load meant less efficiency which in turn led to fewer causes (and the curse of deputy officials!).' This was written about the York courts, where Smith also noted that 'the practice of attracting all

---

[23] N. Landau, *The Justices of the Peace, 1679–1760* (1984), Appendix A.

[24] E. J. Evans, 'Some reasons for the growth of English rural anti-clericalism c. 1750–c. 1830', *Past & Present* 66 (1975), 101.

[25] G. Morgan and Rushton, *The Justicing Notebook (1750–64) of Edmund Tew, Rector of Boldon* (2000), passim.

[26] Ibid., 13–27.

instance causes to York meant that the decline of the courts of the archdeacons of Cleveland, the East Riding and York was swifter than elsewhere in England'.[27] Even so, similar tendencies were clearly at work elsewhere. By the 1830s, many of the lower courts were not functioning at all. Many of those that were still in being were short of experienced and qualified officers. In these circumstances, it is not surprising that more and more litigants made their way to Doctors' Commons. In the southern province of Canterbury the courts that sat in Doctors' Commons handled some 71 per cent of all testamentary business and nearly 70 per cent of all matrimonial business.[28] It is not surprising, therefore, that Doctors' Commons and testamentary and matrimonial affairs should loom so large in the debates after 1830 that led eventually to the final emasculation of the ecclesiastical courts.

The church and its supporters struggled to maintain their legal system, fighting off several attacks upon the powers of jurisdiction of the church courts in the eighteenth century, but it was a losing battle. Their authority was challenged by the gradual erosion of business, by rising rates of contumacy and by the unwillingness of the state to strengthen the weak sanctions that the church had at its command. Existing sanctions, such as those occasional acts of imprisonment for ignoring court dictates and obdurately remaining in a state of excommunication, were undermined by the issue of general pardons. Pardons were issued, for example, in 1672, 1689, 1694 and 1708.[29] Pleas to substitute the writ *de contumace capiendo* for the ancient writ *de excommunicato capiendo* were resisted until 1813, when at last this change, first proposed during the Restoration, was enacted by Parliament. What we will see, however, when we turn next to consider Parliament's role in the decline of the ecclesiastical courts, is that these increased powers, with the consequent commitment of greater numbers of people to prison for contumacy, gave critics a wonderful opportunity to attack the system. It is arguable not only that the Act of 1813 came too late, but also that its passage actually made matters worse for the courts. In the end, it facilitated their dismemberment.

---

[27] Smith, *Pastoral Discipline*, 4.
[28] A. H. Manchester, 'The reform of the ecclesiastical courts', *AJLH* (1966), 54.
[29] Smith, *Pastoral Discipline*, 2; Stone, *Road to Divorce*, 42.

11

THE BILLS OF 1733–1734

The restoration of ecclesiastical jurisdiction in 1660–1 was accompanied by a renewal of criticism of its activities. Tracts were written extolling the supremacy of Parliament over the church, questioning the legality of excommunication and urging those who were cited to appear before the church courts to resist such demands by seeking prohibitions from King's Bench or Common Pleas.[1] Bills attempting to curb clandestine marriages became a regular feature of parliaments from 1666 onwards, providing opportunities on occasion for critics to berate the church courts. In discussing the bill of 1678, for example, one member of the Commons complained that 'a suit about clandestine Marriage may depend in the Ecclesiastical Courts three or four years, and scarce be decided in that time', adding, 'I would have the Tryal of clandestine Marriages be at Common Law.' Another member urged that a clause be added to this bill attempting to speed up their proceedings.[2]

Complaints about real or alleged abuses in the practices of the courts were made in parliament at decadal intervals. A bill 'concerning regulating the Ordinaries, and abuses in Ecclesiastical Courts' was offered to the Commons in 1671.[3] Petitions 'against several Proceedings of Ecclesiastical Courts' were referred to a Commons committee in 1680.[4] A committee of the Lords appointed to investigate irregularities in Westminster Hall was

---

[1] *The Law of England: Or A true Guide For all Persons concerned in Ecclesiastical Courts* (1680); *Excommunication Excommunicated: Or Legal Evidence That the Ecclesiastical Courts have no Power to Excommunicate any person whatsoever for not coming to his Parish-Church* (1680).

[2] A. Grey, *Debates of the House of Commons, From the Year 1667 to the Year 1694* (1763), v, 59–60; Outhwaite, *Clandestine Marriage*, 13–17.

[3] *CJ*, 9, 199.   [4] Ibid., 680–1, 692.

also urged in 1689 to investigate 'what is fit to be redressed in the Ecclesiastical Courts'.[5] The Lords actually passed a bill in 1696 'for better regulating of the Proceedings in the Ecclesiastical Courts', but this failed to progress in the lower house.[6] The Commons returned to the task in 1698, however, with permission being given for two members to prepare a 'Bill to regulate the Proceedings and Process of the Ecclesiastical Courts'.[7] In 1713 the Lords passed, after consultations with the civilians, a bill 'to prevent the too frequent Denunciation of Excommunication, in the Exercise of Ecclesiastical Jurisdiction'. This was returned to them, however, with the addition of two clauses relating to the qualifications of ecclesiastical judges and the taking of exorbitant fees.[8] That there may have been substance to some of the criticisms made of these courts is suggested by the recommendations that surfaced in meetings of Convocation between 1702 and 1715. The clergy in the lower house complained strongly in 1702 about irregularities in the issue of marriage licences, about people remaining excommunicate for lengthy periods and so rendering the sentence 'less awful and effectual than it ought to be', about too frequent commutations of penance and the subsequent private pocketing of the proceeds, about legally unqualified judges being permitted to sit in the courts and about the tendency for fees to creep beyond those specified in the canons of 1604.[9] Such complaints led in 1710 to a Convocation committee recommending that the abuses relating to excommunication would best be remedied by Parliament passing an act that replaced the writ *de excommunicato capiendo* with a writ *de contumace capiendo*, that commutations of penance for cash payments be permitted only with the written consent of the bishop or his deputy and that a register be kept of the uses to which such sums were applied.[10] In 1712 the lower house of Convocation turned its attention more fully to the question of clandestine marriages, recommending in the process that the residential requirements of marriage licences be strictly enforced, a recommendation that would have grossly

[5] *LJ*, xiv, 345.   [6] *LJ*, xv, 704; *CJ*, 11, 526, 529, 533.
[7] *CJ*, 12, 199.   [8] *LJ*, xix, 530, 536, 545, 578, 580–1, 613; *CJ*, 17, 434, 462–6.
[9] E. Cardwell ed., *Synodalia: A Collection of Articles of Religion, Canons, and Proceedings of Convocations* (1842), ii, 711–14.
[10] Ibid., 732–3.

undermined their popularity and thus the profitability of suits brought for their enforcement in the ecclesiastical courts.[11] These recommendations were incorporated into the draft canons of 1714 relating to issuance of such licences where, amongst other things, it was specifically noted that canon 102 of 1604 'hath been frustrated by inserting in such licenses the names of other parish churches or chapels besides those where the parties to be married dwell'.[12] These recommendations reinforced Parliament's then current campaign to curb clandestine marriages and thereby to increase the revenues collectable from the acts of 1695 that imposed taxes on marriage, marriage licences and marriage certificates.[13]

Parliament had passed many statutes that influenced ecclesiastical jurisdiction, though it is true that with the exception of those that specified as felonies behaviour such as buggery and bigamy, most of these statutes granted secular courts a concurrent jurisdiction rather than an exclusive one. This is true, for example, of the 1696 Act that empowered JPs to determine small tithe causes, a measure that led to a marked diminution in such causes in the ecclesiastical courts.[14] No legislation was passed that had as its principal aim the deliberate extinction of jurisdiction in the church courts. This is true even of the Toleration Act. Although it led to the virtual abandonment of church court prosecutions for religious offences, this was an unforeseen consequence of the measure and not its deliberate intention. It is true also of those various statutes that campaigners for the 'reformation of manners' urged should be more actively enforced by the magistrates. As John Disney, an early-eighteenth-century polemicist, pointed out:

Swearing, Drunkenness, Prophanation of the Lord's–Day, and Lewdness, etc., ... are indeed punishable by the Censures of the Church, and the Proceedings of Ecclesiastical Courts; and so they are by the Temporal Laws of the Land. Both the one and the other may severally execute their Authority in such Cases, provided the same individual Offence be not twice punished. The Stat. 4 Jac. I. cap. 5. against Drunkenness, makes

[11] Ibid., 770–5.
[12] Bray, *The Anglican Canons*, 836–7. This, however, probably encouraged the practice that one subsequently encounters of officials inserting in the licence the names of two or more parishes, one of which was the parish of residence.
[13] Outhwaite, *Clandestine Marriage*, 14–15.
[14] 7 and 8 William III, c. 6.

express Provision, that the Ecclesiastical Jurisdiction shall not thereby be abridg'd or restrained, but may still proceed against Offenders by Canon-Law, as usual. The like Provision is made by 1 *Eliz.* Cap. 2. and 3 *Jac.* I. cap. 4 against Absenters from Church; and by 1 *Car.* I. cap. 1. and 3 *Car.* I. cap. 1. against Prophanation of the Lord's-Day. Yet it must be owned, that (wherever the Fault lies) notwithstanding this Power they have, they seldom exert it. Whether they have no Preferments brought before them, or whe-ther they take no Notice of them when they are brought, I can't tell; but so it is in Fact, that the Discipline of the Church, and the Terror of Penance and Excommunication are (thro' some Body's Fault or other) at a very low Ebb, seldom exercised, and little fear'd.[15]

Little is known about the background to those failed parlia-mentary attempts to effect reforms in the church courts. It is likely that such initiatives were frequently sparked off not by inexorably mounting ideological forces but by particular inci-dents, incidents brought to the attention of members of parlia-ment that created opportunities for critics to attack the courts. We get occasional glimpses of such events before 1700,[16] but it is in the eighteenth century that we begin to see clearly the random and opportunistic nature of the assaults that took place periodically on the jurisdiction and practices of the ecclesiastical courts.

On 13 February 1733 the House of Commons received a peti-tion from the 'Gentlemen of the Grand Jury, Justices of the Peace, and other Gentlemen and Inhabitants, now or late of the County of Derby, and elsewhere' complaining about the maladministra-tion of ecclesiastical justice in the consistory court of Lichfield. It complained specifically about unauthorised surrogates granting marriage licences contrary to the canons; about illegal processes, visitations and fees; and about vexatious delays and 'other oppressive Practices'. The document was referred to a parlia-mentary committee headed by Sir Nathaniel Curzon, the MP for Derbyshire.[17] Behind this perhaps familiar set of complaints there lurked a highly specific set of circumstances: in this case involving the clandestine marriage in August 1730 of a twenty-two-year-old army ensign called James MacCulloch and the seventeen-year-old Anna Bella Wilmot, the young daughter of Robert Wilmot, a

---

[15] J. Disney, *An Essay upon the Execution of the Laws against Immorality and Prophaneness* (1708), 16–17.
[16] *CJ*, 9, 680–1; 11, 782.   [17] *CJ*, 22, 37.

gentleman dwelling in Osmaston, situated a mile or so from the town of Derby.[18]

Documents assembled by Wilmot and surviving cause papers at Lichfield enable us to piece together the story in some detail. According to his own testimony, MacCulloch, accompanied by a companion called Hugh Bateman, went to the Virgin's Inn in Derby on the night of Saturday 1 August to drink a bottle of wine. Seeking a third 'agreeable' drinking companion, Bateman nominated, and sent for, Richard Alleyne, a clergyman of St Werburgh's parish, Derby. It was during this drinking session, and while Bateman was out of the room, that MacCulloch aired his plan to marry Anna Bella Wilmot secretly, Alleyne promising to help procure a licence and conduct the marriage. The following day the two conspirators met again, this time in the George Inn in Derby, where they were joined by Henry Cantrell, the Vicar of St Alkmund's in Derby, who came bearing a blank marriage licence and marriage bond – documents which Cantrell proceeded to fill out in their presence. The licence, MacCulloch later recollected, cost him two guineas, of which Cantrell pocketed twenty-five shillings.[19] Although Cantrell told MacCulloch that he was required to swear that the consent of Anna Bella's parents had been given, he allegedly added that 'he could soften it and it would be sufficient to swear that they were not absolutely against it'. Two days later, on 4 August, Alleyne married the pair in a wood called the 'Grove' adjacent to the Wilmot house at Osmaston, the sole witness being a servant 'whose name we do not know'.[20] It was apparently the servant who, during the service, gave the bride away.[21]

The young couple then eloped to London, leaving behind a furious father, Robert Wilmot. A measure of his passion can be gathered from the letter he wrote to his daughter over two months later:

Before you receive the Advantage of a Farthing from me, I am Positively Determined to Punish both Cantrell and Alleyne to the utmost for giving the Finishing Stroaks to the Station you are now in, and also to have your

---

[18] Not to be confused with the other Derbyshire Osmaston, which is near Ashbourne.
[19] DRO, D 3155M/C141.   [20] Ibid., C138.
[21] LRO B/C/5, 1731. This is a bundle of unnumbered documents relating to the cause of Wilmot c. Cantrell.

Marrige Publickly Proved (as to Time and Place) and Consequently to
Redeem your Character as to your Running away from your Mother and
me as a Whore.[22]

He appears to have quickly publicised his intention to prosecute
the two clerics. Indeed so alarmed was Alleyne at this prospect
that he wrote to James MacCulloch four days after the ceremony
in the Grove suggesting that he 'write down to Mr Wilmot to
acquaint him that I did not marry you, but only Joyned your
Hands, upon a Solemn Contract, wherein you Engaged to marry
Each Other and None Else ...'.[23] Alleyne was clearly inviting
MacCulloch to affirm that the ceremony was a mere betrothal, an
espousal *de futuro*, and not one *de presenti*, the ceremony that
created an indissoluble union. The problem with this strategy,
however, was that a licence was not required for a betrothal, as
Alleyne obviously knew when he wrote, 'The Surrogate is in great
Danger (Cantrell I mean) if it be known that he granted the
Licence'.[24] Consequently he urged MacCulloch to obtain another
marriage licence and go through a further marriage ceremony.
This could be managed at St Margaret's, Westminster, where a
licence could be obtained and the ceremony performed, obviating
the need to obtain a licence at Doctors' Commons, the heartland
of ecclesiastical law, wherein dangers obviously lay. Alleyne later
implicitly admitted that his plan to pass off the ceremony as a
mere espousal was a pack of lies. Offering early in October to
Wilmot an 'Exact account of Marriage betwixt Mr MacCulloch
and your Daughter', he acknowledged that the 'Marrige Rites
were Lawfully Solemnized in the upper End of the Grove at
Osmaston by me' on the basis of the licence obtained from Cantrell.[25]

Cantrell also sought to avert prosecution, requesting through
intermediaries an interview with Robert Wilmot in order to clear
his name.[26] Wilmot declined all such overtures, however,
regarding Cantrell, as he wrote to Sir Nathaniel Curzon, as 'a very
Dangerous Man in Conversation, and one that makes no Scruple
to assert Falshood, and to Misrepresent Discourse'.[27]

Nothing could divert Wilmot from his plan to prosecute the
two errant clerics. He diligently compiled accounts of the events
leading up to the ceremony in the Grove and made contact with

[22] DRO, D 3155M/C150.   [23] Ibid., C136.   [24] Idem.
[25] DRO, D 3155M/C148.   [26] Ibid., C143–4.   [27] Ibid., C145.

several bishops and both archbishops advertising the facts of the case. He wrote also to the Master and Fellows of Emmanuel College, the Cambridge college that had educated both Alleyne and, a generation earlier, Henry Cantrell.[28] Alleyne's 'True Character, in all Respects is well known at Emmanuel Colledge', he wrote, for he had recently married his cousin, the daughter of John Alleyne, the rector of Loughborough, without the latter's knowledge or consent.[29]

Exactly a month after the clandestine marriage had occurred, the prosecution of Henry Cantrell for issuing the licence for Anna Bella's marriage without ensuring that parental consent had been obtained got under way in the consistory court at Lichfield, Wilmot's objective being to strip Cantrell of his powers of surrogacy, and two weeks later Wilmot also began the prosecution of Richard Alleyne for conducting a clandestine ceremony.[30] By then, of course, proctors had been sought but they had to be formally admitted in the court; witnesses had to be located and summoned to be examined and articles of accusation had to be prepared. It all took time, though Cantrell's prosecution seems to have taken more time than was customary. The articles eventually drawn against Cantrell accused him of failing to administer a proper oath to James MacCulloch before granting his licence and, indeed, of granting several other licences in 'an illegal and irregular manner'. Two such cases were specifically cited, involving the marriages by licence of Thomas Garrat of Duffield, Derbyshire, and Alexander Sherwyn of Bowton, Derbyshire. It took until the end of March 1731, however, for Garrat and Sherwyn to answer the interrogatories posed on behalf of Cantrell.

Matters could conceivably have been delayed by the death of Edward Chandler, bishop of Lichfield, in November 1730, the illness of Lichfield's chancellor, Dr Henry Raynes, and the frequently enfeebled state of Wilmot's own proctor, the elderly George Hand.[31] Wilmot himself harboured deep suspicions about the judge who actually presided over the case, Raynes's surrogate, Dr Richard Ryder.[32] At the conclusion of the case, Wilmot

---

[28] J. Venn and J. A. Venn, *Alumni Cantabrigienses* (1922), i, 19, 289.
[29] DRO, D 3155M/C140, 141.
[30] LRO, B/C/2/97, fos. 255, 257; DRO, D 3155M/C168.
[31] DRO, D 3155/C157, 160, 161, 164, 167.   [32] Ibid., C179.

accused Ryder of obstruction, complaining to Henry Raynes, 'I
esteem myself to be Used very Unjustly by him.'[33] Wilmot's
lawyer son, Eardley Wilmot, blamed the actual practices of the
court: 'always Unintelligible to all but the Advocates in them'.[34]
Cantrell was, however, a slippery opponent. He used every
opportunity to slow down proceedings, not only challenging all
the charges levelled against him, no matter how hopeless his own
defence was, but also resorting to other, infuriatingly desperate,
delaying tactics. In the summer of 1731, he appears to have hit
upon the fact that in Richard Alleyne's deposition, Wilmot's
daughter was named as 'Anna Bella Wilmott' and he thereupon
deposed 'That no faith or credit at least sufficient in Law be given
to the pretended sayings or Depositions of Richard Alleyne' who
'hath therein sworn falsely and corruptly, for in truth the said
Robert Wilmott never had any Daughter born or baptised by the
name of Anna Bella Wilmott'.[35] As George Hand warned, 'The
Law is grounded upon reason and equity, and gives everyone
Liberty to make the defence, and Cantrel for want of a better Plea,
has made use of this poore Shift, to keep the evil day far off, and
prevent the final determination of his cause this Terme.' He urged
Wilmot to consult an advocate at Doctors' Commons so as to
obtain the best possible advice, a plea he was to reiterate two
months later when he also warned his client that Cantrell would
probably use the next sitting on 28 September to call Wilmot to
explain 'the misnomer in the Certificate, as to your daughters
Christian name'.[36] The certificate referred to was an attested copy
of the entry in the parish register of All Saints Derby indicating
that on 13 October 1712 Wilmot's daughter was baptised with the
name 'Annabella'. Wilmot had subsequently to explain that his
daughter had indeed been baptised as Anna Bella and that the
entry in the register, made some weeks after the christening, 'was
wrote ... by some unskilfull and illiterate person by a mistake'.
He attested that she had always been known as Anna Bella: that
was how she wrote her own name: and, a telling point, that this
was how Cantrell had spelt her name on the licence and bond that
he had filled in. He also asserted that he and his family, dwelling

[33] Ibid., C173.   [34] Ibid., C162.
[35] LRO, B/C/5, 1731: Cantrell's deposition of 6 July 1731.
[36] DRO, D 3155M/C166–7.

as they did so near to Derby, were known to Cantrell, who would also have known that his daughter was marrying without her father's permission[37] Other witnesses were mobilised to support Wilmot's contention that his daughter was indeed known as Anna Bella. Francis Revel of Brockwell Hall, Nottinghamshire, testified to this effect in January 1732, adding that this was because the Wilmots wanted to incorporate the names of both her godparents, one of whom was his mother, into that given to the child.[38] Cantrell continued, however, to deny that she was so baptised and argued that if in the bond and licence she was described as Anna Bella, he was acting on information provided at the time by James MacCulloch.[39]

By this stage, a year and eight months after the wedding, the only judicial decision that appears to have occurred was that the court had decreed the excommunication of MacCulloch and his bride.[40] By 1732 Robert Wilmot's patience was threadbare. He wrote directly to Dr Raynes, the chancellor at Lichfield, complaining about the maladministration of Richard Ryder, Raynes's surrogate, and threatened to complain to a superior court.[41] Cantrell, he later wrote, 'has Ruined many Persons of Good Fortune, and brought much Inconvenience to several Familys, by Granting Licences Illegally, and other Male-Practices'.[42] Several witnesses, including Thomas Garrat and Alexander Sherwyn, who were cited in the original complaint, testified that they had no recollection of signing either bonds or affidavits when obtaining their licences, Cantrell contenting himself on each occasion with getting them to swear on a Bible that nothing could impede the match.[43] Stephen Barton, a baker of Stanley, went further than this. Not only did he declare that he never signed a marriage bond, but on being shown by Wilmot a bond with his name upon

---

[37] LRO, B/C/5, 1731: 'The personal answers of Robert Wilmot', 9 October 1731.

[38] Ibid., dated 25 January 1732.

[39] Ibid., 'The personal Answers of the Reverend Mr Henry Cantrell', dated 6 March 1732.

[40] DRO, D 3155M/C169. MacCulloch subsequently wrote to the churchwardens of Osmoston explaining that in January 1731 he handed over to George Hand, the proctor of Lichfield, the sum of £5 'for Commutation money for excusing me doing Pennance' (ibid., C176). This takes on significance in relation to the parliamentary bill that followed.

[41] Ibid., C173.   [42] Ibid., C175.

[43] LRO, B/C/5, 1731: depositions of Garrat and Sherwyn 30 March 1731 and of John Fanshawe 25 May 1731.

it, he claimed that it was signed 'by the said Mr Cantrell since his prosecution in this Court because the same Name was not of this Deponents hand.'[44] It is clear also that Cantrell was prepared to marry couples in his own church, irrespective of whether they were residents of his parish. He admitted as much when, after completing MacCulloch's licence, he acknowledged that he told him that 'he would add his own Church as the Surrogates usually do'.[45] That he was plying a trade of this sort is suggested by the scale of marriages at St Alkmund's before and after the McCulloch–Wilmot match. In the ten years from 1721 to 1730, at least 481 marriages took place there, an average of 48 per year, which, if the marriage rate was approximately 10 per 1,000 population, would serve a community of near 5,000 people. Derby may have had a population of this size by 1730, but it also had four other parishes. After the event that brought him into court, Cantrell's business shrank noticeably. From 1731 to 1740 only 115 marriages are recorded in the register, an average of 11 a year, much more in line with the church's legal catchment area.[46]

Wilmot was adamant in his objectives, which were, as he explained to George Hand, 'to divest Mr Cantrel of his Surrogacy' and 'to Charge him with Costs'.[47] Brushing aside further pleas from Cantrell for reconciliation, he continually pressed Lichfield officials for a decision.[48] Wilmot was clearly expecting a decision early in July 1732, but his expectations had been dashed in the past and it was not until October that we get a firm indication that a decision had been reached – Curzon commenting in a letter to Wilmot that he was 'glad to hear that you have at last got so just a Sentence'.[49] What precisely that sentence was we do not know, but it is likely that Wilmot realised his objectives, that Cantrell's powers of surrogacy were taken away and that the clergyman had to meet all the costs of the case. This would have amounted to a not inconsiderable sum; Wilmot's court expenses alone came to £38 4s. 5d.[50]

---

[44] Ibid., deposition of 25 May 1731.
[45] Ibid., Cantrell's interrogatories put to MacCulloch.
[46] *Derbyshire Parish Registers*, ed. W. P. W. Philimore, iv (1908).
[47] DRO, D 3155M/C168: draft letter of 20 September 1731.
[48] Ibid., C151, 161, 171–2, 175.   [49] Ibid., C181.
[50] LRO, B/C/5, 1731: 'Expensae litis'.

Exasperated by the tardy nature of the proceedings at Lichfield, Wilmot had begun in late August 1732 to seek signatures for a county petition to be presented to Parliament by Sir Nathaniel Curzon. Sir Simon Every wished it every success, adding in his reply, 'I am no Stranger to the vile abuses committed in their B-Y [Bawdy] Courts and should be glad to see them remedied.'[51] Sir John Rushout thought 'The Impositions and abuses of these Courts are very notorious, and have been universally complained of a long time', adding 'I dare say there will be no want of inclination in the House of Commons to redress those Grievances.'[52] James Cavendish, for one, promised that when it came into the Commons he would give it 'the best attendance' that he could.[53]

On 13 February 1733 the petition was presented to the Commons. Among other matters, it complained:

The Grievances occasioned by the Administration of ecclesiastical Jurisdiction, within the said Diocese, and particularly by the Substitution of Surrogates, not duly qualified, who grant Licences for Marriages, contrary to the Canons of the Church of England, to the Ruin, or the Inconvenience, of many Families, by issuing illegal processes, by illegal Visitations, by the Exaction of illegal and unusual Payments and Fees, by expensive and vexatious Delays, and other oppressive Practices, used in the Episcopal Consistory Court of Lichfield, under the Conduct of the Judge thereof, deputed by the Chancellor of the said Diocese ...

The petition was referred to a committee headed by Sir Nathaniel Curzon.[54] Two days later it was ordered that it should direct its attentions to 'the Abuses and Exactions of the ecclesiastical Courts in general ...'.[55] The timing of the petition was opportune, catching as it did a rising tide of anticlericalism.[56] The committee proceeded to attempt to acquire evidence that the complaints in the petition were well grounded. It ordered the officers of the Lichfield court to submit a list of surrogates, the 'warrant' for the MacCulloch marriage sworn before, and signed by, Cantrell, plus a table of all the fees charged since the reign of Elizabeth.[57]

---

[51] DRO, D 3155M/C180.   [52] Ibid., C182.   [53] Ibid., C183.
[54] *CJ*, 22, 37.   [55] *CJ*, 22, 40.
[56] S. Taylor, 'Whigs, Tories and anticlericalism: ecclesiastical courts legislation in 1733', *Parliamentary History* 19 (2000), 329–55. I am indebted to Dr Taylor not only for his brilliant summary of the politics of this parliamentary session but also for drawing my attention to the importance of the Wilmot papers.
[57] DRO, D 3155M/C284–6.

Curzon was apparently angered when no one appeared to testify to the truth of the complaints in the petition. As Wilmot's son Robert reported, 'They must all be proved very fully', adding the query, 'Where is the licence Cantrel gave?'[58] Some material from Lichfield did eventually arrive but the committee looked at it only on the day before it reported its deliberations to the Commons.[59] Meanwhile, however, the committee attracted polemics such as William Bohun's *A Brief View of Ecclesiastical Jurisdiction*, a tract that complained of the 'Exactions, Extortions and Oppressions, of what are called Spiritual Courts and Jurisdiction', squeezing a near million pounds a year out of 'People's Purses' to support perhaps some 20,000 people.[60]

It was on 9 March 1733 that Curzon reported for the committee. That body proposed that no criminal cause should be commenced without a promoter of the cause who would also have to give security that the prosecution would be pursued; it also recommended that the promoter should bear double the costs if the cause was not upheld. It proposed also that those so accused should be able to seek a prohibition from King's Bench or Common Pleas as a prelude to the transfer of the cause to a secular court where it would be tried by jury. These two proposals, if implemented, would have effectively crippled the prosecutorial function of the church courts. A third proposition advocated removal of the legal disabilities of excommunication but argued for the availability of Chancery 'Writs of Contumacy' to enforce obedience. A fourth resolved that monies paid for commutation of penance should not be paid to church court officials but should be handed over to the overseers of the poor of the parish where the offence was committed. A fifth dealt with rates and assessments for the repair and ornament of churches. A sixth forbade the church courts from compelling wills to be registered and prohibited letters of administration from being required unless specifically requested by those with an interest in an estate. Finally, and Wilmot must have wondered at this stage whether his specific complaints had been totally forgotten, a seventh resolution directed 'That the laws for preventing clandestine Marriages

---

[58] Ibid., C191. [59] Ibid., C194.
[60] W. Bohun, *A Brief View of Ecclesiastical Jurisdiction As it is this Day practised in England, Addressed to Sir Nathanael Curzon, Bart.* (1733).

ought to be amended and made more effectual'. The house ordered that a bill embodying the first six of these resolutions be brought in and that the house should meet in committee to consider the structure of a bill to prevent clandestine marriages.[61]

A month later, on 9 April 1733, a 'Bill for the better regulating the Proceedings of Ecclesiastical Courts' was brought into the Commons and read for the first time. Just over a week later it was read a second time and then committed. At this stage it embodied all but the fifth of the first six resolutions of the Commons committee, the exclusion being dealt with by the introduction of a separate Church Rates bill on 25 April.[62] George Lee, a future dean of the arches and naturally a defender of the courts, thought that the bill ought to have been called 'a Bill to abolish Ecclesiastical Jurisdiction', while the author of *Remarks on a Bill now depending in Parliament*, probably Edmund Gibson, thought that 'if the two first Clauses in the Bill be enacted, there will be neither Presentment nor Prosecutions, and by Consequence neither Excommunication, nor Penance, nor Commutation'.[63]

It was not until mid-May, however, that the committee reported its amendments to the Ecclesiastical Courts bill. These amendments removed or lessened many of the clauses that would effectively have crippled the office side of ecclesiastical jurisdiction. Although we lack a detailed account of the committee's deliberations, a summary tract, perhaps written by Gibson, tells us:

The Bill, as amended by the House of Commons, 1st, Leaves Church-Wardens to Present, as they always have done, without Obligation to give Security of any kind for prosecuting or paying of Costs, 2dly, It leaves the Ecclesiastical Judge to try the Facts by Depositions of Witnesses, as he has always done, without any Recourse to the Temporal Courts. And 3dly, It appropriates the Censure of Excommunication to Spiritual Crimes, and provides a Writ *de Contumace capiendo*, to enforce Obedience in all such Matters of a temporal Nature, as are cognisable by the Ecclesiastical Judge.[64]

It clearly represented a victory for the defenders of the church courts, a group that included an *ad hoc* coalition of Tories and

---

[61] *CJ*, 22, 40, 79–80.   [62] Taylor, 'Whigs', 341.

[63] Taylor, 'Whigs', 338; *Remarks on a Bill Now depending in Parliament, For the better Regulating the Proceedings of the Ecclesiastical Courts* (n.d.), 2.

[64] *An Account of the Bill lately depending in Parliament, for the better Regulating the Proceedings of Ecclesiastical Courts* (n.d.), 1.

Whigs, aided perhaps by government ministers. The amendments were passed and the bill was sent on 18 May to the Lords, where, without ministerial or clerical enthusiasm to hasten it through, it died five days later with the adjournment of Parliament.[65] As the tract just quoted stated,

> those of the Laity who favoured the first Draught, thought it too good with these Amendments; and the Bishops thought it not good enough, without further Amendments; and the Officers of the Ecclesiastical Courts, judged it most convenient that Things should remain as they are. Upon which Accounts, it was dropt in the House of Lords, and went no further than the First Reading.[66]

Curzon's committee, it will be remembered, was also empowered to consider the form that a bill to prevent clandestine marriages might take. The heads of such a measure were duly reported to the Commons on 23 April 1733, and these would have gladdened Wilmot's heart, though in truth there was nothing in their list of suggestions that was inconsistent with prior canon or statute law. The committee suggested that licences were not to be granted without an affidavit declaring the ages, qualities and parishes of both parties being obtained from one of the parties seeking to be married. The person seeking the licence was also required to enter into a bond that would be forfeited if the licence was obtained with a false declaration. No licence was to be granted for the marriage of a person under age without the personal consent of parents or guardians and proof of such consent. The only recommendation not applicable to Wilmot's case was that banning clerics who were in prison from conducting marriages. The first, second and fourth of these recommendations met with the house's approval and a bill was ordered to be prepared. It made, however, no further progress.[67]

The story of the fight to bring about a bill to avoid clandestine marriages has been recounted elsewhere.[68] The fight to bring in a bill to reform the ecclesiastical courts also continued, however, with a 'Bill for the better regulating the Proceedings of the Ecclesiastical Courts' being brought into the Commons late in the parliamentary session on 12 March 1734.[69] This bill, as a tract of that year suggests, broadly espoused the same aims as that of the

---

[65] *CJ*, 22, 147, 153, 156; LJ, xxiv, 274–5; Taylor, 'Whigs', 351–2.
[66] *An Account of the Bill*, 3.   [67] *CJ*, 22, 125.
[68] Outhwaite, *Clandestine Marriage*, chapter 1.   [69] *CJ*, xxii, 262, 281.

previous year.[70] A week later it was read for a second time and committed, but three days later, after a vote of forty-two to thirty-nine, discussion of it was postponed for a month, long enough to kill the bill because Parliament was prorogued on 16 April.[71] The forces mustered to defend the courts successfully resisted this renewed attack.

[70] See *Some Thoughts upon the Last Year's Scheme, for the better Regulating Proceedings in the Ecclesiastical Courts, Put Together on the Occasion of an Appearance of the Revival of it* (n.d.).
[71] CJ, xxii, 281, 288.

12

SNIPS AND REPAIRS: SMALL STEPS TO REFORM, 1753–1813

THE MARRIAGE ACT OF 1753

In 1733, in the wake of Robert Wilmot's complaints about his daughter's clandestine marriage, the House of Commons ordered the preparation of a bill to prevent such unions. The heads of a bill were duly reported, but the initiative came too late in the parliamentary term to make further progress. Pressures to reform the laws that made such unions possible continued, however, with further bills being introduced in the Commons in 1736 and in the Lords in 1740. Both were unsuccessful. Thirteen years later the Commons finally achieved the desired result after considerable debate, with the passage of *An Act for the Better Preventing of Clandestine Marriages*, a measure inextricably associated with then Lord Chancellor, the earl of Hardwicke, a distinguished and active lawyer who had persistently complained about the legal tangles that arose from clandestine unions, especially those that took place in London in the liberties of the Fleet prison, which from the late seventeenth century occupied the type of position in relation to marriage in England that Las Vegas once occupied in relation to divorce in the United States.

Background to the act must take in not only long-standing complaints about the Fleet and other centres for clandestine marriage, but also the publication in 1748–9 of *An Apology for the Conduct of Mrs Teresia Constantia Phillips*, a three-volume autobiography by a serial bigamist who seems also to have slept with a large section of the British peerage. Con Phillips, as she was known, entered into a marriage of convenience in 1722 at the age of fifteen with a soldier called Francis Delafield. This was to protect herself from creditors, having already run up considerable debts this early in her career. Delafield, however, was already

119

married, having joined himself with a woman called Magdalen Yeomans in 1718, the ceremony being performed at a well-known Fleet marriage shop, the 'Hand and Pen', by an equally notorious Fleet parson, the Reverend John Draper. About a year after her 'marriage' to Delafield, Con Phillips met Henry Muilman, the son of a prosperous Amsterdam merchant, and she married him in early 1724. Muilman's attempt to annul this marriage initiated a lengthy and involved series of court cases in the London consistory court, the court of arches, the court of delegates and King's Bench and Chancery.[1] It was in the secular courts where she ran afoul of Hardwicke, who in case after case in the 1730s and 1740s had made clear his opposition to clandestine marriages.[2] He was far from alone. The Phillips–Delafield marriage was also highlighted in an influential tract published in 1750 by Henry Gally, Rector of St Giles in the Fields. Gally began by drawing attention to the way in which 'Women in Debt may, on Purpose to screen themselves from their Creditors, be married to Men, who, they know, are at that Time married to other Women'.[3] Gally continued:

This was the Case of Mrs Phillips, who married De la Field to skreen herself from her Creditors; though she knew that he was then a married Man. And this Marriage produc'd not only the Evil here set forth, but also many others. The Legality of her Marriage afterwards to Mr. Muilman depended upon De la Field's being married to another Woman, when Mrs. Phillips was married to him. And as this Point is said to be not yet decided, the Legitimacy of the Children, which Mr. Muilman has had since by Miss Darnel, remains still in Suspence. De la Field and Mrs Phillips were indeed married by a Licence. But yet their Marriage ought to be reckon'd clandestine, as the Licence, by which they were married, was not granted according to Canon: and so the Marriage was, to all Intents and Purposes, as Clandestine as if the Ceremony had been performed without a Licence. This indeed was the chief Reason that induced me to produce this Instance. For besides its being in Print, and known perhaps to most People, it carries with it full Proof of the ill Effects of uncanonical Licences. As to the general fact here advanced, it is well known to be a common Practice at the Fleet; and that there are Men

---

[1] Her involved matrimonial career is entertainingly related in L. Stone, *Uncertain Unions: Marriage in England 1660–1753* (1992), 236–74.

[2] Outhwaite, *Clandestine Marriage*, 95.

[3] The new husband would then perhaps vanish, as Delafield did, creating a situation in which creditors would have to legally set aside the marriage in order to proceed against the original debtor.

provided there who have each of them, within the Compass of a Year, married several Women for this wicked Purpose.[4]

It is doubtful, however, that the publication of either Con Phillip's *Apology* or Gally's tract was the actual trigger for the launch of the parliamentary bill that later became the Marriage Act, though both publications may have prepared the way for it. The trigger was a Scottish case, *Cochran v. Campbell*, which came on appeal to the House of Lords in January 1753. Two women, Magdalen Cochran and Jean Campbell, fought their way through the Scottish courts, both claiming to be the lawful widow of Captain John Campbell of Carrick, who had died in 1746, and thus to be entitled to his naval pension. Campbell had married both women irregularly and it was the complications that arose from this that exasperated the Lords and led them to order 'That the Judges do prepare and bring in a Bill, for the better preventing of Clandestine Marriages'.[5] The task of framing a bill was entrusted to Sir William Lee, the Lord Chief Justice of the King's Bench, who made such a mess of the task that Hardwicke felt obliged to step in and assume control of the measure.[6]

Section XIII of the Act that was eventually passed stipulated 'That in no Case whatsoever, shall any Suit or Proceeding be had in any Ecclesiastical Court, in order to compel a Celebration of any Marriage *in facie Ecclesiae*, by reason of any Contract of Matrimony whatsoever, whether *per verba de praesenti* or *per verba de futuro*'. Critics of the measure seized on this provision, arguing that it made the bill a seducer's charter, in that jilted lovers would no longer be able to have the promises that were made to them upheld.[7] Despite the fact that marital contract litigation stood poised to disappear, no complaint about the effects on the ecclesiastical courts of the loss of such business has been recorded. Church court officials and their spokesmen in Parliament seem to have kept silent, even though a part of their jurisdiction had been snatched away. This silence is perhaps not surprising since by the mid-eighteenth century spousals cases had virtually disappeared from nearly all the country's diocesan

[4] H. Gally, *Some Considerations upon Clandestine Marriages* (1750), 14–6.
[5] L. Leneman, 'The Scottish case that led to Hardwicke's Marriage Act', *LHR* 17 (1999), 161–9.
[6] Outhwaite, *Clandestine Marriage*, 76–80.
[7] Outhwaite, *Clandestine Marriage*, 84, 89.

courts. From March 1754 onward, jilted lovers could pursue their claims only in the secular courts via *assumpsit* for breach of promise, an action that had been open to plaintiffs since 1674 and that now flowered because the ecclesiastical court alternative was closed.[8]

THE BILL OF 1786 AND THE ACT OF 1787

Parliamentary complaints about the remaining jurisdiction of the courts did not surface again until the mid-1780s. Then, in February 1786, a member of the Commons stated that 'no matter stood more in need of regulation and reform, than the practice of the Ecclesiastical Courts'. He pleaded to be allowed to bring in a bill, the principal objective of which was apparently 'the abolition of the practice of prosecuting for ante-nuptial fornication'. This member, the not inappropriately named Mr Bastard, the MP for Devon, went on to cite several cases where the courts had allegedly behaved oppressively, one of these being a case where a man was apparently prosecuted for prenuptial fornication six or seven years after the death of his wife. Another objective of the proposed bill was to end prosecutions for small tithes in both the church courts and the Court of Exchequer.[9] Bastard's bill *To Prevent frivolous and vexatious Suits in the Ecclesiastical Courts, and for the more easy Recovery of Small Tythes* was presented a week and a half later.[10] Despite the prominence that he gave to suits for prenuptial fornication when requesting permission to introduce his bills, the preamble began with the complaint that suits for defamation were 'generally founded in Malice and Resentment only' and were the cause of great expense to those forced to defend themselves. It went on to complain that expensive costs and charges also awaited those attempting to recover tithe payments in the equity and ecclesiastical courts. To remedy these matters, the bill proposed to limit strictly the term within which defamation cases could be started and to impose both term limits and new

[8] J. H. Baker, *An Introduction to English Legal History*, 4th edn (2002), 393; G. S. Frost, *Promises Broken: Courtship, Class, and Gender in Victorian England* (1995), 14–24.
[9] Cobbett, *Parliamentary History*, xxv, 1053.
[10] Lambert, *Sessional Papers*, xliv, 219–26.

value ceilings for tithe cases, below which the case could not be pursued. Small tithe claims were instead to be heard by one JP acting summarily. Detailed provisions were made for the payments of costs in tithe cases, for rights of appeal and for the recording of judgments at subsequent quarter sessions. Almost as an afterthought, the bill appended provisions imposing new term limits on suits for incontinence or adultery, on brawling in churches or churchyards, and on bringing suits for fornication 'after the Party offending shall have been lawfully married'.

Early in May 1786, however, the bill was found unsatisfactory – 'not prepared in a Proper Manner to answer the Purposes thereby intended' – and John Bastard presented the house with a new bill. This version, similarly entitled, began with a brief preamble, insisting that 'it is proper that the Time within which Suits in the Ecclesiastical Courts may be commenced should be limited' and that 'whereas the Mode of recovering Small Tythes, Offerings, Oblations, Church rates, or other Dues, or Compositions for the same, in the Courts of Equity, Courts of Law, and Ecclesiastical Courts is expensive'. It went on to ask for establishment of time limits for bringing matters involving defamation, fornication, brawling on church premises, adultery, the recovery of tithes etc. before the courts. He sought the abolition of prosecutions for ante-nuptial fornication 'at any Time after the Party offending shall have been lawfully married' and moved an extension of the 1696 Act for the recovery of small tithes to cover church rates and offerings.[11] In this new form it was committed, amendments were made to it, and on 17 May it was sent to the Lords.[12] By this stage, specific time limits had been set: for defamation at three months; for adultery, fornication, the solicitation of chastity (an addition), and brawling on church premises at eight months; and for non-payment of tithes etc. at six years from the time that payment was withheld. In the last of these, defendants were to be given one month's notice of the commencement of such a claim against them. Prosecutions for prenuptial fornication were to be abolished once the parties concerned had been married, and the Act of 1696 was to be duly extended to payments other than tithes.[13]

---

[11] Lambert, *Sessional Papers*, vol. 48, 73–6.
[12] *CJ*, 41, 739–40, 766, 801, 811, 816.
[13] Torrington, *Sessional Papers*, 1781/2–1786, 501–4.

In the Lords, the bill was attacked by the bishops. The bishop of Bangor argued that a limitation of three months in which to sue for defamation was absurdly short, as also was the eight months permitted to commence prosecutions for adultery. The courts should be permitted to continue their present practice of entertaining suits for defamation within a year of the offensive words being spoken. As for solicitation of chastity, 'there was no instance of a suit of that kind having been brought in modern times into the ecclesiastical court'; such suits belonged in the temporal courts, 'where they are tried under the description of actions for seduction'. He also argued that the proposed abolition of prosecutions for prenuptial fornication was unnecessary as no such suits had been brought into the courts at Doctors' Commons within living memory, and, if the situation was different in the country courts, the parties prosecuted could always be relieved on application to the court of arches. Similarly, the law relating to tithes needed no amendments and those proposed would put tithe owners, many of whom were laymen, at a greater disadvantage than they were at present. The archbishop of Canterbury added that the 'dissoluteness of the manners of the age' called for more restraints, not fewer, adding that this bill loosened rather than tightened the law. The bill was consequently defeated.[14]

Opponents of the courts persevered. In February 1787 John Bastard again drew the attention of the Commons to 'those arbitrary and remorseless Ecclesiastical Courts', which, he argued, threw the 'lower classes' into prison for their contumacy in cases of defamation and fornication and prosecuted people for incontinence long after the event. Poor people, he pointed out, could not afford to appeal to the court of arches. Bastard and two Cornish members, Sir William Molesworth and Sir William Lemon, were given leave to bring in a new bill, which they did. Now shorn of its tithe provisions and entitled a *Bill to prevent frivolous and vexatious Suits in Ecclesiastical Courts*, its preamble complained that 'Suits are frequently brought ... for Defamation, when no substantial Injury has been sustained; and such Suits are generally founded in Malice and Resentment only, and, by Reason of the great Expence attending the same, tend to the Ruin and Impoverishment of His majesty's Subjects'. To remedy these

---

[14] Cobbet, *Parliamentary History*, xxvi, 125–8.

complaints it proposed to abolish suits for defamation in the church courts, to impose time limits on the bringing of prosecutions for brawling in church or churchyards and to abolish prosecutions for ante-nuptial incontinence at any time after the offending parties had married.[15] John Bastard by this stage was calling for nothing less than the total abolition of defamation causes. In part, he argued, because all such prosecutions were malicious and partly because there was no penalty other than penance, and what was that but 'merely going to church in a masquerade dress'. Sir James Johnstone condemned all courts that functioned without juries.

In committee the bill was much criticised, as a brief record of one of the committee's meetings indicates.[16] Support for the church tribunals came from some unexpected quarters. John Scott, the future Lord Eldon, argued that they were ancient and, in many respects, useful establishments and he saw no cause for their abolition. Although Eldon's biographer does not say so, his support for the courts may have owed something to family loyalty, for his brother, Sir William Scott, the future Lord Stowell, was already the most redoubtable civilian of his time.[17] Support came also from other legal worthies, such as the Attorney General and the Master of the Rolls. In committee, total abolition of defamation suits was rejected in favour of the imposition of new time limits, the preamble now proposing 'Whereas it is expedient to limit the time for Commencement of certain Suits in the Ecclesiastical Courts'. The bill eventually fixed the terms within which causes had to be pursued at six months for defamation and eight months for fornication and brawling on church premises, and it went on to abolish prosecutions for prenuptial fornication once the parties concerned had married. The bill was sent early in May to the Lords, where it was passed without amendment.[18]

From this point on, prosecutions for ante-nuptial incontinence vanished, and those for fornication dwindled markedly. In Devon, Bastard's own county, the drop was apparently 'substantial'.[19]

[15] Lambert, *Sessional Papers*, xlviii, 333–6.
[16] Cobbet, *Parliamentary History*, xxvi, 1004–9.
[17] R. A. Melikan, *John Scott, Lord Eldon, 1751–1838: The Duty of Loyalty* (1999), 29–30.
[18] *CJ*, 44, 405, 524, 535, 627, 639, 652, 657, 770; 27 George III, c. 44.
[19] A. Warne, *Church and Society in Eighteenth Century Devon* (1969), 78.

That ante-nuptial fornications prosecutions had virtually disappeared before the passage of the 1787 Act may be one reason for
the eventual success that opponents of the courts achieved, but
another is surely that the successful measure, unlike its unsuccessful predecessor, had a small number of strictly limited
objectives. Measures which embodied a whole portmanteau of
grievances were more likely to fail.

THE BILL OF 1812 AND THE ACT OF 1813

Defamation causes continued to come into the church courts,
though in ever-dwindling numbers. It was such a case that
sparked off the next major piece of legislative interference. In
January 1812 Parliament received a petition written on behalf of
Mary Ann Dix (or Dicks), an eighteen-year-old woman from
Bristol. The petition alleged that four years earlier she had been
cited to appear in the consistory court at Bristol to answer a cause
brought for defamation. She complained that she duly appeared at
the right time but no proctor was appointed to defend her, seemingly because she had no money to employ one. She continued
to attend the court for several months, until she went into service
for three months in Bath. During her absence her mother attended the court on Mary's behalf, until the latter was told by the
plaintiff's proctor that the daughter had herself to attend. Mary
eventually did so, until a sentence in the cause was given. She was
ordered to perform penance and to pay costs totalling £12 7s. 11d.
In her petition to parliament, she claimed that she was never told
when and how to perform her penance, and the costs were beyond
not only her own means but also those of her father, who earned
14s. a week as a labourer. For not complying with the sentence she
was eventually declared excommunicate, and to make matters
worse the bill for costs grew to £30. In November 1809, eighteen
months after the case against her began, she was taken on a writ *de
excommunicato capiendo* to Newgate jail in Bristol, where she
apparently still languished, utterly incapable of paying the bill for
costs awarded against her.[20]

---

[20] *CJ*, 67, 15; Hansard, *PD*, xxi, 99–102.

Mary Dix's petition was presented to the Commons by Viscount Folkestone. In the course of a lengthy speech, he berated many of those who presided in the church courts as being 'utterly incompetent to discharge their duties', charged them with imposing 'exorbitant and intolerable' charges and complained that they excommunicated people for 'trifling offences'. He drew special attention to other defamation causes, claiming that such suits were often brought for 'malice and revenge', and sought support for a parliamentary committee to be appointed to inquire into the jurisdiction of the inferior ecclesiastical courts in order to see whether any reform of their practices was desirable.[21]

Other speakers rallied, nonetheless, to defend the church courts. Eldon's brother, Sir William Scott, argued that the problems in the Dix case arose from the defendant's contumacy. The penance imposed in defamation cases, he argued, was not 'grievous': she would not be required to go into a church dressed in a white sheet, but would be asked to seek pardon and forgiveness in a vestry before two or three of the plaintiff's friends. Another prominent civil lawyer, Sir John Nicholl, argued that it was an 'ordinary' case, treated in an 'ordinary' manner. The problems arose from Dix's refusal to appear. The fact that she was a minor was irrelevant, and, as a poor person, she could have pleaded *in forma pauperis*. William Herbert argued that if the ecclesiastical courts had effective authority to enforce their decisions, their costs would be lower, and Nicholl also pleaded for them to have powers to enforce their decisions, ending their reliance on excommunication and the cumbersome procedures that ensued in cases of continued contumacy. The Attorney General himself deflected criticism away from the judges, 'who had merely done their duty', and directed it to the law which they operated, adding weight to Sir William Scott's earlier plea that some alternative punishment to excommunication be instituted. Scott, responding to invitations from several speakers, agreed to bring in a bill to this effect.[22]

This request was not answered promptly, however, and it was not until mid-July 1812 that Scott presented to the Commons his *Bill for better regulation of Ecclesiastical Courts, in that part of the United Kingdom called England, and for the more easy recovery of*

[21] *PD*, xxi, 295–303.   [22] Ibid., 295–319.

Church Rates and Tithes. Although courts were to retain their rights to excommunicate people for spiritual offences, the bill proposed to deal with contumacy by substituting the writ *de contumace capiendo* for the ancient writ *de excommunicato capiendo*. It removed all civil disabilities from those who were excommunicated, apart from a jail sentence for those who refused to seek absolution; even that was not to exceed six months. Scott seized the opportunity also to add further provisions to his bill. It proposed that all the inferior church courts should lose their jurisdiction over contentious causes, it raised the ceiling below which JPs could determine tithe causes, and it proposed that JPs could hear and determine cases in which people refused to pay church rates below a certain value.[23]

The bill came, however, too late in the parliamentary year to make progress, necessitating its reintroduction in April 1813.[24] At that time, although subsequently criticised, and amended in committee, the bill made speedy progress through the Commons and the Lords, receiving the royal assent in mid-July 1813.[25] The act of 1813 maintained the right of the courts to excommunicate offenders but discontinued excommunication for contumacy, substituting writs *de contumace capiendo* obtainable from Chancery for those writs *de excommunicato capiendo* that had earlier been proposed. It also empowered sheriffs to jail offenders until they submitted to the dictates of the courts. The new bill raised the ceiling for tithe cases that could be settled by JPs from the 40s. level laid down by 7 and 8 William III, c. 6, to £10, giving JPs the rights also to hear and resolve refusals to pay church rates below the same value. Action had to be taken within six years of the time when the tithe or other payment fell due.[26] Although Scott's initial proposal to limit the jurisdiction of the minor ecclesiastical courts did not survive, this episode revealed that a reform measure of limited scope, carefully crafted, could get onto the statute book.

[23] Ibid., xxiii, 396, 806–7; *CJ*, 67, 492, 528.
[24] *PD*, xxv, 761–2; *CJ*, 68, 396; *PP*, 1812, I, 487–94, and 1812–13, I, 487–94.
[25] *CJ*, 68, 396, 428, 444, 513, 576–7, 655, 658; *LJ*, xlix, 524, 535, 557, 574, 592, 603, 606; *PD*, xxvi, 311–12, 705–8.
[26] 53 George III, c. 127.

13

ROYAL COMMISSIONS AND EARLY FRUITS,
1815–1832

THE ACT OF 1829

Between 1815 and 1821 several royal commissions were set up to investigate the duties, salaries and emoluments of the various officers involved in the administration of some of the busiest of England's ecclesiastical courts, and these commissioners reported the results of their efforts in two reports in 1823.[1] A more general concern with the costs that operated in the courts continued, however, as suggested by Peel's presentation to the Commons in 1828 of returns from all the ecclesiastical courts in England and Wales that were still operative, the number and nature of causes that were pursued within them and totals of the fees paid to the senior court officials.[2] Petitions were also pressed on Parliament. A Cornish attorney, Thomas Theophilus Hawkey, complained that he was charged £10 by the archdeaconry office in Bodmin for attendance whilst seeking probate and for three copies of a will of twenty-four folios. He himself, as a lawyer, was not allowed to charge more than 4d. per folio for copies of documents, he continued, and if this rate had prevailed in Bodmin he would have had to pay no more than £1 4s. for his copies, plus 6s. 8d. to the registrar for attendance. He also alleged that a widow, seeking in the same office probate of her husband's will, one valued at less

---

[1] Report of the Commissioners For examining the Duties, Salaries, and Emoluments, of the Officers, Clerks and Ministers, of the ... Court of Arches of the Lord Bishop of Canterbury, the Prerogative Court of the same Archbishop, and the Court of Peculiars of the same Archbishop: *PP*, 1823, vii, 27–109; Report of the Commissioners for examining into the Duties, Salaries, and Emoluments, of the Officers, Clerks and Ministers, of the ... Consistory Court of the Lord Bishop of London, and the Court of the Commissary of the same Bishop, ... and the Deaneries of Middlesex and Barking: *PP*, 1824, ix, 25–182.
[2] *CJ*, 83, 234, 384.

than £20, was charged a total of £5, a sum she was not able to pay, requiring her to apply to her parish for relief.[3] A clerical petitioner complained to Parliament about the costs charged by proctors in the consistory court at Exeter.[4] Such was the background to Sir John Nicholl's presentation to the Commons in May 1829 of a *Bill to regulate the Duties, Salaries and Emoluments of the Officers, Clerks and Ministers of certain Ecclesiastical Courts in England.* This, as amended in committee and ultimately approved by both houses, imposed the charges agreed by the commissioners in 1823, insisted that any new charges had to be vetted by the Privy Council, ordered that tables of fees had to be publicly displayed in the offices where business was conducted and laid down certain rules for the appointment of officials in the courts. Concern that contumacy could hinder the speedy conduct of business in the courts revealed itself in the insistence that additional court days could be established where necessary. Delays in the Prerogative Court of Canterbury were countered by ordering that only such holidays as were observed at the government Stamp Office were henceforth to be permitted in that court.[5]

Despite the ultimate successful passage of this act of 1829, critics of the church courts were not satisfied. Joseph Hume declared in the Commons that the courts were 'nests of sinecures which ought to be abolished', and George Dawson observed that 'the stalls of the Augean stable required cleaning'.[6] Hume had earlier attempted unsuccessfully to add an amendment to the bill 'That Proctors appointed to the office of Deputy Registrar, shall not act as Proctors', influenced perhaps by a parliamentary petition reminding the House that deputy registers in Doctors' Commons were in the habit of doing so and were thus 'incompetent persons to tax the bills of other Proctors'.[7] In June 1829 the Commons called for returns of the fees, profits and emoluments of the officers in various ecclesiastical courts, as well as copies of all the bills charged against the suitors in two particular court cases.[8] This was followed in January 1830 by the establishment of a royal commission of inquiry into the state of the ecclesiastical courts in England and Wales. Consisting of the bishops of London,

[3] *CJ*, 83, 466–7.   [4] Ibid., 499.
[5] *CJ*, 84, 289, 291, 307, 311, 326, 348; *PP*, 1829, i, 413–18; 10 George IV, c. 53.
[6] *PD*, n.s. xxi, 1700–01.   [7] *CJ*, 84, 321–2, 389.   [8] *CJ*, 84, 383, 389, 397.

Durham, Lincoln, Exeter and Gloucester, several privy council-
lors, prominent common law judges and four prominent civil
lawyers, the commission was given wide-ranging powers of
inquiry. Its deliberations were to be influenced, however, not only
by Parliament's preoccupations with costs and procedures but
also by contemporaneous concerns about how to deal with errant
clergymen. One such cleric, the Reverend David Griffith Davies,
was involved in a case that came by letters of request from Joseph
Phillimore, the chancellor of the diocese of Oxford, to the court of
arches in 1821.

SAUNDERS V. DAVIES

David Griffith Davies had been the curate of the parish of
Charlbury since 1811, and since 1814 the licensed curate of the
augmented curacy of Ascot under Wychwood, both in Oxfordshire. In addition to his clerical duties Davies ran a school from
his home in Chadlington, a chapelry in Charlbury. To this school
in 1814 came the seventeen-year-old Samuel Beale. This young
scholar lived in Davies's household for about two years before
enrolling in Oxford as an undergraduate. In 1819 Beale returned
to the curate's house, the attraction being neither Davies's wit nor
wisdom but the clergyman's wife Ann. At what particular point
Beale and Ann Davies began to sleep together is not known, but a
succession of female servants testified that they eventually did so
on a regular basis. What is more, Davies appears to have been
totally complicit in the affair. Servants attested that the curate was
often seen conversing with the couple while they were in bed
together and, indeed, was sometimes called in by Mrs Davies to
lace up her stays, Beale presumably being too exhausted to do
anything other than watch. Whether Ann Davies sought solace
with Beale because her husband was frequently drunk and
incapable, or whether Davies took to the bottle because his wife
clearly preferred the attentions of the young lodger to his own, is
also not known. But both parties took to these preferences with
some degree of enthusiasm. One servant testified that she found
Ann's nightgown and cap more often in Beale's room than her
own; another asserted that she went there almost every night.
Sarah Clements, a servant, said that she was frequently sent to get
the curate out of the Sandys Arms, that he would return drunk at

all hours, that he needed help to unlace his boots and that he never went to bed sober. Another witness related that the curate also frequented the kitchen of the Churchill Arms, 'one of the darkest (that is lowest and worst) places in the Country'. He had been seen there 'drinking and singing bawdy songs, some of the grossest that could be heard' and 'as jovial and full of mirth as any of them'. Perhaps he was drunk when he offended the parish clerk in 1821. On his way to conduct a funeral, Davies met the parish clerk who was in conversation with another man, and as the two parties passed each other in the lane the curate was heard to say to his own companion 'in a most irreverent, immoral and indecent manner', 'there's a pretty pair, as the Devil said when he looked at his bollocks'. He was certainly drunk on a number of occasions at meetings of the vestry, as more than one witness recounted, and his conduct of services left much to be desired.

In November 1818 complaints about his behaviour were laid before Dr Cobb, the vicar of Charlbury, but this does not appear to have had any effect. Most of the complaints levelled against him postdated this report. Davies may have been, as one witness related, a 'good natured man', who was 'generous, forgiving, ready to assist anyone at any time', but these qualities should have stopped short of making his wife available to the lodger. He was clearly unfit to be a clergyman. Eventually, in 1821, he was prosecuted for the many offences related above, the case arousing interest not only for its salacious content but also for the fact that it was largely undefended and that the judge, Sir John Nicholl, felt that though the allegations against Davies were overwhelmingly supported by the evidence of eighteen witnesses, he had no power to deprive Davies of his benefice, this power being reserved to his bishop by canon 122 of the canons of 1604. The most he felt able to do was to suspend him for three years and to tax him with the costs of prosecution.[9] What irked reformers of the system was that here was a blatant case of 'drunkenness and profaneness, immorality and irregularity, and indecorum in the performance of divine offices', with the offender being tried and found guilty in the highest ecclesiastical court of the land, but that he could not be deprived of his benefice by sentence of

---

[9] The cause papers for this case are in LPL/H301/1–20; it is reported sub nom. *Saunder* v. *Davies*, 1 Add 291, 162 ER 102 (1822).

the court. Davies, however, was a saint by comparison with Dr Edward Drax Free, whose case played a determining role in the deliberations and recommendations of the 1830 commissioners.

THE CASE OF DR FREE

If the Church of England had run a competition to find the most unsuitable candidate to be a parish clergyman, it would, as Montagu Burgoyne stated in a petition to Parliament in 1825, have been hard pressed to find anyone better qualified than Dr Edward Drax Free.[10] Given in 1808 the living of Sutton, a village of some 300 inhabitants in Bedfordshire, by an Oxford college all too anxious to rid itself of a pathologically irascible, deeply paranoid senior fellow who had become an embarrassment to it, he went on to become notorious and subsequently to become influential in perhaps surprising ways. In the course of two decades following his appointment, Free proceeded to commit an astonishing array of offences, alienating his patrons, his parishioners and the resident gentry family at Sutton, the Burgoynes.

St John's, his former Oxford college, objected to his diversion into his own pocket of £177 paid for 'dilapidations' by the executors of his predecessor as rector of Sutton, to his pocketing a £50 payment from the college for improvement of his rectory, without any alterations to his residence being made, and for his cutting down and selling privately timber belonging to the living. Later he was to strip the lead off the chancel roof, replacing it with tiles, selling the lead to a Cambridge businessman and privately appropriating the profit.

Although at the start of his time in Sutton he appears to have performed his clerical duties satisfactorily, his performance ultimately deteriorated spectacularly, and his parishioners complained of irregular services, of his absence from the parish for lengthy periods, of his failure to perform baptisms and burials without the payment of irregular fees, of his neglect of the churchyard, where he allowed his pigs to root around amongst the graves, of his rudeness and lack of charity, of his grasping attitude towards those

---

[10] A full account of the events that follow is to be found in my *Scandal in the Church: Dr Edward Drax Free, 1764–1843* (1997).

who paid his rents and tithes, and of his constant cheating of those who were unfortunate enough to work for him.

His employees included a succession of young unmarried female housekeepers, all of whom lived alone in the rectory with the much older and highly sexed Dr Free. He was nearly forty-four when he arrived in Sutton and forty-six when he fathered the baby of the first of his housekeepers, Maria Crook. The baby died in a London workhouse where Maria was incarcerated for the birth. Three years later he fathered a child by his second housekeeper, the nineteen-year-old Catharine Siggins. Between the ages of fifty and fifty-four, he produced three more illegitimate children by the third of his female employees, Margaret Johnston. At the age of fifty-eight, he impregnated Maria Mackenzie, though she later miscarried after being physically assaulted by the clergyman. Other housekeepers complained of his attempts at seduction, processes that included him showing them pornographic illustrations and exhibiting his naked torso.

He was constantly involved with the law, either as a litigant or as a defendant. Two years after his arrival in Sutton he physically assaulted a shopkeeper who had presented him with an unsettled bill. For this he was fined at quarter sessions. He was also involved in litigation with the resident gentry family, the Burgoynes, over the precise location of his glebe boundaries. In 1814 he was warned about poaching on Burgoyne land. Obviously determined to exact some sort of revenge, he attempted in 1817 to prosecute Sir Montagu Roger Burgoyne at the Bedfordshire assizes for failing to attend church services at Sutton church over a period of nineteen months. The prosecution failed, if only because witnesses attested that Dr Free was himself absent from Sutton for several months at this time and the church was actually shut up. Relations between the rector and the Burgoynes subsequently went from bad to worse after Free charged Montagu Burgoyne a hundred guineas to create a new vault in which to bury his recently deceased daughter, Frances Campbell. The 1817 episode was not Free's last brush with the law, for in 1823 he was bound over to appear at quarter sessions to answer a charge of assaulting Maria Mackenzie. Later he was to spend time in the King's Bench prison for debt.

Despite his long-sustained record of extreme misbehaviour, Dr Free escaped serious reprimand from the ecclesiastical authorities until 1823, when Montagu Burgoyne organised two presentments against him that were placed before the archdeacon of Bedford. Subsequent events were to expose the weaknesses in the ecclesiastical court system. The archdeacon of Bedford thought initially that his court had the power to pursue the sort of prosecution that was necessary. He had to be told by civil lawyers at Doctors' Commons that this was not the case. The bishop of Lincoln was told that Free's sexual offences were, because of the Act of 1787, out of term and that his remaining offences were 'of such a nature as have been usually corrected by admonition'. The bishop's chancellor thought that the case should have been pursued, initially at least, in his court at Lincoln, but eventually it went, by letters of request, to the court of arches in London, where it opened as *Burgoyne* v. *Free* in October 1824.

The case was plagued thereafter by continual interruptions. The first of these revolved around a quarrel between the bishop of Lincoln's chancellor and the same bishop's commissary as to who should have signed the letters of request. This was not resolved until the end of January 1825. A month later the articles of accusation were presented in court. Some of these articles were rejected by the court, but not enough were discarded to satisfy Free's proctors. The case was interrupted in May 1825 by a writ of prohibition enabling King's Bench to give a ruling on whether or not Free could be charged with fornication, even if the offences were committed more than eight months previously. It took a year to get a ruling in the prosecution's favour. This was followed by a further appeal against the King's Bench judgment to the House of Lords. It was not until November 1826 that the case could be resumed in the court of arches. This was followed almost immediately by Free's proctors appealing to the court of delegates, and in March 1827 also appealing to the House of Lords over an issue relating to costs in King's Bench. It took until July 1828 for the case to be resumed.

In the months that followed, the testimony of witnesses began to be taken, though Free objected that crucial depositions, such as those of the housekeepers, came from persons of notoriously bad character. It was not until mid-June 1829 that Sir John Nicholl, the presiding judge, pronounced sentence against the rector of Sutton. 'Slight offences, accidental irregularities arising from the ordinary infirmities of human nature', said Nicholl, 'might be corrected by admonition or suspension ... but here is a crying grievance – a disgusting nuisance in the parish; no hope exists of bringing back the defendant and his parishioners to entertain those feelings of mutual respect and confidence which ought to subsist'. It was, he continued, his painful duty to deprive him of his living and make him liable for the costs of the case.[11] This stands in marked contrast to his judgment in *Saunders* v. *Davies* eight years earlier, where Nicholl doubted whether he had the power to deprive the clergyman of his living. The serious nature of Dr Free's offences may have been a factor in this reversal of judgments, but advocates had also previously unearthed two seventeenth-century precedents in which it was decided in the court of delegates that the dean of the Arches was not bound by canon 122 and did indeed have powers to deprive.[12] A week after Nicholl's judgment, Free appealed to the court of delegates, a strategy that enabled him to continue in his living until the sentence was confirmed or overturned. Confirmation came eventually in mid-February 1830, more than six years after the formal complaints about his misbehaviour had been laid before the archdeacon of Bedford.

As letters patent establishing the royal commission to inquire into 'the course of proceeding in Suits and other matters instituted or carried on in the Ecclesiastical Courts of England and Wales' were issued only a few weeks before confirmation of Free's sentence by the delegates, and as the pivotal figure in the management of that commission's enquiries was Stephen Lushington – the same advocate who had assisted in Free's prosecution – it is not surprising that the implications of that long-drawn-out case should figure prominently in the commission's enquiries and deliberations. Although that body was chiefly concerned with determining what parts and processes of the church court system might be continued or improved, and what parts might be suppressed, it is clear that it also became preoccupied with the question of how best to prosecute and remove scandalous clerics. In 1838 Henry Philpotts, the bishop of Exeter, went even further in arguing, in the course of a House of Lords debate, that the

---

[11] See *Burgoyne* v. *Free*, 2 Hagg Ecc 456, 492, 162 ER 921, 934 (1829).

[12] See *Pullen* v. *Clewer* and *Rich* v. *Gerard and Loder*, 1 Hagg Ecc (App.) 1–9, 162 ER 760–4. I am grateful for the help of Michael Prichard, who kindly drew my attention to the reports of these cases.

Ecclesiastical Courts Commission had itself been set up because the case of Dr Free had been drawn to the attention of the duke of Wellington, whose government first established that body.

Whether Philpotts was correct or not, the case of Dr Free was constantly alluded to both in the final report of the Ecclesiastical Courts Commission and in the statements of witnesses before it. 'This was a peculiar and an extreme case', the report itself stated, 'in which proceedings for a Prohibition were carried on in the Court of King's Bench, and afterwards by a Writ of Error in the House of Lords; and when the question of Prohibition had been decided against the Defendant, the case was carried by appeal to the Court of Delegates, where the decision of the Court of Arches was ultimately affirmed.'[13]

Joseph Phillimore, an advocate in Doctors' Commons, attested that 'the case of Dr Free ... was an illustration of the extent to which the proceedings in our Courts could be thwarted and impeded by a reference to extrinsic jurisdictions'. Existing modes of prosecuting clergymen, he continued, enabled them to 'extend the proceedings to a great length', though he felt this was not the fault of the church courts.[14] John Dodson, another advocate and one who had assisted Stephen Lushington in prosecuting Free, was another defender of the system, arguing that Free's case was actually dealt with quite promptly in the church courts, the delays being entirely the result of appeals to outside bodies.[15]

Because the report of the commissioners was actually written by Stephen Lushington, it is hardly surprising to find that the body recommended that 'there should exist some Tribunal to which the Clergy should be amenable for any open violation of Morality', and that measures should be taken both to speed up the process of prosecution and to lessen the costs that fell upon prosecutors. Parliaments thereafter witnessed several attempts to put some of the recommendations of the Ecclesiastical Courts Commission onto the statute book.

The subject of clerical delinquency tended to get an airing whenever questions relating to the church courts came up for discussion in Parliament. It was during discussions of the bill that transferred appellate jurisdiction from the court of delegates to the Privy Council, for example, that Lord Wynford drew attention, in

[13] *PP*, 1831–32, 56.   [14] Ibid., 153, 162.   [15] Ibid., 168.

July 1832, to the fact that the bishops were 'subjected to great expense and delay in bringing clergymen to account for any misconduct ... and, that in consequence of such expense and delay, individuals, who were really a disgrace to the church, had been able to retain their situation for a length of time'. A year later, the Lord Chancellor, reviewing the recommendations of the commissioners in respect of clerical misconduct, felt 'It was only necessary for him ... to allude to one or two cases, which must be fresh in their Lordship's remembrance, which had travelled through the whole of those Courts, and even up to that House'.[16] When introducing in 1835 a bill for disciplining of the clergy, Hansard had the Attorney General confusing the former rector of Sutton with a distinguished clerical lawyer in allegedly arguing that 'the case of Dr Coote had been cited as a striking example of delay, expense, and inefficiency'.[17] The case of Dr Free was referred to again when Bishop Philpotts of Exeter complained in 1838 about the proposed transfer of power in cases of clerical delinquency from the bishops to the court of arches. It was, he stated, 'a case long pending in the ecclesiastical courts, and which by the conduct of one of the parties had been transferred from one court to another, until such a delay had taken place, and until such costs were incurred, that hardly any adjudication could lead to a just result'. The proposed changes were supported by the archbishop of Canterbury, moreover, who referred to the case of Dr Free as 'a very sufficient illustration of the evils attending upon the old mode of proceeding in the ecclesiastical courts', and, therefore, of the need for reform.[18]

When reform was eventually achieved in 1840, it was a compromise measure. Bishops were given the power to issue commissions to investigate complaints of scandalous behaviour by the clergy of their dioceses. These commissioners were to examine witnesses to establish whether there was a *prima facie* case for instituting further proceedings. These could occur only if the offences complained of had taken place within the two years preceding the complaint. The limitation of eight months imposed by the Act of 1787 was not to be applicable to clergymen. If the scandalous cleric confessed his guilt, then the bishop could move

---

[16] *PD*, 3rd series xiv, 259; xix, 612.   [17] Ibid., xxvi, 924.
[18] Ibid., xliv, 610–11, 615.

straightaway to a sentence. If, however, he protested his innocence, then legal proceedings could be set in motion, beginning with articles drawn up by an advocate of Doctors' Commons being served upon him. Two weeks later, the accused was to reappear before the bishop, when he would be again given the opportunity to admit the truth of the accusations levelled against him, permitting the bishop to move to an immediate sentence. If, however, he continued to deny the articles, then the case could be tried before the bishop and three assessors, one of whom was to be an experienced advocate in the church courts or a barrister of at least seven years' standing and another a dean of one of his cathedral churches, or his chancellor or else one of the archdeacons of the diocese. The bishop could, however, elect not to try the case in this manner, but instead to send it to the court of appeal of his ecclesiastical province.[19] With this exception, existing ecclesiastical courts were specifically prohibited from instituting suits against clerics 'for any Offence against the Laws Ecclesiastical', an extraordinary removal of their powers of jurisdiction, and one that clearly owed much to the gross delinquency of Edward Drax Free and the weaknesses in the ecclesiastical court system that his long-drawn-out prosecution revealed.

THE ECCLESIASTICAL COURTS COMMISSION AND ITS REPORT

The 1810s and 1820s were characterised by increasing critical scrutiny of the legal system in all its guises. Peel's arrival as Home Secretary in 1822 led to major reforms in criminal law, implementing many of the ideas of earlier reformers such as Romilly and Mackintosh.[20] The court of Chancery, notorious for delays and expenses, was subjected to intense criticism, which Peel deflected with the appointment in 1824 of a royal commission to investigate its procedures.[21] Legal reform was further boosted by Henry Brougham's wide-ranging, six-hour speech to the Commons in 1828, a speech that led 'directly and immediately' to the appointment of two royal commissions – those on the common law and on real property.[22]

---

[19] 3 and 4 Victoria, c. 86.
[20] N. Gash, *Mr. Secretary Peel* (1961), 308–20, 326–41.   [21] Ibid., 321–6.
[22] C. W. New, *The Life of Henry Brougham to 1830* (1961), 391.

The duties, salaries and emoluments of those officiating in the ecclesiastical courts were also, as we have seen, subjected to parliamentary scrutiny in 1823–4 and to legislation in 1829, and in this general climate of review and reform, it should come as no surprise that in January 1830 Wellington's administration established a royal commission to inquire into 'the course of proceeding in Suits and other matters instituted or carried on in the Ecclesiastical Courts of England and Wales … and whether any and what parts thereof may be conveniently and beneficially discontinued or altered, and what (if any) alterations may be beneficially made therein … '.[23] The commission was reissued in July 1830, apparently to take account of episcopal migrations and the need to enlarge the number of enquirers.[24] The commissioners ultimately comprised the archbishop of Canterbury and the bishops of London, Durham, Lincoln, St Asaph and Exeter,[25] together with the chief justices of the court of King's Bench (Lord Tenterden) and of Common Pleas (Sir Nicholas Tindal), Tindal's predecessor at Common Pleas (Lord Wynford), two experienced former colonial lawyers (Sir Codrington Carrington and Robert Fergusson) and four eminent civil lawyers, prominent members of Doctors' Commons (Sir John Nicholl, Sir Christopher Robinson, Sir Herbert Jenner and Stephen Lushington). Between April and December 1830, ably marshalled by Lushington, they interviewed thirty-five witnesses, some of them solicitors practising in the secular courts but mostly senior practitioners in the London and diocesan spiritual courts.

Their report came in two parts. The first – the Special Report – advocated the abolition of the court of delegates and the transfer of appeals to a modified Privy Council. The need to establish a body of delegates anew every time an appeal was presented was thought to produce delays and additional expense. Also, although it was customary for three senior secular lawyers and three civilians to be appointed as delegates, the most senior members of the latter body were frequently the men who had served as advocates

---

[23] *PP*, 1831–2, xxiv, 1–2.

[24] Ibid., 3–4. Both commissions were issued during Wellington's period of office and not 'when the Whigs assumed office' as argued by Stephen Waddams, *Law, Politics and the Church of England: The Career of Stephen Lushington 1782–1873* (1992), 15.

[25] The bishop of Exeter became bishop of Bangor in October 1830.

in the very cases at Doctors' Commons that had led to the appeal, so junior and inexperienced civilians had perforce to be engaged. An additional benefit of the proposed alteration was that the grounds for judgments should in the future be published, helping to formulate general principles and establish uniformity of practice.[26]

The second, and principal, part of the report embraced a whole series of radical proposals, recommendations that were very much in accord with Lushington's personal views of what should happen to the ecclesiastical courts. It proposed that all 'contentious jurisdiction', in other words the litigation pursued between parties, should be transferred to the two provincial courts of Canterbury and York, a proposal that would have ended the pursuit of such causes not only in peculiar courts but also in archidiaconal and consistory courts. Some members of the commission wanted to go further and to suppress entirely the courts at York, transferring all such business to the courts of the southern province, but the commission as a body stopped short of recommending this. The rationale for this radical restructuring was that the volume of business in most of the lower courts was insufficient to maintain a competent body of practitioners in the local courts. The returns obtained from diocesan registries persuaded the commissioners that this was true also of many of the consistory courts: 'the annual amount of Business, and the emoluments of the Judges and other Officers, and of the Practitioners in these Courts, make it impossible in many Dioceses, that efficient Courts can be maintained'.[27] The centralisation of business would, it was thought, create a viable bar. To this end the commissioners also recommended that the judges and other officers of the courts in the two provinces should in the future be paid a salary, rather than being compensated by fees. They were also to discharge their duties in person and not through deputies.

All testamentary causes were to be pursued in the provincial courts of Canterbury and York, and the procedures used in these courts were to be modified so as to admit oral evidence and make use of a jury, thus bringing practice in them into line with common law procedure in testamentary matters. The reason given for these far-reaching modifications was that 'Wills disposing of Real and Personal Estate, or either', should be determined by the same

[26] *PP*, 1831–2, xxiv, 5–8. [27] Ibid., 23.

legal course, irrespective of whether they were brought before a spiritual or a secular court. The commissioners also proposed that the court of arches and the Prerogative Court of Canterbury should be merged, with a similar merger being made at York. To these two provincial courts all extant wills were to be transferred, creating two centralised general registries, and it was there in London and in York that probates and administrations were in future to be sought.

Marital suits were singled out for particular attention – there being 'no department of Ecclesiastical Jurisprudence of more vital consequence to the community'.[28] The commission recommended that 'Suits involving results so serious, and often giving rise to questions of difficulty, will be most safely adjudicated by the Provincial Courts, where the greater experience of the Judges and Practitioners will cause the Law to be administered with less probability of error'.[29] Moreover, trial by jury and the admission of oral evidence were to be permitted in these and other causes conducted before the provincial courts.

Some types of business were to be entirely abolished. Suits for defamation were acknowledged to be rare occurrences in the courts of Doctors' Commons, but they still prevailed 'to a considerable extent' in the diocesan courts.[30] They were thought, however, to have occasioned 'much odium' against the system and also to have led to people being imprisoned for contumacy or their unwillingness to pay costs. Such suits were, therefore, to be withdrawn from the church courts and left to the magistrates at petty sessions.

The commission recommended also that the church courts should lose their entire criminal jurisdiction. This included not only prosecutions for failing to pay church rates, which when followed by jail sentences for contumacy gave critics a stick with which to beat the church courts, but also those for incest, adultery and fornication, causes that were acknowledged to have been rare in the recent past in both the courts at Doctors' Commons and the local, diocesan courts. Any beneficial consequences from such prosecutions were felt to be counteracted by the 'odium they have excited, and the oppression which, in some few instances, has been exercised', though it was felt that incest was so serious an

[28] Ibid., 43.   [29] Ibid., 44.   [30] Ibid., 63.

offence that some punishment at common law should be substituted for its abolition as an ecclesiastical court offence.[31]
Disturbances in church or churchyard were also to be withdrawn
from the jurisdiction of the ecclesiastical courts.

The abolition of criminal prosecutions extended also to the trial
of clergymen for immoral behaviour and serious neglect of duty.
Attention was drawn to 'Some cases of a flagrant nature, which
have occurred of late years, have attracted the attention of the
Public to the corrective Discipline of the Church, as administered
by the Ecclesiastical Courts, and have at the same time exhibited
in a strong light the inconveniences which have attended the
application of the ordinary process of the Courts to such suits',
namely, delays in removing delinquent clergymen and the expense
required in doing so. References to the case of Dr Free followed,
and additional evidence of the impact this case had is to be found
in the proposals offered by the commission. Stretching over five
pages of the report, and embodying thirty-one detailed provisions,
the recommendations of the commissioners were that in future
such cases should be tried before one or more bishops, assisted by
either a civilian advocate or a common law barrister, with appeals
being heard by the archbishop of the province in which the
offence was committed.

The proposals were, therefore, radical. All ecclesiastical courts
other than the provincial ones were to be swept away, as also was
the entire criminal jurisdiction of the system. Two surviving
courts were to be left effectively with testamentary disputes,
probate and administration, and marital causes. Even the disciplining of the clergy was to be taken away from them.

THE ACT OF 1832

The first of the Ecclesiastical Courts Commission's recommendations to be implemented – and this quickly followed the
printing of the commission's report – was that recommending the
abolition of the court of delegates and its replacement as a court of
appeal by the Privy Council. Henry Brougham had touched upon
the subject in his celebrated law reform speech of 1828, when he

---

[31] Ibid., 64.

called the court of delegates 'one of the worst constituted courts which was ever appointed', arguing that 'the course of its proceedings forms one of the greatest mockeries of appeal ever conceived by man'. The majority of those civilians who were appointed as delegates, as he pointed out, were young and inexperienced and they had to pass judgment on the decisions of 'three great judges' – Sir William Scott, Sir John Nicholl and Sir Christopher Robinson – 'the great luminaries of the Civil law'.[32] It was Brougham who, as Lord Chancellor, seized the chance in July 1832 to bring in *An Act for transferring the Powers of the High Court of Delegates, both in Ecclesiastical and Maritime Causes, to His Majesty in Council*. Introduced in the Lords on 5 July, it quickly passed through both houses, receiving the royal assent a month later. In introducing the measure, Brougham took pains to mention that it was one of the recommendations of 'those learned and most respectable individuals, the Ecclesiastical Commissioners'. He rehearsed his earlier complaints, principally that 'frequently barristers [advocates] of not more than one year and a half's standing were called on to preside in this Court of Appeal as Judges'. The alteration would not throw a heavy additional load onto the Privy Council because, he argued, the average number of appeals heard over the past thirty years was no more than three or four per year, though in recent years it had climbed to between eight and ten annually.[33] The quick passage of this measure must have raised the hopes of the 1830 commissioners that further reforms would quickly follow. They were, however, to be severely disappointed.

[32] Hansard, *PD*, 2nd series xviii, 153–4.
[33] Hansard, *PD*, 3rd series xiv, 78–82.

14

REFORM FRUSTRATED

'Sir *R. Inglis* said, whatever other objections there might be to the measure proposed by his right hon. Friend, at least the Government could not be charged with precipitancy in regard to its introduction, for there was no question, he believed, as to which so much had been written and so little done since 1829 as that of the Ecclesiastical Courts.'[1]

Abolition of the court of delegates was the most immediate parliamentary response to the many recommendations of the Ecclesiastical Courts Commissioners, that 'most able and learned body of men', as Lord Brougham described them in a speech in the Lords in 1833. Brougham also lamented the failure of the house to pass his Local Courts Bill. This had made it necessary for him, he argued, to bring forward a measure transferring the jurisdiction of the minor ecclesiastical courts, which he numbered at no fewer than 340, to the diocesan courts. There were disadvantages in such a transfer, he conceded. Some litigants and others would have to travel greater distances to conduct their legal business, an inconvenience that would been avoided had the Lords passed the Local Courts Bill.

The other recommendations of the 1830 commissioners were not forgotten either. The new bill promised to abolish the criminal jurisdiction of the church courts, transforming the offences formerly punishable by them into misdemeanours punishable by the temporal magistracy. Finally, Brougham drew attention to the 'defects of the ecclesiastical jurisdiction exercised by the heads of the Church over clerks who misconducted themselves', reminding

---

[1] Speech on the Ecclesiastical Courts bill in February 1843. Hansard, *PD*, 3rd series lxvi, 330.

his hearers of 'one or two cases ... fresh in their Lordships' remembrance'. To avoid such occurrences in the future, he proposed bringing in the new disciplinary procedures recommended by the commissioners. Nothing came of this initiative, however, for other, more pressing reform matters presented themselves.[2] In 1835, reviewing the history of previous attempts to bring about such reforms, Stephen Lushington said that the reason the bill was not actually brought forward was that a parliamentary committee was then sitting to deal with the admiralty courts and that the whole question of probate was also being independently considered.[3]

In March 1835 a new administration attempted to float a bill embodying many of the same proposals. Introducing the proposed measure in the Commons, Attorney General Pollock paid homage to Lushington, the architect of the 1832 report: 'A more learned and valuable document ... he had rarely met with'. The bill proposed the abolition of the minor courts and the centralisation of business in one court; that court was to retain its jurisdiction over testamentary and marital matters, but lose all remaining jurisdiction, including litigation over tithes and defamation. The power to prosecute criminal offences was also to be withdrawn from the new court, and trial by jury was to be admitted. Lushington welcomed the new proposals, especially the abolition of defamation, explaining that 'It was only in the month of May last that he had himself been compelled ... to send an individual to gaol for defamation'. Others demurred, however, at some of the proposed changes. Whilst welcoming the suppression of the minor courts, Sir John Campbell pleaded for the retention of the diocesan courts, especially for matters of probate. 'It was possible to centralise too much', he argued, 'to bring proceedings too much to London.' Mr Pryme agreed with this, arguing that the establishment of a single institution in London might be convenient for the wealthy testator but that it would be quite

---

[2] Hansard, *PD*, 3rd series xix, 610–13. Brougham later explained that 'there were in the circumstances that then existed, ample reasons why so important a Bill should not be pressed at that moment, for there were then under consideration of this House of Parliament [the Lords], the Bill for opening the East India Trade, the Bill for reforming the Scottish Burghs ...; a Bill respecting the Irish Church, and three or four important Law Bills', Ibid., xxvi, 931–2.

[3] Ibid., xxvi, 926.

inconvenient for poorer men.[4] Although the house gave permission for this bill to be introduced, the change in the ministry led to its being shelved for the moment.[5]

This particular reform bill was accompanied by another, more specialised measure devoted to securing more efficient ways of disciplining discreditable clergymen. Once again the case of Dr Free was raised.[6] Several members in the course of debating these bills also drew attention, as others had before them, to the inadequacies of the law relating to divorce. Proceedings before the Commons and the Lords were, said Sir John Campbell, a 'mere farce' and an expensive one at that. Such cases ought to be tried, he argued, before special judicial tribunals. Cutlar Fergusson, one of the 1830 commissioners, agreed that changes needed to be made in the law and procedures relating to divorce. Present procedures before Parliament were, he thought, a 'matter of jest and merriment'. The whole was a 'disgrace to the country'.[7]

When the *Bill to regulate Ecclesiastical Courts in England and Wales* was reintroduced later in the parliamentary session of 1835, it was preceded and accompanied by a veritable snowstorm of petitions, as at least one member had predicted. Sir John Campbell, by then Attorney General, had warned that the centralisation of probate in London 'would give umbrage to the country solicitors, a very powerful body, who would be sending numerous petitions on the subject to the House'.[8] A little more than a week later they began to arrive.[9] By late July, at least 166 petitions against the bill, containing over 10,000 signatures, had been tabled, and this opposition appears to have persuaded the administration to put off a second reading.[10]

In February 1836 a further attempt was made, this time in the Lords, to introduce a bill consolidating the courts and altering their jurisdiction along the lines proposed in the 1832 report.[11] Once again, however, the bill provoked a flood of petitions, even though reasoned explanations were constantly offered in Parliament to justify suppression of local probate facilities. As Lord Chancellor Cottenham explained, 'This subject had been laboriously investigated by the Ecclesiastical Commissioners, by the Real Property

[4] Ibid., xxvi, 908–24.   [5] *CJ*, 90, 117.   [6] Ibid., 924–6.
[7] Ibid., 915–17.   [8] Ibid., xxvi, 915.   [9] *CJ*, 90, 151, 164–5, 173 *et seq.*
[10] Hansard, *PD*, 3rd series xxix, 1105–7; *CJ*, 90, 375, 437, 516.
[11] *LJ*, 68, 20, 33; Hansard, *PD*, 3rd series xxxi, 324–30.

Commissioners, and by a Committee of the House of Commons, and their decided opinion had been, that it was impossible to effect a due improvement in the Ecclesiastical Courts, leaving to the local courts the power of granting probate.'[12] Despite the torrent of petitions pouring into Parliament, the bill obtained a second reading and was committed.

The strength of the opposition to this Lords bill seems, however, to have provoked several members of the Commons to float a bill of their own, a measure that proposed, amongst other things, the retention of specified consistory and archdeaconry courts for the purposes of probate.[13] The proposal to abolish the consistory courts made it all the more urgent to pass a clergy discipline bill, for abolition of the diocesan tribunals would create obvious problems when a delinquent clergyman had to be tried. *An Act for more effectually enforcing Church Discipline* was consequently brought into the Lords in June. There it languished after a second reading and committal.[14]

The attempts to reform the structure of the ecclesiastical court system subsided temporarily after the failures of 1836, and though some momentum was maintained in relation to the disciplining of the clergy, a further two years were to elapse before a fresh attempt was made to pass a new disciplinary bill. This, framed apparently by Sir John Nicholl, struck out in new directions. Instead of vesting powers in diocesan tribunals composed of bishops and legal advisers, the Lords' bill of July 1838 proposed to hand sole jurisdiction in such matters to the court of arches. The proposal was vigorously attacked in the Lords, especially by the bishop of Exeter, who, lamenting the loss of episcopal authority, complained that the bill was 'the greatest blow that was ever struck against the Church of England'. What is more, as he pointed out, this measure diverged from the recommendations of the 1830 commissioners, whose proposals would 'restore to the bishops that personal jurisdiction which they originally exercised'. Lord Brougham also professed to prefer the bills of previous years, measures that were more in accord with the recommendations of the 1830 commissioners. He drew attention to the 'verbose, and

---

[12] Hansard, *PD*, 3rd series xxxi, 675.
[13] *CJ*, 91, 422, 662; *PP*, 1836. This attempt failed to achieve a second reading.
[14] *LJ*, 68, 423, 503; Hansard, *PD*, 3rd series xxxiv, 998–1000.

antiquated mode' of proceedings in the court of arches, with its reliance on depositions and absence of oral examination of witnesses. Several speakers felt that the bill was introduced too late in the session for it to be examined as closely as it merited. At the archbishop of Canterbury's suggestion, further discussion of it was postponed.[15]

Presentation in February 1839 of a petition from a Welshman imprisoned for non-payment of costs in a suit in the consistory court of St David's provided a fresh opportunity for discussion of the whole subject of reform of the system, a process that Lushington and others averred was being held up by the need to pass a church discipline act.[16] The church discipline bill consequently reappeared and in a form very similar to that which was withdrawn the previous year. It was not surprising, therefore, that it again encountered opposition from the bishop of Exeter.[17] At one point he observed that 'he had never seen so much trash contained within the four corners of any bill'. After spending six weeks in committee in the Lords, it emerged, but too late in the parliamentary session for it to be passed in the Commons.[18]

The reform campaign of 1840 began with mass petitions being presented to the Commons from Protestant dissenters demanding abolition of the ecclesiastical courts and the release of John Thorogood from Chelmsford jail.[19] The latter, a Chelmsford dissenter, had refused to pay a church rate and was consequently summoned to appear before the magistrates, but on so appearing he gave notice that he intended to dispute the validity of the rate. This had the effect of transferring the case to the ecclesiastical court. Thorogood, however, refused to appear before the ecclesiastical tribunal when summoned to do so, and Sir John Nicholl, the presiding judge, set in motion the procedures that sent him to prison.

Alongside this campaign to free Thorogood came a renewed attempt to forge a church discipline bill acceptable to the opponents of a centralised court structure. Lord John Russell reiterated the point that reform of the ecclesiastical courts was being held up by the failure of Parliament to establish a speedy and

[15] Hansard, *PD*, 3rd series xliv, 603–31.   [16] Ibid., xlvii, 536–7.
[17] Ibid., xlvii, 1306–42.   [18] Ibid., xlix, 765–72; l, 262–3.
[19] *CJ*, 95, 85, 121, 249, 297, 307, 324, 360.

cheaper way of ridding the church of delinquent priests. The bishop of Exeter signalled in March 1840 that discussions with his brethren had produced a compromise measure that would eventually be put before Parliament.[20] Three months later *An Act for better enforcing Church Discipline* made its appearance in the Lords. As Lord Chancellor Cottenham indicated, it was a compromise proposal, designed to 'reconcile all the differences which had existed upon the subject'. The net effect of the measure, which speedily passed through both houses, was to establish special commissions, in which the bishops played a significant role, to investigate and try cases of delinquency. A bishop could, however, elect to send a case to his provincial court of appeal, where it would be tried in the normal course of proceeding. With this exception, existing ecclesiastical courts were specifically prohibited from instituting criminal cases against clerics 'for any Offence against the Laws Ecclesiastical'. From 1840, therefore, the ecclesiastical courts lost the power to police the clergy, a highly symbolic manifestation of their waning powers.[21]

Once it was clear that the *Act for the better enforcing Church Discipline* was going to be passed, the way was open for resuming attempts to reform the whole structure of the ecclesiastical courts, though initially matters were complicated by the floating of parallel bills occasioned by the imprisonment of Thorogood. By August 1840 he had been incarcerated for eighteen months, and his case had been taken up by organised dissent, resulting in mass petitions descending on Parliament. Sir John Nicholl launched a bill proposing that a person who refused to pay a church rate below £10 should appear before a magistrate who had power to levy the rate against that person's goods. If, however, the payer questioned the validity of the rate, then the case should go before an ecclesiastical court, but that court too was to be given powers of distraint. Nicholl's bill would have permitted the release of Thorogood once outstanding debts had been cleared. This bill was abandoned, however, in favour of a government reform measure that permitted individuals such as Thorogood to be released if their debtors agreed and if the judges who had sentenced them considered that they had been in prison long

---

[20] Hansard, *PD*, 3rd series lii, 1080–1.
[21] Outhwaite, *Scandal in the Church*, 137–9, explores the Act in greater detail.

enough.[22] An amendment to this bill, however, influenced perhaps by a petition from the ratepayers of Chelmsford, prevented
an individual's release from jail until the debts that put him there
were paid off.[23]

Petitions pleading that dissenters should not have to pay church
rates and that the ecclesiastical courts should be abolished continued to pour into Parliament. Once again the opportunity was
taken to hang such pleas on a particular case. In 1841 the individual commanding Parliament's attention was William Baines of
Leicester, incarcerated in the county jail for non-payment of
church rates.[24] Although the administration was asked whether
reforms were in the offing and the reply was that reform measures
were indeed being prepared, two years were to elapse before a new
government produced a bill to reform the spiritual courts.[25]

Although promises were made again in 1842 that measures
would be submitted to Parliament for the improvement of the
ecclesiastical courts, it was not until 1843 that a fresh attempt was
made to bring in a bill that attempted to put into operation the
various recommendations of the Ecclesiastical Courts Commission. Introducing the bill in the Commons in February 1843, Sir
John Nicholl drew attention to the multiplicity of courts able to
grant probate and the difficulties and legal dangers that were
presented by this. He pointed also to the paucity of contentious
causes litigated in the diocesan courts. Most litigation was being
settled in the courts at Doctors' Commons. This was the prelude
to a scheme in which all peculiar courts were to be abolished,
along with the spiritual jurisdiction relating to tithes, defamation
and brawling in churchyards; all testamentary and marital issues
were to be tried in London, and the consistory courts were to be
left, along with the bishops, to deal with matters relating to clerical discipline and to act as branches of the London court for
probate and administration of property under the value of £300.
The latter provision was clearly an attempt to appease the opposition voiced in the numerous petitions that had poured into
Parliament.[26] This sop was not, however, sufficiently persuasive
to still criticism of the proposed measure. One member

---

[22] Hansard, *PD*, 3rd series lv, 1189–93.   [23] Ibid., lv, 1386–9; *CJ*, 95, 612, 645.
[24] *LJ*, 73, 9; *CJ*, 96, 106, 237, 286.   [25] Hansard, 3rd series lvi, 761.
[26] Ibid., lxvi, 312–25.

complained that the wills of poorer testators were more likely to
be ill drawn than those of the wealthier classes, whose wills were
likely to have been drawn up by a lawyer rather than 'a school-
master, or person of that stamp'. Not only were such wills more
likely to occasion disputes, but these disputes would now be settled in country courts, where the proctors were least likely to be
legally qualified.[27] Others were less specific in their complaints,
few more so than Colonel Sibthorp, the testy member for Lincoln,
who objected that 'It was a measure of what was called "reform" –
a thing which he detested as he detested the devil'.[28]

Over two months were to elapse before the bill received its
second reading, and in that time over a hundred petitions, mostly
from proctors and others practising in local courts, had been
presented against it. Some members of the Commons railed
against the urge to centralise, particularly in relation to probate
and testamentary causes. One MP argued that if there was to be
one central court, why not place it in Northampton, the actual
centre of England. Not a few saw such measures as a plot by
those practising in Doctors' Commons to monopolise for themselves all the profitable church court business. It was 'a dirty
Doctors' Commons job', according to the redoubtable Colonel
Sibthorp. Wills were as safely kept in the country as in London,
it was argued, and costs of consulting them were significantly
lower.

Sir James Graham, the Home Secretary, defending the measure, once again drew attention to its strong intellectual pedigree:

I have then the opinion of three chancellors in favour of the measure,
I have the opinion of the ecclesiastical commissioners in favour of it; I
have the opinion of Attorney-generals on both sides of the House in
favour of it; I have the report of a committee of the House of Lords in
favour of it, I have the report of a committee of the House of Commons
in favour of it.

If the house were to reject this bill, he said, he could not offer any
more acceptable measure.[29] The bill was attacked by some
because it did not go far enough, retaining as it did the diocesan
courts for certain purposes; it was also attacked by those who felt

---

[27] Ibid., 325–9. This objection, however, embodied a misunderstanding, because
any litigation ensuing had to be conducted in London.
[28] Ibid., 335.   [29] Ibid., lxviii, 784–818.

it was too radical in suppressing so many local courts. One member noted that Lord Campbell had once argued that it was often easier for a man to travel to London than to the nearest market town. 'I would like', said Mr Escott, 'to see Lord Campbell with a pair of heavy nailed shoes on his feet, trudging up to London as many a poor man would be obliged to do if this bill should pass into law.'[30] Yet others pleaded for the entire extinction of the church courts. As Peel remarked, 'I scarcely recollect a bill which has had the misfortune ... to meet with vehement opposition from gentlemen who maintain such extremely discordant opinions.'[31] The strength of this opposition was sufficient to produce important modifications in committee to its proposals and ultimately to thwart its progress.

The bill of the following year, which its supporters insisted was essentially that which emerged from the Commons' committee of 1843, proposed to retain the jurisdiction of at least one episcopal court in each diocese throughout England and Wales, although many of the now-customary reform proposals from previous years, such as the introduction of oral examining of witnesses, trial by jury and the abolition of suits for tithes and defamation, were also attached to this bill. Introduced initially in the Lords, it encountered complaints that by retaining the diocesan courts the government had abandoned the proposals of those various commissions and committees that had recommended wholesale culling of the structure. But it was, said the bishop of London, one of its supporters, 'the best Bill which the Legislature was in a condition to pass'.[32] Passed by the Lords, it met sterner opposition in the Commons, where opponents took advantage of the lukewarm enthusiasm of the government for the measure. The prime minister professed that he himself greatly preferred the bill of the previous year and that 'if he thought that the Government could carry the Bill proposed last Session he would certainly have advised his right hon. Friend [Sir James Graham] to persevere in the attempt to carry it through the House'.[33] Pressed in 1845 as to whether it was the government's intention to introduce another bill on this subject, Graham confessed that the experience of the two preceding years led him to despair of 'being able to frame a

[30] Ibid., 1067.   [31] Ibid., 1080.   [32] Ibid., lxiii, 1338.   [33] Ibid., lxxiv, 188.

measure respecting the Ecclesiastical Courts which would be acceptable to the present Parliament'.[34]

Because the government seemed unwilling to launch a new attempt at reforming the courts, it was left to the former Whig Lord Chancellor, Lord Cottenham, to do so. He introduced in the Lords a bill that, he insisted, was identical to that which had emerged from the Lords' select committee of 1836, a bill that he himself had introduced and which had failed because abolition of the diocesan courts at that time would have left the church without fora in which to try delinquent clergymen.[35] Although bishops in the Lords complained in 1845 that they had not been consulted about the measure, it passed that house and was sent to the Commons, where it languished amongst a flurry of hostile petitions.[36]

Petitions pressing for radical reform continued to be presented in Parliament. Members of the Lambeth Association for the Abolition of Ecclesiastical Courts pleaded for abolition, as did the Deputies of the Three Denominations of Protestant Dissenters. The solicitors and legal practitioners of Liverpool pleaded for removal of the distinction between ecclesiastical and civil courts, whilst a surveyor of that city requested that all matrimonial suits be brought in future to the common law courts.[37] In 1848 one member of parliament used such a petition as a means of pressing a motion that 'their continued existence is injurious to the subject, and a scandal to the judicial system of the Country'. The Home Secretary, Sir George Grey, confessed sympathy for the complaints made about the courts, stated that a bill was being prepared but argued that there was insufficient time in the present parliament to consider and pass it.[38] In the event, the promised bill of 1849 did not materialise, and Parliament had to wait until 1852 for the next move.

By then, for over twenty years, reformers had attempted to put the various recommendations of the Ecclesiastical Courts Commissioners into effect. With the sole exception of abolition of the high court of delegates, little or nothing had been achieved. Pressures for change came from many quarters: some came from

[34] Ibid., lxxvii, 169.   [35] Ibid., lxxx, 835–46.
[36] *CJ*, 100, 667, 669, 705, 712, 754.
[37] *CJ*, 101, 1258; 102, 190, 448; 103, 393, 425, 485, 580.
[38] Hansard, *PD*, 3rd series xcix, 100–27.

law reformers frustrated by the increasingly patent inadequacies of spiritual jurisdiction; some came from secular lawyers clearly eager to get a share of what profitable business remained, especially in testamentary matters, though they could not always agree as to where the prospective spoils should go, whether to the common law courts or to the equity courts. Some came from protestant dissenting organizations whose complaints frequently revolved around the iniquity of dissenters being forced to pay church rates and being imprisoned for their failure to do so. Actual cases of imprisonment provided ammunition for their attacks.

Resistance to the attacks came too – and from many quarters. Some bishops objected to the proposed abolition of their diocesan courts, identifying reform with an attack on the power and independence of the church itself. How could they, as bishops, they argued, discipline their own clergy in these circumstances? Those involved in administering justice in the spiritual courts also petitioned Parliament strongly and effectively, often invoking the support of those who feared that the centralisation of justice in London would bear heavily on poorer litigants and testators and on those solicitors and others they were forced to employ. Hostility towards Doctors' Commons frequently arose. It was seen as a nest of patronage and monopoly. Party politics and changes of government sometimes fatally delayed bills, but this was less important than those other forces previously mentioned.

One additional impediment merits serious consideration. Where reforms had been achieved in the past, such as in 1787, 1813 and 1832, they had come from parliamentary bills that fastened on particular facets of the church courts' jurisdiction and procedure, such as prosecuting ante-nuptial fornication, the use of writs *de excommunicato capiendo* and appeals to delegates. The bills that failed, time after time, tended to be comprehensive programmes for reform – attempts to put all or most of the recommendations of the 1830 commissioners onto the statute book in one single measure. Parliament frequently got bogged down in the sheer complexity of wholesale reform; the composition of these bills provided endless opportunities for criticism and for discussion. At least one far-sighted MP saw this as early as 1843. In discussing the bill of that particular year, Mr Elphinstone made a particularly perceptive point: 'I cannot help also suggesting', he said, 'that it would be far more convenient if this bill were divided into four smaller bills – one for wills and administrations, one bill for suits relating to matrimony, one bill for suits relating to ecclesiastical matters, and a fourth bill for the salaries of judges and other officers, and for compensation to such officers as were abolished.'[39] This, a decade or so later, was how success was eventually achieved.

Things began to move forward slowly in 1852. The Commons passed a private member's bill to abolish a part of the criminal jurisdiction of the church courts, but this appears to have sunk in the Lords.[40] Later that year Walpole, the Home Secretary, admitted that the government had no immediate intention of bringing in an ecclesiastical courts bill of its own because it was awaiting a report from the Chancery commissioners as to how best to deal with the complicated questions that related to testamentary matters, a situation that still prevailed the following year.[41] This provoked a further private member's bill, a thoughtfully argued, well-conceived measure that limited itself to transferring probate and testamentary cases with a value of £300 or less to the newly established county courts Common law courts, rather than Chancery, were given those cases of a greater value. After probate had been obtained, all wills were to be transferred to Somerset House, where national indexes were to be maintained, copies of which were to be sent to the various district courts; and one grant of probate was to suffice for the whole of the United Kingdom. The proposals were warmly received but not proceeded with after promises from the government's law officers that reforms were in the offing.[42] From 1854 piecemeal reform measures began to be introduced, though not all of them were government measures.

---

[39] Ibid., lxviii, 1066.   [40] *CJ*, 107, 132, 149, 247, 253.
[41] Hansard, *PD*, 3rd series cxxiii, 295–8; cxxiv, 851.   [42] Ibid., cxxiv, 851–73.

15

REFORMS THICK AND FAST, 1854–1860

Robert Phillimore, both an MP and a civilian practising in the court of admiralty, had on at least one previous occasion attempted to preserve the ecclesiastical courts by advocating measures to strengthen rather than weaken their position.[1] In 1854 he presented a *Bill to alter and improve the mode of taking Evidence in the Ecclesiastical Courts* ... , a bill that permitted the *viva voce* examination of witnesses in the church courts. It quickly passed the Commons and met with approval from lawyers on all sides in the Lords. Lord Campbell confessed to having reservations, fearing that this change would simply prop up, and postpone reform of, institutions 'already doomed'. 'It appeared', he said, 'that those Courts had a charmed life, and were immortal.' He was reassured, however, by the Lord Chancellor's pledge that this measure was 'an instalment of Ecclesiastical Court reform', simply one among a whole raft of reforms that were shortly to be introduced.[2] From the viewpoint of the survival of the ecclesiastical courts, however, Phillimore's bill was a case of too little, too late. It is even doubtful that this measure led to any significant change in court procedure. Parliamentary critics were still complaining two years later that 'if any scheme could have been devised by the wit of man less adapted than another to the bringing forth of the whole truth of a case, it was this mode of written examination and written cross-examination'. The church courts had the authority to conduct

---

[1] Hansard, p. 3rd series cxxiv, 865–70.
[2] *CJ*, 109, 256, 278, 306, 316, 430; Hansard, *PD*, 3rd series cxxxiv, 1080–4, 1090–1; cxxxv, 360–4.

viva voce examinations, but it was 'so rarely exercised as to have become almost a dead letter'.[3]

Robert Phillimore was also responsible for bringing into the Commons the act that less than a year later abolished the church's jurisdiction over defamation. This jurisdiction had long been the subject of complaint, not the least of which came from practitioners within the ecclesiastical courts. Granville Vernon, the chancellor of York and a witness before the 1830 commission, confessed his irritation with such suits and his desire to be rid of them.[4] It was not simply his view that led the commissioners to offer the opinion that 'The proceedings in these Suits have occasioned much odium to the Ecclesiastical Jurisdiction; Imprisonment having in several instances taken place; either from the obstinacy of the party proceeded against, or his inability to obey the sentence of the Court by payment of costs'.[5] Exactly one half of the sixty-eight people imprisoned at the behest of the ecclesiastical courts in the years 1827–9 were incarcerated because of their contumacy in defamation suits.[6] Complaints about such causes and their outcomes were made periodically in Parliament, though with nothing like the frequency with which grievances against laws relating to *bona notabilia* and to church rates were voiced. Lushington 'rejoiced' that the bill of 1835 proposed to take defamation out of the ecclesiastical courts, and in 1848 Edward Pleydell-Bouverie drew attention to what witnesses before the Ecclesiastical Courts Commission had had to say about defamation causes: they were principally causes 'among the lower classes of the people', and these poor litigants sometimes found themselves imprisoned because of their failure to pay the costs of their actions. He went on to assert that 'it was monstrous to inflict such heavy penalties upon persons of a humble class in life, for a comparatively trivial offence'.[7]

---

[3] Hansard, *PD*, 3rd series cxlii, 2017–8.   [4] Waddams, *Sexual Slander*, 56–7.
[5] *PP*, 1831–2, xxiv, 63.   [6] Waddams, *Sexual Slander*, 12.
[7] Hansard, *PD*, 3rd series xxvi, 912; xcix, 108–9.

It was precisely such a case that thrust defamation back into the political spotlight in 1855. In February of that year, Parliament received a petition on behalf of Charlotte Jones, the wife of a collier of Merthyr Tydfil, pleading for the abolition of jurisdiction for defamation in the church courts and her own release from jail.[8] She had been involved in a verbal altercation with another woman, during which she called her a whore, and found herself summoned in September 1853 to appear in the consistory court of Llandaff to answer a charge of defamation. Jones failed to appear on the stipulated day and on three subsequent court days. Her contumacy led eventually to her arrest and imprisonment in April 1854, so that by the time of her petition she had been detained for over nine months.[9]

Phillimore's bill, which proposed not only the abolition of the jurisdiction over defamation but also a retrospective clause permitting the church courts to release people imprisoned for the non-payment of costs, quickly passed the Commons. This retrospective clause, obviously designed to cover cases like that of Charlotte Jones, was struck out in the Lords, but the upper house raised few other objections to the passage of the act. As the bishop of Exeter acknowledged, 'cases of defamation were exceedingly unfit for an Ecclesiastical Court'.[10]

THE DIVORCE AND MATRIMONIAL CAUSES ACT OF 1857

The 1832 report recommended no changes in the laws relating to marriage and separation beyond recommending that cases involving such issues should in future be tried only in the two provincial courts of Canterbury and York. Some individual members of the commission, however, felt strongly that further reforms were necessary. Some were particularly unhappy with Parliament's involvement in divorce proceedings. Cutlar Fergusson, one of the commissioners, argued in the Commons in 1835 that 'the scandal of a Parliamentary divorce – the necessity of applying first to a Court of Law, and then to that House, where such causes were

---

[8] *LJ*, 87, 26.

[9] Waddams, *Sexual Slander*, 3–7, throws invaluable light on this incident and on defamation causes generally.

[10] *CJ*, 110, 95, 100, 316, 324; Hansard, *PD*, 3rd series cxxxvii, 546, 1373–6.

made matter of jest and merriment, and then again to the House of Lords – was a disgrace to the country'. Sir John Campbell complained during the same debate that the 'whole proceeding was a mere farce – a most expensive farce it was true – but a farce that brought no credit at all to any party'. Such matters should, he insisted, be settled before judicial tribunals.[11] Critics drew special attention to the fact that parliamentary divorce was essentially the prerogative of the wealthy. The ability to dissolve a marriage should not be limited, said Sir R. Inglis in 1843, 'to those whose fortune allowed them to spend very large sums on the necessary proceedings'.[12] This message was powerfully reinforced two years later with the publication and wide circulation of Mr Justice Maule's celebrated sentence in 1845 upon a bigamist who came before him at the Warwick Assizes:

Prisoner at the bar, you have been convicted before me of what the law regards as a very grave and serious offence: that of going through the marriage ceremony a second time while your wife was still alive. You plead in mitigation of your conduct that she was given to dissipation and drunkenness, that she proved herself a curse to your household while she remained mistress of it, and that she had latterly deserted you; but I am not permitted to recognise any such plea. You had entered into a solemn contract to take her for better, for worse, and if you infinitely got more of the latter, as you appear to have done, it was your duty patiently to submit. You say you took another person to become your wife because you were left with several young children who required the care and protection of someone who might act as a substitute for the parent who had deserted them; but the law makes no allowance for bigamists with large families. Had you taken the other female to live with you as a concubine you would never have been interfered with by the law. But your crime consists in your having – to use your own language – preferred to make an honest woman of her. Another of your irrational excuses is that your wife had committed adultery, and so you thought you were relieved from treating her with any further consideration – but you were mistaken. The law in its wisdom points out a means by which you might rid yourself from further association with a woman who had dishonoured you; but you did not think it proper to adopt it. I will tell you what that process is. You ought first to have brought an action against your wife's seducer if you could have discovered him; that might have cost you money, and you say you are a poor working man, but that is not the fault of the law. You would then be obliged to prove by evidence your wife's criminality in a Court of Justice, and thus obtain a verdict with damages against the defendant, who was not unlikely to turn out a pauper. But so

[11] Hansard, *PD*, 3rd series xxvi, 915, 917.   [12] Ibid., lxvi, 831.

jealous is the law (which you ought to be aware is the perfection of reason) of the sanctity of the marriage tie, that in accomplishing all this you would only have fulfilled the lighter portion of your duty. You must then have gone, with your verdict in your hand, and petitioned the House of Lords for a divorce. It would cost you perhaps five or six hundred pounds and you do not seem to be worth as many pence. But it is the boast of the law that it is impartial, and makes no difference between the rich and the poor. The wealthiest man in the kingdom would have had to pay no less than that sum for the same luxury; so that you would have no reason to complain. You would, of course, have to prove your case over again, and at the end of a year, or possibly two, you might obtain a divorce which would enable you legally to do what you have thought proper to do without it. You have thus wilfully rejected the boon the legislature offered you, and it is my duty to pass upon you such sentence as I think your offence deserves, and that sentence is, that you be imprisoned for one day; and in as much as the present assizes are three days old, the result is that you will be immediately discharged.[13]

Such criticism led to the setting up in 1850 of a royal commission on divorce, under the chairmanship of Lord Campbell. Its report, issued three years later, proposed to preserve the existing law relating to divorce but to administer the law in a different way, transferring jurisdiction to a new secular court. This would make it unnecessary for plaintiffs to resort to three separate tribunals – an ecclesiastical court, a common law court and Parliament – in order to obtain marital freedom. The following year saw the first attempt to put some of these recommendations into effect with Lord Chancellor Cranworth's Divorce and Matrimonial Causes Bill. This bill preserved the conservatism of the law relating to divorce, declining for example to offer husbands and wives parity of treatment in relation to adultery. It departed from the recommendations of the Royal Commission, however, in allocating causes of divorce *a vinculo* to a single new court to be based in London, sending all other matrimonial causes to Chancery. Doubts about the capacity of an already overburdened Chancery's ability to deal with an additional load of cases, misgivings about the judicial composition of the new court and the lateness of the parliamentary session halted progress on the bill. When Cranworth withdrew it, he also openly

---

[13] I have taken the version of this speech that is reproduced in R. Phillips, *Putting Asunder: A History of Divorce in Western Society* (1988), 416–17.

confessed the strategy the government had embarked upon. On various occasions, he admitted, he had 'expressed his belief that the most effectual way of accomplishing a reform of the Ecclesiastical Courts was to deal with the subject by separate Bills, and not to have one great measure that would present many points of attack, and be open to many objections from different quarters'.[14] Separation of aims did not lessen, however, the intensity of the attacks that were launched against subsequent attempts to effect changes in divorce procedures.

When eventually, in 1856, the divorce bill was reintroduced by Cranworth, it proposed the establishment of a separate tribunal to try all marital causes rather than handing some of them to Chancery. The issue of financially inequitable access to divorce was still the prime focus of the bill. As the Lord Chancellor stated, 'The object of the Bill was to render proceedings for divorce less complicated, less difficult, and less expensive than now'.[15] Lord Lyndhurst and other critics complained, however, that the bill was inequitable in other ways, particularly in giving wives fewer legal rights than husbands. Husbands, for example, could divorce their wives for adultery on the part of the wife, but wives could not divorce their husbands for adultery alone. The plea had to be one of aggravated adultery, which custom had decreed occurred only where the husband's adultery was compounded with the sin of incest. Lyndhurst was sceptical also of the excuse that legal conservatives had offered in denying women the same legal rights as men, that this would open the floodgates, producing a rush of divorces. This had not happened, he argued, in Scotland. He added that it was 'monstrous' that the law should be so different in different parts of the kingdom. Support for Lyndhurst's plea that the divorce laws should be considered more widely by a select committee came from Lord Brougham, who pleaded that women should be given the same rights as men, not only in respect of adultery but also in respect of desertion, as was the case in Scotland.[16]

Cranworth's bill emerged from the select committee greatly modified. It proposed to rectify many of the legal disabilities faced

[14] Hansard, 3rd series cxxxiv, 128, 935–46, 1436–40. Stone is in error in suggesting that this bill proposed to hand all matrimonial cases to the new court: *Road to Divorce*, 369–70.

[15] Hansard, 3rd series cxliii, 236.   [16] Hansard, 3rd series cxliii, 401–27.

by women who were legally separated from their husbands, and although it stopped short of granting women the same rights as men in respect of adultery, Lyndhurst pushed the committee into accepting that women could divorce their husbands when adultery was accompanied by cruelty and bigamy as well as incestuous adultery. Though it was not proposed to abolish actions for criminal conversation, they were no longer to be necessary preludes to securing a divorce. Lord Campbell urged the house to accept the bill, which was 'an immense improvement on the law of marriage and divorce', arguing that the country was not prepared to accept anything more radical. Opponents such as Viscount Dungannon sided with the bishop of Oxford, however, in arguing that 'if the means of dissolving the marriage tie were made more generally accessible, an extent of immorality and collusion, which it was fearful to contemplate, would be developed among the lower classes of society'.[17] Fears of this sort, along with alarms about possible collusive actions, led the committee to accept the bishop of Oxford's amendment, which provided that persons divorced for adultery should be forbidden from subsequently marrying the person with whom the adultery had been committed.[18] This was not acceptable to Cranworth, however. He thought that the proviso would do more damage than good. He also reminded the house that though the Lords customarily inserted in their private divorce bills a proviso that such lovers were not subsequently to intermarry, the House of Commons invariably struck out such limitations when the bills came to them. 'Such a clause', he argued, 'would either encourage the adulterer to abandon the woman, marry some one else, and enter society ... or it would lead to the guilty parties living together, not in a state of marriage.'[19] His arguments failed to win the day and on this basis the bill was sent to the Commons, where hostility to this provision and its late arrival in the session combined to deter progress.[20]

Undeterred by this failure, the Lord Chancellor reintroduced the bill in February 1857, though with significant alterations. He omitted, for example, the stipulation that the guilty party in a divorce action should not be able to marry the lover, and he introduced a clause permitting wives to petition for a divorce if

---

[17] Ibid., 1968–87.   [18] Ibid., cxliii, 251.   [19] Ibid., 308.   [20] Ibid., 710.

the husband's adultery was accompanied by desertion for two years. Conservative critics lamented both changes, whilst more progressive ones regretted that *crim.con.* actions were not to be abolished and that wives were not to be given the same rights as their husbands to divorce their partners for adultery alone. Cranworth also proposed that couples should be able to separate by deeds that gave wives rights to all property that they subsequently acquired.[21] Campbell regarded this as equivalent to divorce without the intervention of a legal tribunal, and, as such, a dangerous proposal.[22] Opponents of the bill argued moreover that the establishment in London of a single divorce court would do nothing to bring divorce to the poor living in far-flung counties and that it could hardly offer cheap litigation if the court was to be composed of the Lord Chancellor and other legal dignitaries. Although the bill was read a second time, it fell with the dissolution of Parliament in late March.[23] Back it came in May 1857. Though many bishops argued against various of its provisions and lawyers such as Lyndhurst continued to press for sexual parity in relation to adultery, the bill eventually passed in the Lords.

Opponents in the Commons, a group that included Gladstone, responded initially by attempting to put off the second reading of the bill, arguing that its introduction in late June made it impossible for the house to give the measure the sort of seriously detailed examination it undoubtedly merited, particularly as Parliament had also to accommodate other pressing concerns, such as the probate bill and the Indian Mutiny. Palmerston, the prime minister, would have none of this, however, vowing that he would keep the house in session for 'as long as may be necessary to dispose of the important measures before us'.[24] Critics argued also that there was no popular clamour for such a measure and that a considerable number had signed petitions against some of its provisions, especially that which permitted divorced couples to remarry in church. Marriage, they argued, was essentially indissoluble and asking the clergy to wed divorced individuals, and especially the guilty ones, was an affront to their consciences. A clergyman, argued one, 'ought rather to strip off his gown, and resign his living, than be the instrument of prostituting the holy

---

[21] Ibid., cxliv, 432–5.   [22] Ibid., 1031.
[23] Ibid., 1685–721.   [24] Hansard, *PD*, 3rd series cxlvii, 413.

service of the Church by converting an adulteress into a bride.'[25]
Others denied that the legal procedures outlined in the bill would
bring the costs of divorce within the reach of people of humble
means, and even if it did, this was not to be encouraged because it
would simply increase the number of divorces that were likely to
occur. 'Under the present system', said one member, 'the process
was tedious and expensive, and it was precisely because this Bill
proposed to render the process easier that he objected to it.'[26]

Similar arguments were deployed against the proposals to
widen the opportunities presented to women to seek legal reme-
dies against their husbands. When attempts to halt the second
reading of the bill failed, opponents turned their attention day
after day, and night after night, through a sultry August to picking
critically at the bill's clauses in committee. Offering amendment
after amendment, opponents seized every opportunity to delay its
progress. How, asked one member, would it affect people residing
in India? Another asked whether the jurisdiction extended to the
Isle of Man. The Attorney General, on whom fell the principal
responsibility for steering the bill through the Commons, was
severely provoked at times by the nature of the debate. Stung by
criticism that the composition of the court was too exalted and its
location in London too inconvenient for provincial suitors, he
somewhat sarcastically suggested that four persistent critics –
Henley, Malins, Warren and Collins – should form themselves
into a 'little auxiliary sub-committee', devising ways to enlarge the
court and make it accessible to all persons.[27] This suggestion was
immediately seized upon and opponents used it as a device to
wring from the government a series of alterations in the bill,
eventually giving jurisdiction in cases of legal separation to assize
court judges and to magistrates at quarter sessions while retaining
a vinculo divorces within the new central court, though not before
considerable time had been spent discussing the merits of alternative jurisdictions in the newly established county courts. Nit-
picking abounded. Women, according to the bill, were to be
allowed to sue for divorce on the grounds of adultery when it was
accompanied by incest or cruelty or desertion, and to this it was
proposed to add bigamy. But what, asked Sir William Heathcote,
if the bigamous man was arrested coming from the church before

[25] Ibid., 838.   [26] Ibid., 767.   [27] Ibid., 1169.

adultery had taken place? The Attorney General's proposed solution, to use the phrase 'adultery and bigamy combined', led another member to point out that the husband might commit bigamy with one person and adultery with another.[28]

Opponents of the measure constantly pleaded for definitions. A plea for the term 'desertion' to be defined led one member to respond in exasperation that he 'thought the Committee had been occupied for hours in the profitless task of splitting straws'.[29] At the end of one sitting on 13 August, Palmerston exclaimed, 'I certainly congratulate the opponents of this Bill on the success with which they have, for ten hours, contrived to exercise their ingenuity upon three lines of a clause.' He warned them that they would return 'and sit here day by day, and night by night, until this Bill is concluded.'[30]

The proposed abolition of the action for criminal conversation also gave rise to considerable debate. Sir Denham Norreys threatened to move that the title of the bill be altered to 'An Act for the encouragement of Adultery', unless something was substituted in its place. The government's proposed solution was the imposition of a fine on the adulterer, but this in turn outraged those who argued that adultery had never been a crime punishable at law, but merely an ecclesiastical offence.[31] Debate continued in meeting after meeting until, on 21 August, the bill finally passed the Commons and was returned to the Lords. There, renewed attempts to postpone immediate consideration of bill failed by the margin of two votes. The Lords went on to reject the jurisdiction the Commons gave to the quarter sessions in cases of legal separation but agreed to the most of the amendments introduced in the Commons – though in the case of one amendment the government had to resort to the counting of proxy votes.[32]

This bill passed in the Lords because its provisions were conservative in nature; because the government threw its weight behind the bill; because lawyers on all sides were adamant that the existing system was inequitable and, in the case of *crim. con.* suits, also embarrassing; and because the bench of bishops was divided on many counts. Some, such as the bishops of Oxford and Salisbury, fought tenaciously to scupper the bill, but others were prepared to

---

[28] Ibid., 1561–3.   [29] Ibid., 1593.   [30] Ibid., 1602.   [31] Ibid., 1739, 1840.
[32] Ibid., 1962–71, 2005–67.

support it. Although on the occasion of its third reading in the Lords seven bishops voted against the bill, five eventually voted for it.[33] Though a redoubtable amalgam of conservative church-men, including evangelicals such as Gladstone, Roman Catholics and other supporters of the ecclesiastical courts fought tenaciously against the bill and various of its provisions, the government's substantial majority and Palmerston's determination to see matters through to a conclusion carried them through the storm. The bill was yoked with that relating to probate. Much effort had been invested in both measures. The failure of one might well imperil the other, and the failure of both would almost certainly have clogged up parliamentary proceedings for years to come.

The precise content of the Divorce and Matrimonial Causes Act of 1857, and its consequences for divorce and separation in England, are subjects that have been amply considered else-where.[34] What matters here is that the ancient jurisdiction of the ecclesiastical courts in matrimonial causes had finally came to an end.

THE PROBATES AND LETTERS OF ADMINISTRATION ACT OF 1857

An Act to amend the Law relating to Probates and Letters of Administration in England was introduced in the Lords on the same day as that relating to divorce, illustrating that the two were conceived as a package of ecclesiastical court reforms.[35] Critics of the ecclesiastical courts had continued from the early 1850s to press the case for ending the confusions that arose from the church's law relating to probate. After one such parliamentary outburst in 1853 by Robert Collier, the member for Plymouth, the Solicitor General acknowledged that 'they were all agreed as to one thing, that the abuses of the Ecclesiastical Courts were intolerable, and could no longer be suffered to exist', though Robert Phillimore, for one, still felt that the system could be

---

[33] The debates marking its passage through the Lords are in Hansard, 3rd series cxlv, 483–538, 779–832, 912–30, 1096–100, 1403–20, 1657–65; cxlvi, 200–35.

[34] O. R. McGregor, *Divorce in England* (1957); A. Horstman, *Victorian Divorce*; Phillips, *Putting Asunder*; Stone, *Road to Divorce*.

[35] *LJ*, lxxxix, 22.

reformed rather than abolished.[36] Collier rose to his own chal-
lenge, however, in attempting a few weeks later to bring in a bill
transferring the testamentary jurisdiction of the church courts to
the courts of common law and to the county courts, arguing that if
this business, the 'pabulum and nutriment' of the civilians, was
taken from them, their courts would eventually wither away too.
The government pleaded that they were awaiting the report of a
commission looking into such matters and that when that report
was received they would bring in their own measure.[37] This they
did the following year, but the scheme to transfer the ecclesiastical
jurisdiction of the ecclesiastical courts to Chancery, and to treat
the wills of personal and real property identically, encountered
serious opposition.

The next year, 1855, saw a change of direction. This time the
government proposed to establish a new Court of Probate and
Administration to deal with both real and personal estates, separate from Chancery but modelled upon it. These features were
enough, however, to stifle its progress in the parliamentary
committee set up to consider it. The opposition drew attention
also to the need for the government to present simultaneously a
bill removing matrimonial causes from the church courts. Failure
to do this would leave the spiritual tribunals with too little business to keep a separate legal profession in being.[38] This failure
prompted Collier to attempt in February 1856 again to bring in
his bill. His diatribe against the ecclesiastical courts is worth
reproducing:

At present we have 372 Ecclesiastical Courts in this country – episcopal,
archiepiscopal, diaconal, archidiaconal, rectorial, manorial, and peculiars
of every description – presenting such a grotesque and motley array as
was disgraceful to the country. The characters of the Judges [Collier later
admitted he meant registrars] were equally varied, comprising bishops,
lawyers, old women, rectors, lords of manors, colonels in the army, boys
and girls, exercising their functions by deputies and deputies' deputies,
and with their offices settled in remainder two or three deep. In the
present state of the law, a will was, *prima facie*, provable in the
jurisdiction where the testator had dwelt at the time of his death; but if it
turned out that he had *bona notabilia* to the extent of £5 out of the district,
the probate so obtained was utterly worthless, and it was necessary to take

[36] Hansard, *PD*, 3rd series cxxiv, 851–75.   [37] Ibid., cxxviii, 1231–51.
[38] Ibid., cxxxviii, 1429–64; cxliv, 427; *PP*, 1854–5, VI, 233–70.

out a probate in the Court of the Archbishop of the province ... But when he had got the metropolitan probate, if it turned out that he had *bona notabilia* out of that jurisdiction, he must get the other Archbishop's probate; and even then that probate was not good enough for Scotland or Ireland.

What is more, he pointed out, one set of rules applied to real property and another to personalty. He drew attention to the case of *Nicholls* v. *Remigo*, where the testator was found to be insane in the ecclesiastical court but sane by the verdict of a jury in a common law court, the end result being that Nicholls got the realty and Remigo the personalty, though there was in reality little left of either after the lawyers took their share. Collier proposed to rationalise the system so that only one grant of probate needed to be obtained throughout the kingdom. That was to be in the district where the testator died; he advocated handing probate jurisdiction relating to property below £300 to the county courts and jurisdiction over property above £300 either to Chancery or to a newly established central court, to establish a central register of wills at Somerset House; and to employ ecclesiastical court registrars as registrars of wills in the county courts. It was a thoughtful scheme, forcefully argued, but it foundered once again on the government's determination to bring in its own bill, as well as on divisions among lawyers as to where the spoils arising from the 25,000 wills and administrations, involving £50 million worth of personal property, should go. As Phillimore pointed out, the church courts partly survived because the lawyers squabbled amongst themselves, 'the Common Law lawyer saying there was nothing like the Common Law Courts, and the Equity lawyer that there was nothing like the Court of Chancery'.[39]

The year 1856 witnessed several attempts to reform the laws relating to probate and administration. In March, one month after Collier had introduced his own bill, the government introduced its promised measure. This proposed to abolish the jurisdiction of the ecclesiastical courts, vesting it instead in a new court of probate and administration to be located in London or Middlesex. The county courts, however, were to be given jurisdiction over estates worth less than £200.[40] Dissatisfaction with these

---

[39] *CJ*, 111, 28, 30, 54, 332; Hansard, *PD*, 3rd series cxl, 384–406.
[40] Hansard, *PD*, 3rd series cxli, 219–20; *PP*, 1856, vi, 557–611.

proposals seems to have led Sir Fitzroy Kelly and two other members to introduce their own testamentary and matrimonial causes bill. It also proposed to establish a court of probate in London or Middlesex, a court that was to have jurisdiction over all wills, and not just those dealing with personal property – though as with the government's bill, the county courts were to be given jurisdiction to deal with estates of less than £300 in value.[41] One consequence of this plethora of testamentary bills was that a second reading of the government's own bill was delayed, the Solicitor General promising modifications in proposals in exchange for Collier and Kelly not proceeding with their own measures.[42] But this also created problems, with some members objecting that the bill they were being asked to discuss was not the one originally introduced. Originally the central court was to have jurisdiction over all wills, those dealing with real estate as well as personal estate, and it was to employ common law procedures, but the bill now proposed the creation of local probate facilities, based on the county court districts; these were to deal with probates and administrations involving personal estates of less than £1,500. These modifications to the bill were welcomed by Kelly and Collier, though the latter had doubts that a new court was necessary, believing that the county courts and courts of common law were perfectly well equipped to deal with such business. Others, such as Malins, persisted in arguing that such business should be given to Chancery, no longer burdened with a backlog of cases and perfectly able to deal with contentious causes of this type. Yet others, including Robert Phillimore, thought the ecclesiastical courts were perfectly competent to deal with contentious matters, which amounted to a tiny fraction of all wills proved. The courts needed only to be secularised. Although the bill was read a second time late in June 1856, its committal came too late in the parliamentary term for the bill to be passed.[43] In mid-July, the government conceded that there was no hope of passing such a complex measure in the time remaining to them.[44]

It was not until February 1857 that the government moved again, but this time in the Lords, and concurrently with its divorce bill, *An Act to amend the Law relating to Probates and*

[41] *PP*, 1856, vi, 419–66.   [42] Hansard, *PD*, 3rd series cxlii, 1227–8.
[43] Ibid., 1995–2042.   [44] Ibid., cxliii, 679–82.

Letters of Administration in England. Once again there was to be a central court of probate. However, because of critical pressures against over-centralisation, the new bill proposed that some thirty district courts should be established, incorporating the diocesan will registries, to deal with estates valued at less than £1,500. Any grant of probate from these courts was to be valid throughout the kingdom. Contentious jurisdiction was to be largely confined to the metropolitan court, though county courts were to be allowed to settle disputes in estates with a value below £200. Probate was not envisaged for real property, but where caveats were entered respecting the sanity of testators one court decision was to determine the matter for both forms of estate.[45]

The dissolution of Parliament meant that this bill had to be reintroduced, along with the divorce bill, in May 1857.[46] The probate bill quickly passed the Lords and on its introduction to the Commons it met with widespread approval. The framers of the bill had learned the lessons of previous failures: local as well as metropolitan facilities for probate and litigation were to be provided, the central court was to be independent of Chancery and there was to be compensation for many of those in the ecclesiastical courts who suffered loss of office or business, though there were differences of opinion over who exactly should be compensated and how generous such compensation should be.[47] In committee, some provisions encountered serious criticism, but remarkably few amendments of substance were offered or effected. Much less time was devoted to it than to the divorce bill and it failed to arouse the passions its companion measure did. The Commons, revealing strong anti-metropolitan sentiments, removed the value restraints on probates obtained in the district courts and also threw open the new courts to solicitors and barristers, refusing to give advocates and proctors a monopoly of practising in them.

Such bills had been before them year after year since 1853 and both houses were exhausted and keen to see some measure of reform in this complex area.[48] As the Lord Chancellor said when the amendments by the House of Commons came back to the

---

[45] Hansard, *PD*, 3rd series cxliv, 422–32.
[46] Ibid., cxlv, 384–98, rehearses some of the complex history of previous legislative attempts.
[47] Ibid., cxlvi, 451–95.   [48] Ibid., cxlvi, 974–1020, 1288–322; cxlvii, 1777–81.

Lords, 'if they were to wait in the hopeless endeavour of making the two Houses agree upon every point of detail in a bill like the present, they would never pass the measure at all'.[49] But this did not occur. The bill was passed and the ecclesiastical courts lost their most profitable forms of business.

THE ACT OF 1860

The final measure of which we must take note has perhaps a symbolic importance. In April 1860 Edward Pleydell-Bouverie brought into the Commons a bill to abolish defamation in the ecclesiastical courts of Ireland and to abolish suits for brawling in churches or church yards in the ecclesiastical courts of England and Ireland, pleading that he had been approached to do the former by Irishmen anxious to see a measure for their country similar to the one that he and Phillimore had introduced five years earlier for England and Wales. It appears to have passed the Commons with little debate, raising alarms only in the Lords, where the bishop of Exeter lamented the encroachment by the state on the spiritual realm and on spiritual sanctions. His opposition was not enough to stop the bill, however, and in fact it sailed through both houses.[50] It meant that the church courts had lost their sole remaining jurisdiction over the laity. They became courts with a strictly limited range of functions: they could, in certain circumstances, correct misbehaving clergy; they entertained requests for faculties and they could still issue marriage licences that dispensed with the calling of banns. Everything else had disappeared. The stripping of ecclesiastical jurisdiction was virtually complete.

As that far-sighted MP Mr Elphinstone had predicted in 1843, reform was eventually managed by introducing and passing separate bills to cover particular parts of the system. The complexity of the issues and the heated nature of the debates accompanying the probate and divorce bills underlined the wisdom of this strategy. Rather than attempt wholesale reform of structures and jurisdiction within the context of an omnibus bill, one problem after another was addressed. Reconciling desires for

---

[49] Ibid., cxlvii, 1781.   [50] Ibid., clvii, 1807–8; clviii, 1074–85; clix, 321–2.

local probate facilities with equally powerful pressures for centralisation of facilities had proved a particularly tough nut to crack, and ultimately it was dealt with by compromise. Parliament became heartily sick of debating these issues year after year. Divorce touched powerful nerves, as the prolonged and passionate debates in Parliament attested. This too could have run on and on, but yoking it to the probate bill was a clever strategy. Its supporters pointed out that if a probate act was passed and the divorce bill failed, the courts would be left with too little business to maintain a professional group of ecclesiastical lawyers. This, coupled with sheer exhaustion amongst MPs, secured the consent that led to the virtual eradication of a jurisdiction the English church had held for centuries.

SELECT BIBLIOGRAPHY

EARLY TREATISES, TRACTS, AND EDITIONS OF COURT RECORDS

Acts and Ordinances of the Interregnum, 1642–1660, ed. C. H. Firth and R. S. Rait (1911).

The Anglican Canons 1529–1947, ed. Gerald Bray (1998).

The Archdeacon's Court: Liber Actorum 1584, ed. E. R. Brinkworth, Oxfordshire Record Society 23 and 24 (1942 and 1946).

Before the Bawdy Court: Selections from Church Court Records, ed. Paul Hair (1972).

Bohun, William, *A Brief View of Ecclesiastical Jurisdiction as it is at this day practised in England, Addressed to Sir Nathanael Curzon, Bart.* (1733).

Burn, Richard, *Ecclesiastical Law*, 1st edn (1763).

The Commission for Ecclesiastical Causes in the Dioceses of Bristol and Gloucester, ed. F. D. Price (1972).

Disney, J., *An Essay upon the Execution of the Laws against Immorality and Prophaneness* (1708).

Documentary Annals of the Reformed Church of England, ed. Edward Cardwell (1844).

Documents Illustrative of English Church History, ed. H. Gee and W. J. Hardy (1910).

An Episcopal Court Book for the Diocese of Lincoln 1514–1520, ed. Margaret Bowker, Lincoln Record Society 61 (1967).

Excommunication Excommunicated: or Legal Evidence that the ecclesiastical courts have no power to excommunicate any person whatsoever for not coming to his parish church (1680).

Gally, Henry, *Some Considerations upon Clandestine Marriages*, 2nd edn (1750).

Gouge, William, *Of Domesticall Duties* (1622).

The Law of England: Or a True Guide for all Persons Concerned in Ecclesiastical Courts (1680).

Lawton, George, *A Brief Treatise of Bona Notabilia* (1825).

Puritan Manifestoes, ed. W. H. Frere and C. E. Douglas (1954).

A Record of the archdeaconry courts of Buckinghamshire during part of 1521, in *Records of Buckinghamshire*, ed. F. W. Ragg, 10 (1916), 304–31.

Select XVI Century Causes in Tithe, ed. J. S. Purvis, Yorkshire Archaeological Society, Record Series 114 (1949).

174

A Series of Precedents and Proceedings in Criminal Causes, ed. William Hale (1847).

Swinburne, Henry, *A Briefe Treatise of testaments and last willes* (1590).

Synodalia: A Collection of Articles of Religion, Canons, and Proceedings of Convocations, ed. Edward Cardwell (1842).

MODERN SECONDARY WORKS

Adair, Richard, *Courtship, Illegitimacy and Marriage in Early Modern England* (1996).

Addy, John, *Sin and Society in the Seventeenth Century* (1989).
  Death, Money and the Vultures: Inheritance and Avarice, 1660–1750 (1992).

Albers, J. M., 'Seeds of contention: society, politics and the Church of England in Lancashire, 1689–1790', unpublished PhD thesis, Yale University (1998).

Allman, C. T., 'The civil lawyers', in *Profession, Vocation and Culture in Later Medieval England*, ed. Cecil Clough (1982), 155–80.

Amussen, Susan, *An Ordered Society: Gender and Class in Early Modern England* (1988).

Anglin, Jay, 'The Essex Puritan movement and the "bawdy" courts, 1577–1594', in *Tudor Men and Institutions: Studies in English Law and Government*, ed. Arthur Slavin (1972), 171–204.

Arkell, Tom, 'The probate process' and 'Interpreting probate inventories', in *When Death Do Us Part*, ed. Tom Arkell, Nesta Evans and Nigel Goose (2000), 3–37, 72–102.

Baker, J. H., *An Introduction to English Legal History*, 4th edn (2002).
  Monuments of Endlesse Labours: English Canonists and Their Work 1300–1900 (1988).

Beaver, Dan, ' "Sown in dishonour, raised in glory": death, ritual and social organization in northern Gloucestershire, 1590–1690', *Social History* **17** (1992), 389–419.

Bennett, Austin, *The Jurisdiction of the Archbishop of Canterbury: An Historico-Juridical Study* (1958).

Berman, Harold, *Law and Revolution I: The Formation of the Western Legal Tradition* (1973).
  Law and Revolution II: The Impact of the Protestant Reformations on the Western Legal Tradition (2003).

Bevilacqua, Antonio, *Procedure in the Ecclesiastical Courts of the Church of England* (1956).

Bonfield, Lloyd, 'Normative rules and property transmission: reflections on the link between marriage and inheritance in early modern England', in *The World We Have Gained*, ed. Lloyd Bonfield, R. Smith and K. Wrightson (1986), 155–76.

Boulton, Jeremy, 'Itching after private marryings? Marriage customs in seventeenth-century London', *London Journal* **16** (1991), 15–34.

Bowker, Margaret, *The Secular Clergy in the Diocese of Lincoln 1495–1520* (1968).

'The Commons' Supplication against the Ordinaries in the light of some archidiaconal acta', *TRHS*, 5th series **21** (1971), 61–77.

The Henrician Reformation: The Diocese of Lincoln under John Longland 1521–1547 (1981).

'Some archdeacons' court books and the Commons' Supplication against the Ordinaries of 1532', in *The Study of Medieval Records: Essays in Honour of Kathleen Major*, ed. D. A. Bullough and R. L. Storey (1971), 282–316.

Brand, Paul, *The Origins of the English Legal Profession* (1992).

Brigden, Susan, 'Tithe controversy in reformation London', *JEH* **32** (1981), 285–301.

Brinkworth, E. R. C., 'The Laudian church in Buckinghamshire', *University of Birmingham Historical Journal* **5** (1955–6), 31–59.

Shakespeare and the Bawdy Court of Stratford (1972).

Brooks, C. W., *Pettyfoggers and Vipers of the Commonwealth* (1986).

Brown, Sandra, *The Medieval Courts of the York Minster Peculiar* (1984).

Capp, Bernard, 'The double standard revisited: Plebian women and male sexual reputation in early modern England', *Past & Present* **162** (1999), 70–100.

Carlson, Eric Josef, *Marriage and the English Reformation* (1994).

'The origins, function, and status of the office of churchwarden', in *The World of Rural Dissenters, 1520–1725*, ed. Margaret Spufford (1995), 164–207.

Chapman, Colin, *Ecclesiastical Courts, their Officials and their Records* (1992).

Churchill, E. F, 'Dispensations under the Tudors and Stuarts', *EHR* **34** (1919), 409–15.

Churchill, Irene, *Canterbury Administration: The Administrative Machinery of the Archbishop of Canterbury illustrated from original records* (1933).

Clark, Richard, 'Why was the re-establishment of the Church of England in 1662 possible? Derbyshire: a provincial perspective', *Midland History* **8** (1983), 86–105.

Clegg, Cyndia, *Press Censorship in Jacobean England* (2001).

Coffey, John, *Persecution and Toleration in Protestant England 1558–1689* (2000).

Collinson, Patrick, *From Iconoclasm to Iconophobia: The Cultural Impact of the Second English Reformation* (1986).

Cooper, J. P., 'The supplication against the Ordinaries reconsidered', *EHR* **72** (1957), 616–41.

Coppel, Stephen, 'Wills and the community: a case study of Tudor Grantham', in *Probate Records and the Local Community*, ed. Riden (1985), 71–90.

'Willmaking on the deathbed', *Local Population Studies* **40** (1988), 37–45.

' "To bring them up in the fear of God". Guardianship in the diocese of York, 1500–1668', *Continuity and Change* **10** (1995), 9–32.

'Popular religion and the parish register, 1538–1603', in *The Parish in English Life 1400–1600*, ed. Katherine French, Gary Gibbs and Beat Kümin (1997), 94–111.

Baptism and Spiritual Kinship in Early Modern England (2002).

Cox, Jane, *Hatred Pursued Beyond the Grave* (1993).

Crankshaw, David, 'Preparations for the Canterbury provincial Convocation of 1562–63: a question of attribution', in *Belief and Practice in Reformation England*, ed. Susan Wabuda and Caroline Litzenberger (1998), 60–93.

Cross, Claire, *Church and People, 1450–1660: The Triumph of the Laity in the English Church* (1976).

Davies, C. S. L., 'The Pilgrimage of Grace reconsidered', *Past & Present* **41** (1968), 54–76.

Davies, Julian, *The Caroline Captivity of the Church* (1992).

Dean, David M., *Law-Making and Society in Late Elizabethan England* (1996).

Derrett, J. D. M., *Henry Swinburne (?1551–1642) Civil Lawyer of York* (1973).

Doe, Norman, *Fundamental Authority in Late Medieval English Law* (1990).

Duncan, G. I. O., *The High Court of Delegates* (1971).

Dunning, R. W., 'The Wells consistory court in the fifteenth century', *Proceedings of the Somersetshire Archaeological and Natural History Society* **106** (1962), 46–61.

Easterby, William, *The History of the Law of Tithes in England* (1888).

Elliott, Vivien B., 'Single women in the London marriage market: age, status and mobility, 1598–1619', in *Marriage and Society*, ed. Brian Outhwaite (1981), 81–90.

Ellis, I. P., 'The Archbishop and the usurers', *JEH* **21** (1970), 33–42.

Elton, G. R., 'The Commons' supplication of 1532: parliamentary manoeuvres in the reign of Henry VIII', *EHR* **66** (1951), 507–34.

'The supplication against the Ordinaries reconsidered', *EHR* **72** (1957), 616–41.

The Tudor Constitution: Documents and Commentary (1962).

Reform and Renewal (1973).

Emmison, F. G., *Elizabethan Life: Morals and the Church Courts* (1973).

Evans, Eric J., 'Some reasons for the growth of English rural anti-clericalism c. 1750–c. 1830', *Past & Present* **66** (1975), 84–109.

The Contentious Tithe (1976).

'Tithes', in *The Agrarian History of England and Wales, 1640–1750*, **5**:2 (1985).

Evans, Nesta, 'Inheritance, women, religion and education in early modern society as revealed by wills', in *Probate Records*, ed. Riden (1985), 53–70.

'The occupations and status of male testators in Cambridgeshire, 1551–1800', in *When Death Do Us Part*, ed. Tom Arkell, Nesta Evans and Nigel Goose (2000), 176–88.

Fincham, Kenneth, *Prelate as Pastor: the Episcopate of James I* (1990).

Fletcher, A. and MacCulloch, D., *Tudor Rebellions*, 4th edn (1997).

Fox, Adam, 'Ballads, libels and popular ridicule in Jacobean England', *Past & Present* **145** (1994), 47–83.

Foyster, E. A., *Manhood in Early Modern England: Honour, Sex and Marriage* (1999).

French, Katherine, *The People of the Parish* (2001).

Frost, G. S., *Promises Broken: Courtship, Class, and Gender in Victorian England* (1995).

Gash, Norman, *Mr Secretary Peel* (1961).

Gibson, William, '"Good Mr Chancellor," The Work of Dr John Audley, Chancellor of York', *Yale University Library Gazette* **73** (1998), 32–46.

Goldberg, P. J. P., *Women, Work, and Life Cycle in a Medieval Economy* (1992).

Goose, Nigel and Nesta Evans, 'Fertility and mortality in pre-industrial English towns from probate and parish register evidence', in *When Death Do Us Part*, ed. Tom Arkell, Nesta Evans and Nigel Goose (2000), 189–212.

'Wills as an historical source', in *When Death Do Us Part*, ed. Tom Arkell, Nesta Evans and Nigel Goose (2000), 38–71.

Gowing, Laura, *Domestic Dangers: Women, Words, and Sex in Early Modern London* (1996).

Greaves, Richard, *Society and Religion in Elizabethan England* (1981).

Green, I. M., *The Re-Establishment of the Church of England, 1660–1663* (1978).

Haigh, Christopher, 'Anticlericalism and the English Reformation', in *The English Reformation Revised*, ed. C. Haigh (1987), 56–74.

English Reformations: Religion, Politics and Society under the Tudors (1993).

The English Reformation Revised (1987).

Reformation and Resistance in Tudor Lancashire (1975).

'The troubles of Thomas Pestell: Parish squabbles and ecclesiastical politics in Caroline England', *Journal of British Studies* **41** (2002), 403–28.

'Slander and the church courts in the sixteenth century', *Transactions of the Lancashire and Cheshire Antiquarian Society* **78** (1975), 1–13.

Hall, Hubert, 'Some Elizabethan penances in the diocese of Ely', *TRHS*, 3rd series, **1** (1907), 263–77.

Heal, Felicity, 'Clerical tax collection under the Tudors: the influence of the Reformation', in *Continuity and Change: Personnel and Administration of the Church in England 1500–1642*, ed. Rosemary O'Day and Felicity Heal (1976), 215–37.

Of Prelates and Princes: A Study of the Economic and Social Position of the Tudor Episcopate (1980).

Helmholz, R. H., *Marriage Litigation in Medieval England* (1974).

Canon Law and the Law of England (1987).

Roman Canon Law in Reformation England (1990).

The ius commune in England: Four Studies (2001).

The Canon Law and Ecclesiastical Jurisdiction from 597 to the 1640s (Oxford History of the Laws of England, i, 2004).

Hembry, Phyllis, *The Bishops of Bath and Wells, 1540–1640* (1967).

Hill, Christopher, *Economic Problems of the Church from Archbishop Whitgift to the Long Parliament* (1956).

Society and Puritanism in Pre-Revolutionary England (1966).

Liberty Against the Law: Some Seventeenth-Century Controversies (1996).

Hockaday, F. S., 'Withington Peculiar', *Transactions of the Bristol and Gloucestershire Archaeological Society* **40** (1917), 89–113.

'The consistory court of the diocese of Gloucester', *Transactions of the Bristol and Gloucestershire Archaeological Society* **46** (1924), 195–287.

Horstman, Allen, *Victorian Divorce* (1985).

Hoskins, W. G., 'Harvest fluctuations and English economic history, 1480–1619', *Agricultural History Review* **12** (1964), 28–43.

Houlbrooke, Ralph, 'Persecution of Heresy and Protestantism in the diocese of Norwich under Henry VIII', *Norfolk Archaeology* **35** (1972), 308–26.

'The decline of ecclesiastical jurisdiction under the Tudors', in *Continuity and Change: Personnel and Administration of the Church in England 1500–1642*, ed. Rosemary O'Day and Felicity Heal (1976), 239–257.

Church Courts and the People during the English Reformation, 1520–1570 (1979).

The English Family, 1450–1700 (1984).

'The making of marriage in mid-Tudor England: evidence from the records of matrimonial contract litigation', *Journal of Family History* **10** (1985), 339–52.

Death, Religion and the Family in England, 1480–1750 (1998).

Hughes, E., 'The English stamp duties, 1664–1764', *EHR* **56** (1941), 234–64.

Hunt, Alan, *Governance of the Consuming Passions: A History of Sumptuary Law* (1996).

Ingram, Martin, 'Spousals litigation in the English ecclesiastical courts, c. 1350–c. 1640', in *Marriage and Society: Studies in the Social History of Marriage*, ed. R. B. Outhwaite (1981), 35–57.

'Religion, communities and moral discipline in late sixteenth and early seventeenth-century England: case studies', in *Religion and Society in Early Modern Europe, 1500–1800*, ed. Kaspar von Greyerz (1984), 177–93.

Church Courts, Sex and Marriage in England, 1570–1640 (1987).

' "Scolding women cucked or washed": a crisis in gender relations in early modern England?', in *Women, Crime and the Courts in early modern England*, ed. Jennifer Kermode and Garthine Walker (1994), 48–90.

'Puritans and the church courts, 1560–1640', in *The Culture of English Puritanism, 1560–1700*, ed. Christopher Durston and Jacqueline Eales (1996), 58–91.

'Reformation of manners in Early Modern England', in *The Experience of Authority in Early Modern England*, ed. Paul Griffiths, Adam Fox and Steve Hindle (1996), 47–88.

'Law, litigants and the construction of "Honour"; Slander suits in early modern England', in *The Moral World of the Law*, ed. Peter Coss (2000), 134–60.

'Regulating sex in pre-Reformation London', in *Authority and Consent in Tudor England: Essays presented to C.S.L. Davies*, ed. G. W. Bernard and S. J. Gunn (2002), 79–95.

Jacob, W. M., 'Clergy and society in Norfolk, 1707–1806', unpublished PhD thesis, University of Exeter (1982).

Lay People and Religion in the Early Eighteenth Century (1996).

James, Margaret, 'The political importance of the tithes controversy in the English Revolution, 1640–60', *History* **26** (1941), 1–18.

Jardine, Lisa, 'Why should he call her whore? Defamation and Desdemona's case', in *Addressing Frank Kermode*, ed. Margaret Tudeau-Clayton and Martin Warner (1991), 124–53.

Jones, M. D. W., 'The ecclesiastical courts before and after the Civil War: the office jurisdiction in the dioceses of Oxford and Peterborough, 1630–1675', unpublished BLitt thesis, Oxford University (1977).

Jones, W. J., *The Elizabethan Court of Chancery* (1967).

Kelly, Michael, 'The submission of the clergy', *TRHS*, 5th series **15** (1965), 97–119.

Kemp, E. W., *Introduction to Canon Law in the Church of England* (1957).

Kennedy, W. P. M., *Elizabethan Episcopal Administration* (1924).

Kerridge, Eric, *Usury, Interest and the Reformation* (2002).

Kettle, Ann, 'My wife shall have it: marriage and property in the wills and testaments of later medieval England', in *Marriage and Property: Women and Marital Customs in History*, ed. Elizabeth Craik (1984), 89–103.

Kinnear, M., 'The correction court in the diocese of Carlisle, 1704–1756', *Church History* **59** (1990), 191–206.

Kitching, Christopher, 'Probate during the Civil War and Interregnum', *Journals of the Society of Archivists* **5** (1976), 283–93, 346–56.

Landau, Norma, *The Justices of the Peace, 1679–1760* (1984).

Lander, Stephen, 'Church courts and the Reformation in the diocese of Chichester, 1500–58', in *Continuity and Change: Personnel and Administration of the Church in England 1500–1642*, ed. Rosemary O'Day and Felicity Heal (1976), 215–37.

Lathbury, Thomas, *A History of the Convocation of the Church of England from the Earliest Period to 1742* (1853).

Lehmberg, Stanford E., *The Reformation Parliament, 1529–1536* (1970).

Leneman, Leah, 'The Scottish case that led to Hardwicke's Marriage Act', *LHR* **17** (1999), 161–9.

Levack, Brian, *The Civil Lawyers in England, 1603–1641: A Political Study* (1973).

Macfarlane, Alan, *Witchcraft in Tudor and Stuart England* (1970).

Reconstructing Historical Communities (1977).

Marriage and Love in England 1300–1840 (1986).

Maguire, Mary H., 'Attack of the common lawyers on the oath *ex officio* as administered in the ecclesiastical courts in England', in *Essays in History and Political Theory*, ed. Carl Wittke (1936), 199–229.

Maitland, F. W., *Roman Canon Law and the Church of England* (1898).

Major, Kathleen, 'The Lincoln diocesan records', *TRHS*, 4th series **22** (1940), 39–66.

Makower, Felix, *The Constitutional History and Constitution of the Church of England* (1895).

Manchester, A. H., 'The reform of the ecclesiastical courts', *AJLH* **10** (1966), 51–75.

Marchant, Ronald, *The Puritans and the Church Courts in the Diocese of York 1560–1642* (1960).

The Church under the Law: Justice, Administration and Discipline in the Diocese of York 1560–1640 (1969).

Marsh, Christopher, 'In the name of God? Will-making and faith in early modern England', in *The Records of the Nation*, ed. G. H. Martin and Peter Spufford (1990), 215–49.

'"Departing Well and Christianly"; Will-making and Popular Religion in Early Modern England', in *Religion and the English People*, ed. Eric Josef Carlson (1998), 201–44.

Popular Religion in Sixteenth-Century England (1998).

McGregor, O. R., *Divorce in England* (1957).

McIntosh, Marjorie, *Controlling Misbehavior in England, 1370–1600* (1998).

Meldrum, Tim, 'A women's court in London: defamation at the Bishop of London's consistory court, 1700–1745', *London Journal* **19** (1994), 1–20.

Melikan, Rose A., *John Scott, Lord Eldon, 1751–1838: The Duty of Loyalty* (1999).

Milson, S. F. C., 'Richard Hunne's *Praemunire*', *EHR* **76** (1961), 8–82.

Morris, P., 'Defamation and sexual reputation in Somerset, 1733–1850', unpublished PhD thesis, University of Warwick (1985).

Muldrew, Craig, *The Economy of Obligation: The Culture of Credit and Social Relations in Early Modern England* (1998).

Neale, J. E., *Elizabeth I and her Parliaments, 1584–1601* (1957).

New, C. W., *The Life of Henry Brougham to 1830* (1961).

Newsom, G. L., *Faculty Jurisdiction of the Church of England*, 2nd edn (1993).

O'Day, Rosemary, 'The Law of Patronage in early modern England', *JEH* **26** (1975), 247–60.

'The role of the registrar in diocesan administration', in *Continuity and Change: Personnel and Administration of the Church in England 1500–1642*, ed. Rosemary O'Day and Felicity Heal (1976), 77–94.

The English Clergy: The Emergence and Consolidation of a Profession 1558–1642 (1979).

O' Day, Rosemary and Heal, Felicity, (eds), *Continuity and Change: Personnel and Administration of the Church in England 1500–1642* (1976), 21.

O'Hara, Diana, *Courtship and Constraint: Rethinking the Making of Marriage in Tudor England* (2000).

Outhwaite, R. B., (ed.), *Marriage and Society: Studies in the Social History of Marriage* (1981).

Inflation in Tudor and Early Stuart England, 2nd edn (1982).

'Sweetapple of Fledborough and clandestine marriage in eighteenth-century Nottinghamshire', in *Transactions of the Thoroton Society of Nottinghamshire for 1990* 94 (1991), 35–46.

Clandestine Marriage in England 1500–1850 (1995).

Scandal in the Church: Dr Edward Drax Free, 1764–1843 (1997).

Owen, D. M., *The Records of the Established Church in England* (1970).

Church and Society in Medieval Lincolnshire (1971).

'Ecclesiastical jurisdiction in England, 1300–1550', in *Materials, Sources and Methods of Ecclesiastical History*, ed. Derek Baker (SCH 11, 1975), 199–247.

Parker, Kenneth, 'Richard Greenham's "spiritual physicke": the comfort of afflicted consciences in Elizabethan pastoral care', in *Penitence in the Age of Reformations*, ed. Katharine Lualdi and Anne Thayer (2000), 71–83.

Peters, Christine, 'Gender, sacrament and ritual: the making and meaning of marriage in late medieval and early modern England', *Past & Present* **169** (2000), 63–96.

Peters, Robert, 'The administration of the archdeaconry of St Albans, 1580–1625', *JEH* **13** (1962), 61–75.

Oculus Episcopi: Administration in the Archdeaconry of St. Albans 1580–1625 (1963).

Phillips, Roderick, *Putting Asunder: A History of Divorce in Western Society* (1988).

Pollock, Frederick and Maitland, F. W., *The History of English Law before the Time of Edward I*, 2nd edn (1898, repr. 1968).

Potter, J. M. 'The ecclesiastical courts in the diocese of Canterbury, 1603–1665', unpublished MPhil thesis, University of London (1973).

Price, F. Douglas, 'An Elizabethan church official – Thomas Powell, chancellor of Gloucester diocese', *Church Quarterly Review* **128** (1939), 94–112.

'Gloucester diocese under Bishop Hooper, 1551–3', *Transactions of the Bristol and Gloucestershire Archaeological Society* **60** (1939), 51–151.

Pruett, John, *The Parish Clergy under the Later Stuarts* (1978).

Quaife, G. R., *Wanton Wenches and Wayward Wives* (1979).

Riden, Philip (ed.), *Probate Records and the Local Community* (1985).

Ritchie, Carson I. A., *The Ecclesiastical Courts of York* (1956).

Rodes, Robert, Jr., *Lay Authority and Reformation in the English Church: Edward I to the Civil War* (1982).

Law and Modernization in the Church of England: Charles II to the Welfare State (1991).

Ruddock, R. P., 'Women, witchcraft, and slander in early modern England: cases from the church courts of Durham, 1560–1675'; *Northern History* **18** (1982), 116–32.

'"The eye of the bishop": Nottingham causes in the archdeacon's court, 1760–1795, a study in decline', unpublished MS thesis, University of Nottingham (1997).

Sharpe, J. A., 'Crime and delinquency in an Essex parish 1600–1640', in *Crime in England 1550–1800*, ed. J. S. Cockburn (1977), 90–109.

Defamation and Sexual Slander in Early Modern England: The Church Courts at York (1980).

'"Such disagreements betwyx neighbours": litigation and human relations in early modern England', in *Disputes and Settlements: Law and Human Relations in the West*, ed. John Bossy (1983), 167–87.

Witchcraft and women in seventeenth-century England: some Northern evidence', *Continuity and Change* **6** (1991), 179–99.

Sheehan, Michael, 'The formation and stability of marriage in fourteenth-century England: evidence of an Ely register', *Mediaeval Studies* **33** (1971), 228–63.

Sheils, W. J., *The Puritans in the Diocese of Peterborough 1558–1610* (Northamptonshire Record Society 30, 1979).

'"The right of the Church"; the clergy, tithe and the courts at York, 1540–1640', in *The Church and Wealth*, ed. W. J. Sheils and Diana Wood (*SCH* 24, 1987), 231–55.

Shoemaker, R. S., *Prosecution and Punishment: Petty Crime and the Law in London and Rural Middlesex, c. 1660–1725* (1991).

Slatter, M. D., 'The records of the Court of Arches', *JEH* **4** (1953), 139–53.

Smith, David L. 'The Root and Branch petition and the Grand Remonstrance. From Petition to Remonstrance', in *The Theatrical City: Culture, Theatre, and Politics in London, 1576–1649*, ed. David L. Smith, Richard Strier and David Bevington (1995), 209–23.

Smith, *M. G., Pastoral Discipline and the Church Courts: The Hexham Court 1680–1730* (1982).

Spalding, J. C., 'The *Reformatio legum ecclesiasticarum* of 1552 and the furthering of discipline in England', *Church History* **39** (1970), 162–71.

Spurr, John, *The Restoration Church of England, 1646–1689* (1991).

Squibb, G. D., *Doctors' Commons* (1977).

Stieg, Margaret, *Laud's Laboratory: The Diocese of Bath and Wells in the Early Seventeenth Century* (1982).

Stone, Lawrence, *The Crisis of the Aristocracy 1558–1641* (1965).

The Family, Sex and Marriage in England, 1500–1800 (1977).

Road to Divorce: England 1530–1987 (1990).

Uncertain Unions: Marriage in England 1660–1753 (1992).

Strier, Richard, 'From diagnosis to operation', in *The Theatrical City: Culture, Theatre and Politics in London, 1576–1649*, ed. David L. Smith, Richard Strier and David Bevington (1995), 224–43.

Sykes, Norman, *From Sheldon to Secker* (1959).

Takahashi, Motoyasm, 'The number of wills proved in the sixteenth and seventeenth centuries', in *The Records of the Nation*, ed. G. H. Martin and Peter Spufford (1990), 187–213.

Tarver, Anne, *Church Court Records: An Introduction for Family and Local Historians* (1995).

'The consistory court of the diocese of Coventry and Lichfield and its work, 1680–1830', Unpublished PhD thesis, University of Warwick (1998).

Tate, W. E., *The Parish Chest: A Study of the Records of the Parochial Administration in England*, 3rd edn (1969).

Taylor, S., 'Whigs, Tories and anticlericalism: ecclesiastical courts legislation in 1733', *Parliamentary History* **19** (2000), 329–55.

Thomas, Keith, *Religion and the Decline of Magic* (1971).

'The Puritans and adultery: the Act of 1650 reconsidered', in *Puritans and Revolutionaries*, ed. D. Pennington and K. Thomas (1978), 99–111.

Till, B. D., 'The administrative system of the ecclesiastical courts in the diocese and province of York', unpublished typescript, Borthwick Institute, York (1963).

Trumbach, Randolph, *Sex and the Gender Revolution* (1998).

Tyler, Philip, 'The significance of the ecclesiastical commission at York', *Northern History* **2** (1967), 27–44.

'The Church Courts at York and Witchcraft Prosecutions 1567–1640', *Northern History* **4** (1969), 84–109.

Underdown, David, 'The taming of the scold: the enforcement of patriarchal authority in early modern England', in *Order and Disorder in early modern England*, ed. A. Fletcher and J. Stevenson (1985), 116–36.

Usher, Roland, *The Rise and Fall of the High Commission* (1913, repr. with new Introduction by Philip Tyler, 1968).

Waddams, S. M., *Law, Politics and the Church of England: The Career of Stephen Lushington 1782–1873* (1992).

Sexual Slander in Nineteenth-Century England: Defamation in the Ecclesiastical Courts 1815–1855 (2000).

Wall, Alison, 'For love, money or politics? A clandestine marriage and the Elizabethan court of Arches', *Historical Journal* **38** (1995), 511–33.

Ware, Sedley L., *The Elizabethan Parish in its Ecclesiastical and Financial Aspects* (1908).

Warne, Arther, *Church and Society in Eighteenth Century Devon* (1969).

Webster, Tom, *Godly Clergy in Early Stuart England* (1997).

Wenig, Scott, *Straightening the Altars* (2000).

Weske, Dorothy B., *Convocation of the Clergy* (1937).

Whitaker, W. B., *Sunday in Tudor and Stuart Times* (1933).

Whiteman, Anne, 'The re-establishment of the Church of England, 1660–1663', *TRHS*, 5th series **5** (1955), 111–31.

Witte, John, Jr., 'Anglican Marriage in the Making', in *The Contentious Triangle: Church, State, and University*, ed. Rodney Petersen and C. A. Pater (1999), 241–59.

Wood, A. C., 'Nottinghamshire Penances (1590–1794)', *Transactions of the Thoroton Society of Nottinghamshire* **48** (1944), 52–63.

Woodcock, Brian, *Medieval Ecclesiastical Courts in the Diocese of Canterbury* (1952).

Wrightson, Keith, and David Levine, 'Infanticide in European history', *Criminal Justice History* **3** (1982), 1–20.

Poverty and Piety in an English Village: Terling, 1525–1700, 2nd edn (1995).

Wrigley, E. A., and Schofield, Roger, *The Population History of England 1541–1871* (1981).

Wunderli, Richard, *London Church Courts and Society on the Eve of the Reformation* (1981).

INDEX

A Brief View of Ecclesiastical Jurisdiction (by William Bohun,1733), 115
Abortion, 59
Acts of Parliament (where titles given in full): *An Act for more effectively enforcing Church Discipline* (1840), 148, 150; *An act for payment of tithes* (1549), 30; *An Act for the Better Preventing of Clandestine Marriages* (1753) ('Lord Hardwicke's Marriage Act'), ix, 119; *An act for the prevention of frauds and perjuries* (1676), 90; *An Act for transferring the Powers of the High Court of Delegates, both in Ecclesiastical and Maritime Causes, to His Majesty in Council* (1832), 144; *An Act to amend the Law relating to Probates and Letters of Administration in England* (1857), 167, 170–1; *For the true payment of tithes and offerings* (1540), 29; *For tithes to be paid throughout this realm* (1535), 28; *see also* Divorce and Matrimonial Causes Act (1857); Statute of Frauds (1677); Toleration Act (1689)
Addy, J., 34n.
Administration (of estates), 7, 19, 34, 54, 66, 67, 89, 90, 97, 115, 142, 151–2, 156, 167–9; *see also* Probate
Admiralty courts, 146
Adultery, 5, 6, 42, 44, 59, 60, 62, 70, 74, 76, 81, 123, 124, 142, 160, 161, 162, 163, 164, 165, 166
Advocates: *see* Lawyers (Church courts)
Advowson, 24

Alleyne, John, rector of Loughborough, Leicestershire, 110
Alleyne, Richard, vicar of St Werburgh's, Derbyshire, 108, 109, 110, 111
An Apology for the Conduct of Mrs Teresia Constantia Phillips (by Constantia Phillips, 1748–9), 119, 121
Apparitors, 9, 10, 21, 57, 63, 64, 66, 73, 82, 100
Appeals/Appellate courts, 4, 15, 94, 100, 121, 123, 137, 140, 143, 144, 150; *see also* Chancery court; Court of Arches; Court/High Court of Delegates; Divorce courts; House of Lords (as court); Privy Council (as court)
Archbishop's courts, 4, 69, 74, 76, 143; *see also* Audience courts; Provincial courts
Archdeaconry/Commissary courts, 2, 3, 4, 7, 16, 21, 48, 57, 74, 75, 76, 84, 98, 100, 101, 127, 141, 148, 168; Barnstaple, 83; Bedford, 135; Bodmin, 129; Buckingham, 41; Cambridgeshire, 2; Canterbury, 2, 58; Carlisle,100; Chichester,16, 17, 100; Cleveland, 103; Coventry, 83, 100; Doncaster, 58; Durham, 100; Essex, 2; Gloucester, 100; Hereford, 100; Huntingdonshire, 2; Kelvedon, Essex, 2; Leicestershire, 2; Lichfield, 83, 100; Lincoln,18; London, 59, 60; Norwich, 59, 60; Nottingham, 56, 84, 91, 92, 93; St Albans, 54; Salisbury, 58; Staffordshire, 2; Suffolk, 21, 34, 54, 56; Surrey, 2;

Hipwell, Margerie, of London, 46
Hooper, John, bishop of Gloucester
  (March–April 1851), of Gloucester
  and Worcester (1852–4), 71
Hopkins, Margery, of Oxford, 46
Houlbrooke, Ralph, 17, 19, 28, 41, 50,
  59, 69
House of Commons (as court), 147,
  159
House of Lords (as court), 121, 135,
  137, 147, 159, 161
Howley, William, archbishop of
  Canterbury (1826–56), 140, 149
Hume, Joseph, MP, 130
Hundred courts, 6

Idolatory, 5
Imprisonment, 14, 72, 73–4, 77, 85,
  103, 117, 126, 128, 142, 149–51, 155,
  158, 159, 161
Incest, 59, 72, 142, 162, 165
Income: *see* Church court fees/income
Infanticide, 59
In forma pauperis pleas, 127
Inglis, Sir Robert, MP, 145, 160
Ingram, Martin, 43, 44, 50, 63, 72n.,
  100/101n.
Instance causes, vii, 10, 10n., 11, 15,
  16, 17, 18, 19, 20, 21, 22, 27, 31, 35,
  41, 48, 53, 54, 64, 69, 74, 79, 80, 84,
  86, 87, 94, 96, 98, 103; *see also* Breach
  of faith/*Fidei laesio* causes;
  Defamation/Slander causes; Marital/
  Matrimonial causes; Probate;
  Testamentary/Wills business;
  Tithes/Tithe causes

Jacob, W. M., 100/101n.
James I, petition to, 75–6
James II, 82
  Declaration of Indulgence of 1687,
  81, 82
Jenner (otherwise Jenner-Fust), Sir
  Herbert, lawyer Doctors' Commons,
  140
Jesuits, 77
Johnston, Margaret, of Sutton,
  Bedfordshire, 134
Johnston, Sir James, MP, 125
Jones, Charlotte, of Merthyr Tydfil, 159
Jones, W. J., 70
Judges (Church courts), 9, 10, 13, 53,

63, 65, 66, 99, 105, 110, 135, 141,
  149, 150, 156, 168
Judges (Common law courts), 127, 129,
  131, 135, 136, 140, 142, 149, 160–1
Justices of the Peace/Magistrates, 28,
  63, 87, 88, 100, 101, 102, 106, 107,
  123, 128, 142, 149, 150; *see also*
  Magistrates' courts

Kaye, John, bishop of Lincoln
  (1827–53), 140
Kelly, Sir Fitzroy, MP, 170

Laud, William, archbishop of
  Canterbury (1633–45), 19, 58, 76,
  77, 78
Law, Edmund, bishop of Bangor, 124
Lawyers (Church courts), 38, 53, 54,
  54n., 65, 98, 102, 129, 139, 140–1,
  143, 155, 173
Lawyers (Civil courts), 38, 73, 50,
  54n., 72, 73, 75, 97, 111, 152,
  155, 171
Leach, Edward, of Milton,
  Cambridgeshire, 36
Lee, George, 116
Lee, Sir William, lord chief justice of
  the King's Bench, 121
Lemon, Sir William, MP, 124
Levack, Brian, 72
Long Parliament, 78
Lushington, Stephen, MP, lawyer
  Doctors' Commons, later dean of
  arches, 136, 137, 140, 141, 146, 149,
  158
Lyndhurst, first Baron (John Copley),
  lord chancellor (1834–5, 1841–6),
  162, 163, 164

MacCulloch, James, of Derbyshire,
  107–10, 112–14, 112n., 113n.
Macfarlane, A., 2
Mackintosh, Sir James, 139
Mackenzie, Maria, of Sutton,
  Bedfordshire, 134
Magistrates: *see* Justices of the Peace/
  Magistrates
Magistrates' courts, 63, 87, 100, 101,
  102, 123, 128, 145, 149, 150, 165; *see
  also* Justices of the Peace/Magistrates
Malins, Sir Richard, MP, 165
Manorial courts, 6, 168